# PROTECTION BY PERSUASION

## *International Cooperation in the Refugee Regime*

ALEXANDER BETTS

CORNELL UNIVERSITY PRESS
ITHACA AND LONDON

First published 2009 by Cornell University Press
Printed in the United States of America

Library of Congress Cataloging-in-Publication Data

Betts, Alexander, 1980–
   Protection by persuasion : international cooperation in the refugee regime / Alexander Betts.
        p. cm.
   Includes bibliographical references and index.
   ISBN 978-0-8014-4824-9 (cloth : alk. paper)
   1. Refugees—International cooperation.  2. Refugees—Government policy.  3. Refugees—Protection.  4. Office of the United Nations High Commissioner for Refugees.  I. Title.

   HV640.B485   2009
   362.87'6—dc22           2009024185

Cornell University Press strives to use environmentally responsible suppliers and materials to the fullest extent possible in the publishing of its books. Such materials include vegetable-based, low-VOC inks and acid-free papers that are recycled, totally chlorine-free, or partly composed of nonwood fibers. For further information, visit our website at www.cornellpress.cornell.edu.

Cloth printing        10   9   8   7   6   5   4   3   2   1

# CONTENTS

# ACKNOWLEDGMENTS

This book is the culmination of ten years of thinking about the politics of refugee protection. The journey began unexpectedly in 1999. As an undergraduate with a long summer holiday, little to do, and less money, I discovered an opportunity to do volunteer work in a reception center for asylum seekers and refugees in a small town in the Netherlands. Refugees had come to my attention during the Kosovo crisis, but until my visit to the center in Heerenween, I had had little understanding of their situation.

What I took from my experience in the Netherlands was far greater than what I was able to contribute. While there, I simply helped to build a playground and organize activities for the children. But the experience proved to be the greatest introduction to world politics I could ever have hoped for. I spent long evenings talking to people who had experienced conflict or persecution firsthand in Bosnia, Iraq, Iran, Pakistan, former Zaire, China, Rwanda, and Liberia. These people were able to explain to me some of the major conflicts and atrocities of the post–Cold War era.

Many of the people I met were far more talented and qualified than I was ever likely to be, and it struck me as unjust that the world would confine such people to reception centers with no right to work and few opportunities, often for several years.

On my return home, I was eager to learn more. I went to libraries—including the Refugee Studies Centre library in Oxford—to try to understand better why these people were in this situation and what, if anything, could be done about it. It seemed to me a deeply political issue and surely the consequence of choices made by people in positions of power. I wanted to understand the underlying causes of flight, the reasons why political choices were made that led to such apparently limited solutions, and what other alternatives might exist. What I discovered during my first foray into the literature, however, was that there had been extremely little work on the politics of refugee protection. With few notable exceptions, political science and international relations, the very disciplines likely to shed light on the power relations, interests, and ideas that shaped the situation of refugees, had largely shunned the study of asylum and refugee protection.

Beginning with an undergraduate dissertation on refugee protection as a global public good, which was eventually published in the *Journal of Refugee Studies,* I started to consider the forces that shape the relationship between global politics and refugee protection. I found my undergraduate degree in economics inadequate for explaining the questions I was interested in. I went to the University of Oxford, combining the study of international politics with the opportunities offered by the presence of the Refugee Studies Centre. There I discovered an ideal environment in which to work toward bridging the gap between the study of world politics and forced migration. One of the major outcomes is this book. It is the first small installment in my paying back the very considerable debt I owe to people I met at the asylum reception center in Heerenween.

During the thinking about, research for, and writing of this book, I have received significant support from a wide range of people within Oxford and beyond. Oxford is the perfect place to study the relationship between international relations and forced migration. Not only does it have the top-ranked Department of Politics and International Relations in Europe, but it is also a hub for the study of migration and forced migration. My associations with colleagues at the department; the Refugee Studies Centre; the Global Economic Governance Programme; the International

Migration Institute; and the Centre on Migration, Policy and Society have played an important role in the development of this book.

My first word of thanks goes to Gil Loescher and James Milner, who have influenced much of my thinking on the relationship between refugees and international politics. They have been mentors, friends, and colleagues throughout my time in Oxford, and they have been a constant source of inspiration through their work, ideas, and commitment to the area. Of all my friends and colleagues in Oxford, Anne Roemer-Mahler may know this work better than anyone. She has spent many hours reading and discussing various iterations of the manuscript. I cannot name everyone, but discussions with and feedback from other colleagues have either directly or indirectly contributed. I am especially grateful to Stephen Castles, Matthew Gibney, Guy Goodwin-Gill, Jason Hart, Eva-Lotta Hedman, Esra Kaytaz, Anna Lindley, Paul Martin, Walter Mattli, Kalypso Nicolaides, Gillian Peele, Jochen Prantl, Martin Ruhs, Devi Sridhar, Jennifer Welsh, and Ngaire Woods.

Outside Oxford, others have played an important role in helping me to develop the ideas in the book. Susan Martin has been a constant source of advice and useful historical information relating to my case studies. I am grateful to Anna Schmidt for many conversations about both issue linkage and the refugee regime. I have had numerous influential discussions on burden-sharing with Eiko Thielemann, who gave me the opportunity to present my undergraduate work at the London School of Economics and to publish my first journal article. I am grateful to Joe Nye for making the time to have dinner with me at Wadham to discuss the relationship between cross-issue persuasion and soft power and for encouraging me with "I think you are on to something." I also thank Bob Keohane for pushing me hard on the conceptual framework and encouraging me to clarify how my ideas fit in with the existing literature on issue linkage. Rey Koslowski read the entire manuscript, providing constructive feedback and sage advice on how to frame my argument. I am grateful to Sarah Cross (my intellectual doppelganger), who also read the entire book meticulously and provided suggestions on the title.

I spent nearly six months working at UNHCR Headquarters in the second half of 2005. That period enabled me to conduct interviews, undertake archive research, and engage in some participant observation. While at UNHCR, I received significant support from Anita Bundegaard,

Beverley Byfield, Jeff Crisp, Erika Feller, Brian Lander, Pablo Mateu, and José Riera. I am most grateful to Jean-François Durieux for engaging me in an ongoing dialogue on the role of UNHCR in world politics. Initially as the person who brought me to UNHCR to work on Convention Plus and later as a colleague in Oxford, he has been a constant source of insight and intellectual debate.

I am also grateful to my excellent students, especially those in my International Relations and Forced Migration course, who have constantly inspired me with their challenging questions. If I had the space to name them all, I would. I thank B. S. Chimni and Neil MacFarlane, who as my doctoral examiners provided constructive feedback that subsequently influenced the writing of this book.

Nick Van Hear and Andrew Hurrell, as my doctoral supervisors and later as colleagues, have played a significant role in helping to transform an initial set of ideas into a more or less coherent argument. Nick has been a constant source of advice, encouragement, and support on forced migration. He has helped me to establish many of the networks and contacts that have made my research and its dissemination possible. Andrew has inspired many of the conceptual ideas in the book and has shaped my understanding of the discipline of international relations more than anyone else.

I am grateful to the Economic and Social Research Council, the Rose Research Fellowship at Lady Margaret Hall, the Hedley Bull Research Fellowship Fund at the Department of Politics and International Relations, and the MacArthur Foundation for financial support at various stages of the research and writing of this book. I am also immensely grateful to Roger Haydon at Cornell University Press, who is the best editor I could have hoped for. He has contributed greatly to nurturing this project, explaining to me the difference between a thesis and a book, and bluntly telling me when things could be better. To the extent that this project now resembles a book, he deserves the credit.

I am thankful to my parents who, in contrasting ways, have made me who I am. My late dad, John, inspired me with his enterprise, vision, and determination right until the very end. Last, and most important, I thank my mum, Hilary, whose unconditional love, support, and wisdom have gotten me through the difficult times.

A. B.

# ABBREVIATIONS

| | |
|---|---|
| 4Rs | repatriation, reintegration, rehabilitation, and reconstruction |
| AfP | Agenda for Protection |
| ASC | Asamblea de la Sociedad Civil |
| ASEAN | Association of Southeast Asian Nations |
| AU | African Union [formerly OAU] |
| CASWANAME | Central Asia, South-West Asia, North Africa, and the Middle East |
| CCA | Common Country Assessments |
| CGDK | Coalition Government of Democratic Kampuchea |
| CIREFCA | Conferencia Internacional sobre los Refugiados Centro-americanos (International Conference on Central American Refugees) |
| CIS | Commonwealth of Independent States |
| COMPAS | Centre on Migration, Policy and Society |
| CPA | Comprehensive Plan of Action |

| | |
|---|---|
| CPU | Convention Plus Unit |
| DAC | Development Assistance Committee |
| DANIDA | Danish International Development Assistance |
| DAR | development assistance in relation to refugees |
| DIIS | Danish Institute for International Studies |
| DLI | development through local integration |
| DPKO | UN Department of Peacekeeping Operations |
| EC | European Community |
| EEC | European Economic Community |
| EPAU | UNHCR Evaluation and Policy Analysis Unit |
| ExCom | UNHCR Executive Committee |
| FNLA | Frente Nacional de Libertação de Angola (National Liberation Front of Angola) |
| Forefem | First Regional Forum on Gender Focus in Working with Refugee, Returnee and Displaced Women |
| GCIM | Global Commission on International Migration |
| GFMD | Global Forum on Migration and Development |
| HST | hegemonic stability theorem |
| ICARA | International Conference(s) on Assistance to Refugees in Africa |
| ICRC | International Committee of the Red Cross |
| ICVA | International Council of Voluntary Associations |
| IDPs | internally displaced persons |
| IFRC | International Federation of the Red Cross |
| IGC | Intergovernmental Consultations on Migration, Asylum and Refugees |
| IOM | International Migration Organization |
| I-PRSPs | Interim Poverty Reduction Strategy Papers |
| IR | international relations |
| ISM | Irregular Secondary Movements [strand] |
| JSU | UNHCR Joint Support Unit |
| LPDR | Lao People's Democratic Republic |
| MAN | Migration-Asylum Nexus [project] |
| MDGs | Millennium Development Goals |
| MIAs | U.S. soldiers missing in action |
| MPLA | Movimento Popular de Libertação de Angola (Popular Movement for the Liberation of Angola) |
| NGOs | nongovernmental organizations |

| | |
|---|---|
| OAS | Organization of American States |
| OAU | Organization of African Unity |
| ODA | Overseas Development Administration |
| ODC | Overseas Development Council |
| ODP | orderly departure procedure |
| OECD | Organisation for Economic Cooperation and Development |
| OPEC | Organization of the Petroleum Exporting Countries |
| PEC | Special Programme of Economic Cooperation for Central America |
| PRK | People's Republic of Kampuchea |
| PRODERE | Programa para los Desplazados (Development Programme for Displaced Persons, Refugees and Returnees in Central America) |
| PRS | Poverty Reduction Strategy |
| PRSPs | Poverty Reduction Strategy Papers |
| QIPs | UNDP Quick Impact Projects |
| RAD | refugee and development [debate] |
| RBLAC | Regional Bureau for Latin America and the Caribbean |
| RSC | Refugee Studies Centre |
| RSD | refugee status determination |
| SFM | Swiss Forum on Migration |
| SPCP | Strengthening Protection Capacity Project |
| SRV | Socialist Republic of Vietnam |
| TDA | Targeting Development Assistance [strand] |
| UNDAF | UN Development Assistance Framework |
| UNDG | UN Development Group |
| UNDP | UN Development Programme |
| UNHCR | Office of the UN High Commissioner for Refugees |
| UNICEF | UN International Children's Emergency Fund |
| UNITA | União Nacional para a Independência Total de Angola (National Union for the Total Independence of Angola) |
| USAID | U.S. Agency for International Development |
| USCRI | U.S. Committee for Refugees and Immigrants |
| USSR | Union of Soviet Socialist Republics |
| WFP | UN World Food Programme |
| ZI | Zambia Initiative |

# PROTECTION BY PERSUASION

# INTRODUCTION

Refugees are people who cross international borders to flee conflict and persecution. Historically, refugees have been one of the most visible human consequences of significant conflicts and atrocities. From the Second World War to the proxy conflicts of the Cold War to contemporary conflicts in Iraq and Afghanistan, people have been forced to leave their countries of nationality. Similarly, large-scale human rights abuses and repressive dictatorships have forced refugees to flee in search of international support. Once they leave their country of origin, refugees are in need of international protection—that is, the willingness of other countries to ensure that they have access to a basic set of rights and that they are eventually able to return home or to be permanently integrated into another society or state.

Ensuring that refugees receive access to protection matters both for human rights and for international security. People whose own states are unable or unwilling to guarantee their rights need to have access to food, shelter, safety, and a set of legal entitlements. When the assumed relationship between citizen and state has broken down, protection ensures that another state can stand in as a substitute supplier of the rights normally guaranteed by the country of origin. It also ensures that people whose relationship with their own state has broken down can be reintegrated into the state system and so do not become a source of instability. By guaranteeing that all refugees have access to a state and a set of rights, protection reduces the likelihood that people will fall outside the state system and so become a potential source of threat.

Crucially, international cooperation is a necessary condition for protection. This is so because, whereas the benefits of protection—in terms of guaranteeing human rights and security—accrue to the entire international community, the costs are borne by whichever state opens its borders or chooses to financially contribute to protection. This means that individual states will generally be willing to contribute to refugee protection only insofar as there is a guarantee that other states will reciprocate in contributing to refugee protection. Otherwise, states will have a great incentive not to contribute and to, instead, free-ride on the provision of other states.

This makes it important to understand the conditions under which international cooperation takes place in the provision of refugee protection. Yet this issue has rarely been explored by scholars of international relations (IR). Exploring when and why states are prepared to contribute to refugee protection is important not only because of its significant human rights and security implications but also because it presents a distinct and interesting puzzle for IR.

As with many other policy fields—trade, climate change, and health—an international regime has emerged to facilitate sustained international cooperation. The main elements of the refugee regime are the 1951 Convention on the Status of Refugees and the Office of the United Nations High Commissioner for Refugees (UNHCR). The 1951 Convention provides a definition of who is a refugee and the rights to which refugees are entitled, whereas UNHCR is mandated to work toward ensuring protection and long-term solutions for refugees and has supervisory responsibility for ensuring that states meet their obligations under the 1951 Convention.

In spite of the existence of the regime, international cooperation on protection is not unproblematic. The regime sets out two core norms: asylum, which relates to the obligations of states to provide protection to refugees who are in their territory, and burden-sharing, which relates to the obligations of states to contribute to the protection of refugees who are in the territory of another state. Whereas the norm of asylum is well established and is based on a strong legal and normative framework, the norm of burden-sharing is subject to a very weak legal and normative framework. Given that the overwhelming majority of world refugees come from and remain in the global South, the disjuncture between these norms has significant consequences. It means that Southern states that neighbor on conflict-ridden or human rights–abusing countries have an obligation to provide asylum to people who arrive on their territory but that Northern states that remain outside of the refugees' region of origin have no obligation to contribute to the protection of refugees who remain in the South. Contributions to burden-sharing are discretionary and voluntary. The regime has, consequently, been characterized by what can be described as a North–South impasse, in which Northern states have had very little incentive to cooperate on burden-sharing and Southern states have had very little ability to influence the North. This impasse has had significant negative consequences for refugees' access to protection and durable solutions.

Faced with this impasse, UNHCR has convened a series of conferences to facilitate cooperation and to address long-standing or mass-influx refugee situations in the South. During the last thirty years, the main such initiatives have been the International Conferences on Assistance to Refugees in Africa (ICARA I and II) of 1981 and 1984, the International Conference on Central American Refugees of 1987–1995, the Comprehensive Plan of Action for Indochinese Refugees of 1988–1996, and the Convention Plus initiative of 2003–2005. In the absence of clear norms on burden-sharing, these conferences have been ad hoc bargaining processes and have had their own unique institutional design. In each case, UNHCR has been faced with the task of trying to persuade Northern states to voluntarily contribute to supporting refugee protection in the South even in the absence of any clear normative or legal obligation to contribute to burden-sharing.

Under certain, albeit rare, conditions, the impasse has been overcome and the conferences have led Northern states to voluntarily contribute to refugee protection in the South. But what is particularly interesting about the refugee regime is that the interests that have motivated those contributions have come from outside of the refugee regime. The contributions of Northern states to burden-sharing have not been based on altruism or a concern with refugee protection per se; rather, they have been based on a perception that refugee protection is related to their wider interests in other issue areas, notably immigration, security, and trade. When the perception of this relationship has been present, cooperation has taken place; when it has been absent, cooperation has been extremely limited.

Based on this observation, I argue in the book that a particular concept—cross-issue persuasion—is useful for explaining when cooperation has taken place. *Cross-issue persuasion* can be formally defined as the conditions under which an actor A can persuade an actor B that issue area X and issue area Y are linked as a means of inducing actor B to act in issue area X on the basis of its interest in issue area Y. In the case of the refugee regime, international cooperation has depended on Northern states' being persuaded that refugee protection in the South is linked to their wider interests in, for example, migration, security, and trade. It is the perception of these wider relationships that has provided incentives for Northern burden-sharing by expanding the perceived benefits that accrue to those states from contributing to protection in the South.

My analyses of the four initiatives convened by UNHCR to facilitate North–South burden-sharing highlights the conditions under which the UNHCR successfully used cross-issue persuasion to influence the behavior of states. First, there needed to be an underlying structural relationship between the issue areas. Second, UNHCR also had to assume the agency to either change these structural interconnections or to recognize and effectively communicate their existence to states. When these conditions were fulfilled, UNHCR was able to influence the beliefs of Northern states about the causal relationship between refugee protection in the South and their wider interests.

In addition to highlighting the conditions under which international cooperation has taken place in the refugee regime, cross-issue persuasion has more general implications for world politics. In this book, I build on the existing IR literature on issue linkage to highlight when and how substantive linkages among issue areas come to matter for the politics of a given issue area. I demonstrate how a given actor (in this case UNHCR) can create, change, or simply recognize and effectively communicate substantive linkages to persuade other actors to change their behavior.

This has significant practical and theoretical significance for world politics because it identifies the role of substantive linkages as a neglected resource of power. Using cross-issue persuasion does not rely on having significant economic or military resources. It simply relies on being able to influence the perception of the target actor about the causal relationship between issue areas. As the case studies presented here show, this does not require hard power, but may be achieved through, for example, the provision of information, playing an epistemic role, argumentation, or institutional design. In that sense, changing or articulating substantive linkages may represent a means through which weaker actors can influence the behavior of militarily or economically stronger actors.

## Refugee Protection

Under international refugee law, a *refugee* is defined as a person who, "owing to a well-founded fear of being persecuted for reasons of race, religion, nationality, or membership of a particular social group or political opinion, is outside of country of his nationality and is unable or, owing to such fear, is unwilling to avail himself of the protection of that country" (Goodwin-Gill and McAdam 2007, 573). Because of their well-founded fear of persecution and the fact that they have crossed an international border, refugees are often colloquially referred to a "human rights violations made visible" (Loescher 2001a, 185). During the twentieth and early twenty-first centuries, wherever there has been violent conflict, crimes against humanity, or other serious rights violations, people have needed to flee across international borders in search of international protection.

The number and distribution of refugees have varied with changing patterns of global conflict and with the emergence and collapse of repressive dictatorships. Significant numbers of refugees were displaced by the collapse of states in the aftermath of the First World War and as a result of the Holocaust in Europe during the Second World War. During the early Cold War, large numbers of refugees fled communist countries to seek asylum in Europe and North America. And, during the 1960s, many people in the developing world were displaced by the colonial liberation wars in Africa, so that by 1975 there were estimated to be around 2.4 million refugees in the world. With the Cold War proxy conflicts that took place in Africa, Latin America, and Southeast Asia, this number increased to 10.5 million by 1985 and to 14.9 million by the end of the Cold War. The new wars of the post–Cold War era, particularly in the former Yugoslavia and parts of sub-Saharan Africa, contributed to a dramatic upsurge in the number of refugees, which reached a peak of 18.2 million in 1993 (Benz and Hasenclever 2008; Loescher et al. 2008; UN High Commissioner for Refugees [UNHCR] 2008).

Gradually, with the resolution of the conflicts of the 1990s, the number of refugees began to drop, so that it was 9.9 million by 2006. But, with violence in Iraq, Afghanistan, and Sudan, this number again began to increase, reaching 11.4 million by 2007. These 11.4 million people mainly come from Afghanistan, Sudan, Burundi, the Democratic Republic of the Congo, Somalia, Vietnam, Palestine, Iraq, and Azerbaijan (UNHCR 2008). The overwhelming majority of these refugees are hosted in camps and settlements in the developing world. In addition, there are over 5 million Palestinian refugees in the Occupied Territories and the Middle East, many of whom are the descendants of those originally displaced in 1948 (Dumper 2008). It is also estimated that there are around 26 million internally displaced persons (IDPs) who are in a refugee-like situation but who have not crossed an international border (Phuong 2005; Weiss and Korn 2006).

Normally, within the nation-state system, sovereign states are assumed to have the primary responsibility for guaranteeing the human rights of their citizens. A key function of the state is to ensure that its citizens have access to a range of civil, political, economic, and social rights. In the case of refugees, the inability or unwillingness of the country of origin to guarantee these rights has compelled them to seek access to those rights in another state. In other words, they are in need of international protection.

*International protection* refers to two different sets of needs that refugees have: the right to asylum and a timely resolution of their predicament. Refugees have a right to asylum and to access to human rights while in exile. Both international refugee law and international human rights law set out the right of refugees not to be forcibly returned to a state in which they may face persecution (*nonrefoulement*) and the civil, political, economic and social rights that refugees should have while in exile (Goodwin-Gill and McAdam 2007, 421–61; Turk and Nicholson 2003). Second, an important element of protection is the access of refugees to a timely resolution (durable solution) to their predicament; that is, rather than refugees' remaining indefinitely in a state of limbo without citizenship or residency, they should be fully reintegrated into a state. This may be within their country of origin (repatriation), within the interim host state (local integration), or within another state (resettlement) (Chimni 1999; Hathaway 2005, 913–90; UNHCR 2006, 129–52).

Ensuring that refugees have access to protection matters for both human rights and international security. On the one hand, it ensures that people who are politically persecuted because of their beliefs or identity, or who face ethnic cleansing, genocide, or other crimes against humanity, are able to leave their countries and have somewhere else to go. It guarantees that people whose own governments—because of state collapse or civil conflict—are unable or unwilling to protect their citizens' rights can access those rights in another country. It serves as a corrective to a state system that fails to ensure that people have access to basic rights and freedoms.

On the other hand, the availability of protection also contributes to international stability. It ensures that people whose rights cannot be met by their own state are nevertheless reintegrated into a state within the international system. Without access to protection, those fleeing persecution would be stateless. Finding a collective means of addressing their plight avoids the possibility that such people may fall outside the state system and become a source of instability or a threat to state security. Ensuring refugees have access to rights and are reintegrated into a state and society reduces the likelihood that they will spread conflict or will be recruited by radical organizations or terrorist groups (Lischer 2005; Salehyan and Gleditsch 2006; Stedman and Tanner 2003).

The willingness of states to contribute to refugee protection cannot be taken for granted. It relies on states' being prepared to bear the costs of short-term hosting and long-term reintegration, without which protection would not be available. States can contribute to refugee protection in two principal ways: they may admit refugees into their territory and accord them rights (asylum), or they may contribute to supporting refugees who are not in their territory but who are on the territory of another state, either financially or by offering resettlement places for the refugees (burden-sharing). In either case, this requires that a state allocate scarce resources toward assisting noncitizens—this is a cost that many states are reluctant to bear.

One of the great political challenges to ensuring that protection is available is that, although the costs of refugee protection fall on each individual contributing state, its benefits—in terms of upholding human rights values and international security—are available to all states, whether they themselves contribute to protection or not. It has been argued that refugee protection is a global public good, the benefits of which, once provided, extend to all other states, irrespective of who bears the cost of provision. Rather like street lighting in domestic politics, the benefits of refugee protection are available to all states in international society, regardless of whether they make a contribution to providing the good. Because the benefits of refugee protection are collectively available to all states, whereas the costs fall on whichever states contribute, there are strong incentives for states not to contribute significantly to refugee protection but, rather, to shirk individual responsibility and free-ride on the contributions of other states. The consequence of the disjuncture between the collective nature of the benefits and the individual nature of costs means that, in the absence of international cooperation, refugee protection will be underprovided for relative to what states would have provided had they acted collectively (Betts 2003; Suhrke 1998; Thielemann 2003).

This means that refugees' access to protection depends on international cooperation. The contribution of each state is dependent on the guarantee that other states will also be prepared to contribute. Without coordination to ensure that all states provide asylum on a similar basis, and without collaboration to ensure that burden-sharing is available to compensate states that host a disproportionately high number of refugees, there will be a failure of collective action. In other words, even though there may be a collective incentive to ensure that refugees do have access to protection, when acting individually it will be rational for states to understate their preferences and free-ride on the contributions of other states.

That is why states created a global refugee regime in the aftermath of the Second World War. They recognized that a set of formal institutions was required to regulate the responses of states to refugees and to ensure that all states shared responsibility for providing refugee protection. By creating a common set of standards and an institutional framework to oversee their implementation, the aim was to ensure that states contributed equitably to refugee protection, which they recognized was in their collective interest. The regime that was created, however, was only half complete.

## The Global Refugee Regime

A *regime* is generally defined as implicit or explicit "principles, norms, rules, and decision-making procedures" around which the expectations of actors converge in a given area of IR (Krasner 1983, 2). Regimes regulate the behavior of states in specific issue areas. For example, there are international regimes governing trade, climate change, nuclear nonproliferation, heath, and security. They are created or emerge to facilitate international cooperation among states in the given issue area (Hasenclever, Mayer, and Rittberger 1997; Keohane 1982). They generally fulfill this role by, for example, establishing common standards of behavior and providing information and surveillance on the compliance of participating states.

In creating a refugee regime, states were not acting purely altruistically. Rather, they were creating a regime to meet their interests through collective action. The *Travaux Preparatoires* for the 1951 Convention on the Status of Refugees reveal that the negotiating states had a dual concern that guided their negotiation of the regime. First, they were concerned with international order. Ensuring that European refugees were afforded protection and promptly reintegrated within states was seen as a means of contributing to stability and security in Europe (Lauterpacht and Bethlehem 2003, 136). Second, they were concerned with justice. There was widespread acknowledgment of the significant and unprecedented human consequences of the Second World War, and establishing a refugee regime was seen as a way of promoting values of human rights within the context of the emerging United Nations system. A refugee regime, it was believed, would ensure that all states made a collective contribution to overcoming a common problem.

The centerpiece of the regime is the 1951 Convention on the Status of Refugees. It emerged in the immediate aftermath of the Second World War and was originally conceived as a means of coordinating the responses of states to refugees displaced in Europe by the war. It was not until 1967 that the Protocol to the Convention extended its geographical scope to the rest of the world. The 1951 Convention sets out the definition of who is a refugee and what rights people who meet that definition have vis-à-vis states. The 1951 Convention has subsequently been supplemented by various regional treaties, such as the 1969 Organization of African Unity (OAU) Convention in Africa, the 1984 Cartagena Declaration in Latin America, and the 2004 European Asylum Qualification Directive.

To oversee the implementation of the refugee regime, states created UNHCR, a specialized UN agency focusing on refugees. Although UNHCR began with only a temporary mandate and a very small staff, it has subsequently expanded to become a significant international organization with a large permanent bureaucracy. The 1950 Statute of the Office of the United Nations High Commissioner for Refugees set out the mandate of UNHCR. Its central role is to oversee the implementation of the 1951 Convention. Under Article 35 of the 1951 Convention, it is explicitly given supervisory responsibility for the implementation of the convention. Since the 1950s, the UNHCR mandate has had two core components: (1) to ensure refugees' access to their rights while in exile and (2) to ensure refugees' timely access to durable solutions (Loescher, Betts, and Milner 2008).

As the main international organization with responsibility for refugees, UNHCR has a very particular role in world politics. It works to ensure that refugees receive access to international protection; however, it is highly constrained in its ability to fulfill that role. It has very little material power to influence states and is dependent on a relatively small number of Northern donors to fund its activities. Nevertheless, UNHCR has sometimes been able to exert some degree of autonomous influence on how states respond to refugees. This autonomous influence has generally relied on persuasion based either on the moral authority derived from its statute and the 1951 Convention or on an appeal to and channeling of the interests of states into a commitment to refugee protection (Loescher 2001b; Loescher, Betts, and Milner 2008).

Over time, the work and mandate of UNHCR have evolved. Until 1967, with few exceptions, its work was mainly geographically confined to Europe, focusing on the protection and resettlement of those displaced by the Second World War. From the late 1960s, UNHCR played an increasing role in ensuring protection in the developing world in, first, the anticolonial liberation wars and, later, the proxy conflicts of the Cold War. It nevertheless had a relatively small field staff and fiercely guarded its character as a nonpolitical and exclusively humanitarian actor, focusing its work mainly on legal advice and on building protection capacity in accordance with its surveillance role as set out in the 1951 Convention.

By the 1980s, asylum was becoming increasingly political with the emergence of South-North asylum movements, and UNHCR was called on by donors to fulfill new tasks in the developing world, such as determining refugee status and running quasi-permanent refugee camps. In the 1990s under the leadership of High Commissioner Sadako Ogata, UNHCR underwent a massive expansion, reaching a budget of $1.3 billion by 1996 and a staff of over 5,000. It increasingly took on a role in providing humanitarian assistance to people fleeing the new wars in the former Yugoslavia and sub-Saharan Africa, focusing increasingly on its care and maintenance role, expanding its involvement in repatriation operations, and even engaging in the protection of IDPs (Barnett and Finnemore 2004; Loescher, Betts, and Milner 2008, 48–59).

By the early 2000s, UNHCR faced growing institutional competition. Whereas previously UNHCR had been the main international actor working on any aspect of human mobility, other international organizations (such as the International Migration Organization, IOM) and informal networks (such as the Intergovernmental Consultations on Migration, Asylum, and Refugees, IGC) emerged to address state issues such as asylum and irregular migration. Faced with institutional competition and the possibility of states' engaging in forum-shopping, UNHCR has needed to increasingly compete to make itself relevant to states, taking on a growing range of roles including IDP protection and even considering a role in the protection of some groups of irregular migrants (Betts 2009; Crisp 2008; Guterres 2008).

Many have argued that the gradual shift from being a mainly legal and nonpolitical actor between the 1950s and 1970s to a more politicized humanitarian actor since the 1980s has gradually compromised the moral authority of UNHCR (Goodwin-Gill 2000). Others suggest that the expansion of the work and mandate of the UNHCR has been necessary to ensure its ongoing relevance to states (Cohen 2006). Whichever position we take in this debate, it is clear that, over time, persuasion based on moral authority has become ever less viable and UNHCR has relied ever more on its ability to appeal to and meet the interests of powerful states to ensure a commitment to refugee protection (Loescher, Betts, and Milner 2008).

The principal norms within the refugee regime—asylum and burden-sharing—have contrasting legal bases. Asylum is a widely accepted and clearly defined norm. Once refugees reach the territory of a state, most states recognize that they have certain obligations toward them. The principle of *nonrefoulement* (that states cannot forcibly return a refugee to a state in which he or she might face a well-founded fear of persecution) has become so widely accepted that it is now argued to be part of international customary law (Lauterpacht and Bethlehem 2003). It is clearly defined in Article 33 of the 1951 Convention and supplemented by international human rights law. Furthermore, the range of civil, political, economic, and social rights that a state must accord to refugees on its territory are clearly set out in both the 1951 Convention and are complemented by international human rights law (Gorlick 2000; McAdam 2007).

In contrast, there is no clearly defined normative framework for burden-sharing. The principle of burden-sharing is by far the weakest aspect of the refugee regime. From a normative and legal perspective, there are few obligations on states to contribute to refugee protection beyond their territory. To the extent that norms exist in relation to global burden-sharing, they remain weak and underdeveloped. On a global level, only the preamble to the 1951 Convention and the Conclusion 85 (1998) of the UNHCR Executive Committee (ExCom) offer nonbinding guidance in relation to the need for a more equitable allocation of international responsibility for refugee protection (Milner 2009; Thielemann 2003). Consequently, burden-sharing is an entirely discretionary act subject to the voluntary contributions and interests of each state.

In the sense that the regime sets out a clear normative framework regulating asylum but not burden-sharing, it may be regarded as half complete. The regime establishes that states have obligations toward refugees who reach their territory but not toward those who remain in the territory of another state. This disjuncture between the normative scope of the principles of asylum and burden-sharing has had practical consequences for the distribution of responsibility for refugee protection. In particular, it has meant that, historically, Southern states, because of their greater proximity to refugees' countries of origin, have had responsibility for hosting and protecting the overwhelming majority of world refugees.

Generally, refugees come from conflict-ridden or human rights–abusing states, and such states are invariably located in the global South. Because refugees often lack the means to travel great distances in search of protection, they usually seek asylum in nearby neighboring states. These Southern host states have an obligation under the refugee regime to admit refugees to their territory and to ensure that they have access to protection. In contrast, states outside the region—particularly Northern states—have no clearly defined normative obligation to contribute to the protection of refugees who remain in the South. Rather, because the regime gives them obligations only toward refugees who reach their territory, it implicitly creates an incentive for Northern states to try to contain refugees within the refugees' region of origin so as to avoid incurring such an obligation. The absence of clear norms on burden-sharing thereby contributes to a situation in which the states with the least capacity to contribute to refugee protection have the greatest responsibility.

## The North–South Impasse

North–South relations are central to explaining the international politics of refugee protection (Chimni 1998; Castles 2004).[1] Whereas Southern states have historically hosted the overwhelming majority of world refugees, Northern states have few clearly defined obligations to contribute to the protection of refugees in the South. So, as noted, those states with the least capacity to host refugees have the greatest responsibility to do so. In addition, this has meant that the politics of protection has been characterized by a North–South impasse: Southern states have had de facto responsibility for refugee protection, but Northern states have had little obligation or incentive to share this responsibility. This impasse has had significant implications for refugees' access to protection and long-term solutions.

Southern states have hosted the overwhelming majority of world refugees. Refugees are more often than not from Southern states. Given their limited means and entitlement to travel long distances, the majority have sought asylum in neighboring countries within their region of origin. For example, the majority of Afghan refugees have been hosted in neighboring Iran and Pakistan, the majority of Burundian refugees have been hosted in neighboring Tanzania, and the majority of Liberian refugees have been hosted in neighboring Guinea. With relatively porous borders, limited capacity to deport, and a clearly defined legal obligation not to forcibly return refugees to their countries of origin if they face persecution, these neighboring states have had little choice other than to host refugees. Beyond

---

1. Clearly the world does not neatly divide into a North-South dichotomy, and there is enormous diversity among both Northern and Southern states. Nevertheless, the dichotomy does capture an important dynamic of the international system. In the refugee context, the *North* can be regarded as comprising the industrialized third-party asylum states, which are generally outside the refugees' regions of origin and exert a relative degree of border-control and extraterritorial influence. The *South,* on the whole, comprises the refugee-producing, transit or first-asylum host states within the refugees' regions of origin. For analyses and discussions of the North–South dichotomy, see Doty (1996); Duffield (2001); Fawcett and Sayigh (1999); Krasner (1985).

fulfilling their limited obligations to host refugees, however, these states are rarely willing or able to extend significant rights to the refugees they host or to work toward long-term solutions. Instead, under economic and political pressure to privilege their own citizens, they have invariably resorted to hosting refugees in confined camps and settlements in often insecure border regions (Crisp 2003b; Milner 2009).

Northern states, meanwhile, have had little obligation to contribute to protection or durable solutions for refugees who remain in the South. Although the refugee regime has the explicit assumption of burden-sharing, this is a vague and ill-defined obligation. The absence of a clear, binding obligation of burden-sharing means that, in practice, the contributions of Northern states to support refugee protection in the South are entirely discretionary and are allocated purely in accordance with the interests of contributing states. This means that the financial contributions of Northern states for protection in the South have been extremely limited compared to refugees' needs. Given that their only clear legal obligation has been territorial asylum, Northern states have, in fact, had a perverse incentive to allocate resources toward border control to prevent refugees and asylum seekers from reaching their territory instead of supporting protection in the South (Crisp 2003a).

This structural situation has had significant implications for the international politics of refugee protection. The majority of the contemporary multilateral debates on refugee protection polarize along North–South lines. Southern states consistently appeal for greater burden-sharing, whereas Northern states consistently earmark their limited contributions to the UNHCR annual budget or to resettlement quotas in accordance with their own priorities and interests. This dynamic is present in the UNHCR annual budget negotiations, the debates in its annual ExCom discussions, and its special programs. It has also been a dynamic that has undermined a range of attempts by UNHCR to facilitate international cooperation to overcome long-standing refugee situations in the South.

The North–South impasse has wider significance because of its human consequences. One of the clearest manifestations of the North–South impasse is the persistence of protracted refugee situations, in which refugees are often confined to enclosed camps and settlements for many years with limited access to their most basic rights; in a protracted refugee situation, refugees have remained in this intractable state of limbo for more than five years. In 2004, even excluding the large number of Palestinians in this situation, there were thirty-three protracted refugee situations involving around 5.5 million people, or 61 percent of world refugees. The main protracted refugee situations involve Afghans in Pakistan (960,000) and Iran (950,000), Burundians in Tanzania (440,000), Somalis in Kenya (154,000), and Burmese in Thailand (120,000). The average length of their stay in exile is seventeen years. Such situations emerge from the absence of refugees' access to durable solutions. Without the ability to return home or the opportunity to integrate locally or to be resettled abroad, refugees have to remain in exile indefinitely. These long-term refugee situations are the result of a failure of North–South cooperation; Southern states have justified long-term encampment on the grounds that they have received insufficient Northern support to enable them to countenance alternatives (Loescher and Milner 2005; Loescher, Betts, and Milner 2008).

The majority of refugees who do not have access to durable solutions spend many years remain confined in insecure refugee camps and settlements. Such long-term encampment has become the norm in the responses of states to refugee protection. In long-term encampment, refugees often have very poor-quality protection. They have limited access to freedom of movement, few educational or training opportunities, and no right to work. They are generally left dependent on international humanitarian assistance for their most basic care and maintenance. Furthermore, it has been well documented that many refugee camps are insecure and subject to violence, both because of their insecure location and because long-term encampment often leads refugees to develop negative coping strategies. The confined conditions in which refugees live for such long periods have led advocates to describe the phenomenon as *refugee warehousing*. It has been argued by the U.S. Committee for Refugees and Immigrants that this practice of long-term encampment represents "a denial of rights and a waste of humanity" (Smith 2004, 38).

It is partly because of this general impasse and its consequences that UNHCR has historically initiated a number of multilateral processes, based around international conferences. These ad hoc processes have attempted to address specific regional mass-influx or protracted refugee situations. Analyzing these processes is worthwhile because they offer useful insights into the conditions under which the North–South impasse can be and has been overcome.

## UNHCR's Conferences

Given the half-complete nature of the global refugee regime, UNHCR plays a very contrasting role in asylum as opposed to burden-sharing. In asylum, given the existence of a relatively strong legal framework, much of UNHCR work involves providing legal advice, implementation, and surveillance of the compliance of states with their 1951 Convention obligations. In burden-sharing, in contrast, given the absence of a clear normative framework guiding the contributions of states to burden-sharing, the UNHCR role is one of political facilitation. It must work to persuade states to voluntarily contribute, either financially or through resettlement quotas, to the protection of refugees who remain in other parts of the world.

Given that UNHCR has no permanent source of funding, it has historically appealed to donors to voluntarily contribute to refugee protection through the UNHCR annual budget or its ad hoc special appeals. The commitments of states to provide places for resettlement have been similarly short-term in nature, with states generally announcing their resettlement targets annually in the Tripartite Consultations on Resettlement. In both of these areas, the contributions of states have been entirely voluntary and at their own discretion. The short-term and unpredictable nature of these commitment to burden-sharing has placed UNHCR in an extremely precarious position. Without any binding obligation to contribute to burden-sharing, states have selected their priority areas and earmarked their contributions to UNHCR projects and programs in accordance with their own perceived interests.

UNHCR has therefore had to respond to new refugee emergencies, mass-influx situations, and long-standing refugee situations through ad hoc appeals that have focused on persuading states to cooperate in providing refugee protection. On a small scale, this has simply involved the UNHCR External Relations Department's compiling special appeals and sending them to interested donor and resettlement countries for consideration. In the case of large-scale and intractable refugee situations, UNHCR has occasionally convened special initiatives, using international conferences, as a means of facilitating international cooperation and burden-sharing. The ad hoc initiatives and conferences that UNHCR has convened provide a wealth of empirical material for understanding the international politics of refugee protection.

Such ad hoc initiatives have been the basis for UNHCR attempts to facilitate international cooperation to address long-standing refugee situations. The four main initiatives launched during the last thirty years are the International Conferences on Assistance to Refugees in Africa (ICARA I and II), which took place in Geneva in 1981 and 1984; the Conferencica Internacional sobre los Refugiados Centroamericanos (International Conference on Central American Refugees; CIREFCA), which was an initiative that was focused around a 1989 conference held in Guatemala City but which in practice ran between 1987 and 1995; the Comprehensive Plan of Action (CPA) for Indochinese Refugees, which was focused around a 1989 conference held in Geneva but which in practice ran between 1988 and 1996; and the Convention Plus initiative, which was a global initiative that was focused around five main conferences held in Geneva between 2003 and 2005.

ICARA I and II were African state–initiated conferences to seek compensation from Northern donor states for the infrastructural costs of having hosted large rural refugee populations throughout much of the 1970s. The ICARA process was based in two one-off Geneva-based pledging conferences convened in 1981 and 1984, at which the African states solicited financial contributions to support a range of development projects that would be jointly implemented by UNHCR and the United Nations Development Programme (UNDP). These projects were intended to simultaneously benefit local populations and to promote the self-sufficiency and local integration of refugees (Betts 2004; Gorman 1986, 1987, 1993).

The Indochinese CPA, agreed on in Geneva in 1989, was an initiative that was intended to address the long-standing exodus of the Indochinese boat people mainly leaving Vietnam and seeking asylum in Southeast Asian states and Hong Kong. It was conceived as a follow-up to a previous 1979 agreement in which Northern states beyond the region had committed to resettle all new arrivals from Indochina provided that the states in the region maintained the principle of first asylum. The 1989 CPA was a response to the breakdown of this previous agreement. It set out a three-way political agreement for international cooperation among the country of origin, the host states of first asylum in the region, and the third-party countries outside the region to end the exodus and clear the refugee camps and detention centers of the region (Jambor 1992; Robinson 1998, 2004; Towle 2006).

CIREFCA, agreed to at a Guatemala City conference in 1989, addressed the situation of refugees and other displaced people in the aftermath of Central American Cold War civil conflicts. CIREFCA was jointly implemented by UNHCR and UNDP and was considered to be part of the wider regional peace process and postconflict reconstruction process. Based on the financial commitment of mainly European states, it developed a series of integrated development projects that facilitated access to sustainable repatriation, local integration, and self-sufficiency for refugees (Betts 2008).

Finally, the UNHCR Convention Plus initiative was a Geneva-based initiative held between 2003 and 2005 that was intended to lead to the development of a normative framework for global burden-sharing. The development of the framework was conceived as a North–South dialogue. It divided the intergovernmental debates into three areas considered to be insufficiently addressed by the 1951 Convention: the strategic use of resettlement, the targeting of development assistance, and irregular secondary movements of refugees. The UNHCR intention was that the resulting framework would then be applied to address specific protracted refugee situations within a given regional context, beginning with pilot projects such as the CPA for Somali Refugees (Betts and Durieux 2007; Durieux and Kelley 2004).

All four initiatives had in common that they were attempts by UNHCR to facilitate North–South cooperation to overcome long-standing refugee situations in particular regions. In each case, UNHCR was attempting to persuade Northern states to commit to greater levels of burden-sharing, either through money or resettlement, to overcome specific protracted refugee situations in the South. All were led by UNHCR and were focused around UNHCR Headquarters in Geneva as the locus of North–South interaction. In the first three initiatives, the aim was to facilitate a Northern commitment to support refugee protection and access to durable solutions for refugees in a specific region: Africa, Central America, and Southeast Asia. In the final initiative, Convention Plus, the aim was to supplement the existing 1951 refugee convention by facilitating an interstate agreement on the creation of a normative framework for burden-sharing that could then be applied to specific protracted refugee situations in various regions.

The four initiatives are particularly interesting because they highlight the conditions under which UNHCR has been able to facilitate international cooperation and to overcome the North–South impasse. In terms of their ability to promote North–South cooperation, two of the initiatives can be regarded as successes and two as failures. The ICARA conferences and Convention Plus are widely recognized as failures; both polarized along North–South lines and failed to lead to significant additional burden-sharing. In contrast, CIREFCA and the Indochinese CPA, the initiatives that focused on Central America and on Southeast Asia at the end of the Cold War, overcame the North–South impasse and thereby helped to overcome two long-standing regional refugee situations. Unpacking the reasons for the differences in the relative success of the initiatives is extremely important both for understanding the international politics of refugee protection and for identifying the conditions under which international organizations such as UNHCR are able to facilitate North–South cooperation. In this book, I therefore examine these four main examples of UNHCR ad hoc initiatives to facilitate North–South cooperation, exploring the conditions under which they have achieved success or failure in overcoming the North–South impasse.

The global refugee regime has been characterized by a North–South impasse. This has been a significant political obstacle to ensuring refugees' access to effective international protection. Overcoming the impasse has, therefore, been a major challenge for UNHCR as the organization responsible for facilitating international cooperation in relation to refugee protection. Under certain rare conditions, the North–South impasse in the global refugee regime has been overcome—despite the absence of a binding normative obligation on states to contribute to the protection of refugees beyond their own territory, Northern states have sometimes been persuaded to voluntarily contribute to supporting the protection of refugees in the South.

The reason for the contributions of these Northern states was not the altruistic concern with the welfare of refugees per se; rather, their voluntary contributions to refugee protection were motivated by their own interests. Crucially, however, these interests were not derived from within the global refugee regime; the most relevant politics for refugee protection came from outside of the refugee regime. The contributions of Northern states to refugee protection were motivated by a perceived relationship between their contributions to refugee protection and their wider interests in other issue areas such as security, migration, trade, foreign policy, development, and peace-building.

When states had wider interests in other issue areas and perceived them to be connected to refugee protection, they were sometimes persuaded to contribute to refugee protection beyond their territory. When these wider interests were absent or only tenuously connected to the refugee issue, states rarely had a clear incentive to voluntarily contribute to supporting refugee protection. For example, in the two successful case studies explored in the book, Northern states were prepared to contribute to the protection of Central American and Indochinese refugees not because of an altruistic concern with the welfare of those refugees per se but because they were persuaded that the refugee protection issue was inextricably intertwined with their wider interests in areas such as security, migration, and trade. The Southern states in these regions were similarly persuaded to cooperate on the basis of their wider interests. In the case studies of the ICARA and Convention Plus initiatives, the participating states were not successfully persuaded that the issue of refugee protection was connected to their wider interests.

In other words, the way in which refugee protection has been packaged in relation to other issue areas in interstate bargaining determined how states perceived and, therefore, responded to refugee situations. When UNHCR was able to appeal to a wider set of interests and make these either an explicit or implicit part of the multilateral negotiations, it was able to persuade states to voluntarily contribute to refugee protection on the basis of their own perceived interests. Northern states were willing to contribute to supporting protection in the South insofar as UNHCR connected it to their wider interests in the negotiation process. So, in the two successful case studies, the contributing states were motivated by their interest in wider issue areas; in the two failed case studies, refugee protection was either addressed in isolation or its proposed linkages to other issue areas were not perceived as credible.

To explain when and how the politics of other issue areas influenced the willingness of states to contribute to refugee protection, I develop a new concept—*cross-issue persuasion*. This concept builds on the existing IR literature on issue linkage (Aggarwal 1998; Haas 1980/1994, 1990; Keohane 1982; Martin 1993; McGinnis 1986; Stein 1980; Young 1996). *Issue linkage* is the way in which issues come to be combined during interstate negotiations. It has been identified as a means of facilitating international cooperation by including enough issues in the negotiations that all the actors can derive payoffs from cooperation. Issue linkage has been identified as especially important for North–South relations because it may provide an incentive for Northern states, for example, to cooperate on an issue on which they would otherwise have little interest (Bhagwati 1984; Ravenhill 1990). By linking issues in which Northern states have an interest to those in which they have little interest, an organization such as UNHCR may induce them to cooperate on the latter. Linkage changes the payoffs that actors derive from cooperation, making cooperative outcomes more likely.

The issue-linkages literature generally focuses on instrumental interstate bargaining and examines the mechanisms by which different issues come to be packaged in negotiations. It broadly offers two types of linkage: tactical linkages and substantive linkages (Aggarwal 1998; Haas 1980/1994, 1990). The first refers to a situation in which two issues that may be entirely unrelated are combined simply on the basis of horse-trading and conditionality. The second refers to a situation in which two issues are combined on the basis of having a substantive relationship to one another, either material, ideational, or institutional. It relates to the causal relationship between action in one area and consequences in another area.

The literature on substantive linkage remains particularly underdeveloped. There are many substantive linkages between different issues and issue areas. Some of these go ignored or unperceived and have little impact on politics; others—such as the relationship between migration and development or between the environment and development (i.e., sustainable development)—become extremely influential in world politics. The question of how these substantive relationships between issues and issue areas come to matter for the politics of a particular policy field remains underexplored. Cross-issue persuasion allows an examination of this question. It helps to shed light on the conditions under which an actor—in this case, an international organization—can create, change, or simply recognize and effectively communicate substantive linkages between issue areas as a means of influencing the behavior of another actor.

In this book, I identify the conditions under which cross-issue persuasion has been successfully used to promote North–South cooperation. I argue that the ability of UNHCR to successfully persuade states that refugee protection is linked to other issue areas in which the states have wider interests is dependent on two crucial factors: structural conditions and agency conditions. That is, for UNHCR to successfully appeal to the interests of a state in another issue area, first, the proper *structural conditions* must be in place; in other words, there has to be a structural relationship between refugee protection, on the one hand, and the other issue areas, on the other. An actor cannot simply induce action by a state in one issue area by appealing to its interests in another issue area. For the linkage to be effective, there must be a structural relationship between the two issue areas; they must be connected by ideational, institutional, or material[2] structures. Second, there must be the appropriate *agency conditions;* that is, just having the proper structural conditions is not enough—UNHCR also has to play an active role. Often the structural relationships are ambiguous or go unrecognized; UNHCR must either recognize and effectively communicate the existence of these structural relationships to the participating states or effect a change in these relationships. UNHCR has been able to alter, draw on, and communicate these substantive linkages through, for example, its epistemic role, its institutional design, argumentation, or the provision of information.[3]

In addition to shedding light on the international politics of refugee protection, I suggest in this book that the study of the refugee regime has wider implications for understanding world politics. It highlights the important role that cross-issue persuasion can play, not only in facilitating North–South cooperation but also as a source of power for a range of weaker actors in world politics, including international organizations, Southern states, and nongovernmental organizations (NGOs). The book therefore serves as an in-depth case study of the role of cross-issue persuasion in world politics. It offers an exploration of the conditions (in terms of structures and agency) under which international organizations (and other actors) can appeal to the interests of states in wider issue areas as a means of influencing their behavior.

---

2. This book does not explore material interconnections in detail for two reasons. First, it is methodologically almost impossible to ascertain the real empirical relationship between two issue areas at a given time in the past; second, material structures are mediated through perception and how relationships between issue areas are perceived is far more significant for explaining state behavior. Nevertheless, material interconnections are clearly an important aspect of how two issue areas are connected.

3. The claim that cross-issue persuasion has mattered for the politics of protection is falsifiable; it can be tested through our being able to reject two null hypotheses: (1) that altruism was the basis of contributions and (2) that UNHCR was irrelevant to the interstate bargaining process.

# 1

# The International Politics of Refugee Protection

The causes and consequences of human displacement are highly political, and refugee issues are by definition international in scope. People who flee persecution by crossing international borders generally do so because of political causes such as conflict or internal repression. The influx of refugees into a state has implications for security and the distribution of resources within that state. Furthermore, refugees' access to protection while in exile and long-term solutions to their plight are a consequence of political decisions and nondecisions.

Nevertheless, despite the inherently political and international nature of refugee protection, there has been surprisingly little attempt by academics working on refugee-related issues to draw on IR theory to understand the international politics of refugee protection. Nor has there been much attempt by IR to bring issues of refugee protection into the discipline and to explore what they can offer for the reconsideration of IR theory. In contrast to the work that has been done in issue areas such as the environment, human rights, and trade, refugee protection has largely been invisible within mainstream IR.

Only isolated pockets of scholarship have emerged, drawing selectively on insights from different areas of IR. There have been some theoretical attempts to examine refugee issues from a state security or human security perspective (Milner 2000; Newman and Van Selm 2003; Weiner 1996), the international political economy of the refugee regime (Castles 2004), the relationship between conflict and displacement (Lischer 2005; Salehyan and Gleditsch 2006; Stedman and Tanner 2003), the role of UNHCR (Barnett and Finnemore 2004; Loescher 2001b; Loescher, Betts, and Milner 2008), and the position of refugees in relation to the state system (Haddad 2008). Yet much of the work on the politics of refugee protection has come from lawyers or sociologists rather than political scientists. Generally, the most acclaimed work on the IR of refugee protection has been historical and descriptive rather than drawing on the conceptual tools provided by IR (Gordenker 1987; Loescher and Monahan 1996; Skran 1995; Zolberg, Suhrke, and Aguayo 1989). Few mainstream IR scholars have devoted time to considering the international politics of refugee protection,[1] and in forced-migration studies, the majority of the work has been from the perspective of the displaced and draws mainly on disciplines such as anthropology, geography, and sociology.

Yet exploring the international politics of refugee protection is extremely important both for theory and practice. From a theoretical perspective, analyzing an unexplored area of world politics has great potential for challenging and developing the core concepts of IR. Refugee protection is an issue that potentially offers insights for a range of key themes in IR, such as international cooperation, the role of international organizations, globalization, security, and conflict. From a practical perspective, anyone who wishes to understand or influence the behavior of states toward refugees must first understand the conditions under which states are and are not willing to contribute to refugee protection. Although many people who work with refugees and forced migrants might argue for the need to take a grassroots perspective and understand the experiences of the displaced, analyzing forced migration at the level of the state and interstate

---

1. Notable exceptions include Michael Barnett, James Fearon, Jack Snyder, Steve Stedman, and Thomas Weiss.

politics is at least as important for anyone who wishes to understand the reasons why refugees do or do not receive access to international protection (Landau 2007).

## Refugee Protection as a Global Public Good

In the little academic work that exists on international cooperation in the refugee regime, it has been suggested that refugee protection is a global public good (Suhrke 1998). A *public good* is a good that has the properties of nonexcludability and nonrivalry. In other words, once provided, the benefits conferred by the good (1) cannot be excluded from all the other members of the community and (2) do not diminish or become scarce when enjoyed by another actor. In domestic politics, a classic example of a public good is street lighting. Because of their characteristics, public goods such as street lights present a particular challenge to ensuring that they are adequately provided. Although all members of a community would want street lights and might be prepared to pay their share, no one individual would be prepared to provide the street lights alone knowing that everyone else would benefit without paying. When public goods such as street lights are not provided by a central authority, they are likely to be underprovided relative to the community members' collective interest because, individually, people have a strong incentive to free-ride on other people's contributions. In domestic politics, the collective action failure that results from public goods is generally addressed by the state; governments pool the resources of citizens and ensure that public goods are provided.

At the global level, in the absence of a world government, the provision of global public goods presents a greater challenge. As with domestic public goods, such as street lights, global public goods are characterized by nonexcludability and nonrivalry. And, as with the citizens in our domestic public goods example, states may value the provision of a good and, acting collectively, would choose to provide the goods but not be prepared to provide it unilaterally if they believe that their contribution is not tied to the contributions of other states and that they can simply free-ride on the contributions of other states. Consequently, the overall level of provision will be suboptimal relative to how states would have acted had their actions been coordinated. This disjuncture between how states act collectively and how they act independently is referred to as collective action failure. It is commonly illustrated using the game theoretical analogy of the Prisoner's Dilemma, which highlights the divergence between how actors behave when they coordinate their behavior and how they behave when they make decisions individually (Olson 1965).

In world politics, a number of issues that are global in scope (that is, that affect all states) have been identified as global public goods. The provision of goods such as climate-change mitigation, the eradication of communicable disease, the international monetary system, global security, nuclear nonproliferation, and asteroid risk mitigation have all been analyzed from the perspective of global public goods. These issues have in common that, because their benefits are available to all states, irrespective of which states provide the goods, states have a tendency to free-ride on the contributions of other states rather than contributing to the cost of provision themselves. The challenge for policymakers has therefore been how to devise institutions at the global level that ensure that collective action failure is overcome and that these goods are provided (Barratt 2008; Boyer 1993; Kaul, Grunberg, and Stern 1999).

In general, the international politics of refugee protection has not been integrated into the mainstream study of global public goods. One of the very few exceptions to this general absence of conceptual work on the international politics of refugee protection is the path-breaking work of Astri Suhrke, who has argued that the provision of refugee protection may be considered a global public good. Because refugee protection is collectively valued by states but the benefits it provides are available to all states, irrespective of who provides, Suhrke suggests that states tend to free-ride on the provision of other states. As she explains, this means that, because the costs of providing protection are borne by individual states but the benefits accrue to all states even if they do not contribute, the refugee regime is likely to be characterized by collective action failure (Suhrke 1998).

Indeed, the availability of refugee protection can be thought of as providing two nonexcludable benefits to states: order and justice. Both of these benefits were explicitly recognized as the reason that it was important to create a global refugee regime at the time of the negotiation of the 1951 Refugee Convention. Refugee protection contributes to international order;[2] it ensures that individuals whose rights are not provided by their own nation-state can be reintegrated into the nation-state system. From the perspective of states, the availability of refugee protection is therefore of value because it prevents people who cross boundaries to flee conflicts and human rights abuses from becoming stateless. This reduces the likelihood that they, in turn, become a source of conflict or insecurity. The absence of effective refugee protection has been associated with the recruitment of refugees by guerrilla movements and terrorist organizations, for example (Juma and Kagwanja 2008; Lischer 2005; Morris and Stedman 2008; Zolberg, Suhrke, and Aguayo 1989). Refugee protection also contributes to international justice;[3] it ensures that, even when states cannot or will not ensure the human rights of their citizens, these values are nevertheless upheld through their being accorded to refugees by another state. Because both these benefits are available to other states, even if they do not actually contribute to refugee protection themselves, international order and justice may be thought of as the public benefits that come from the provision of refugee protection.

In practice it is unlikely that these nonexcludable benefits will accrue equally to all members of the international community. Some states— especially those with greater proximity to a given refugee outflow—will benefit more greatly from a neighboring state's contribution to refugee protection than would a more distant or disinterested state. In other words, the benefits of refugee protection are more likely to be a regional public good than a global public good. Nevertheless, the public goods concept is valuable insofar as it highlights that the partly nonexcludable nature of many of the benefits of protection may lead to free-riding.

## The Refugee Regime as a Prisoner's Dilemma

The public-goods nature of the benefits of international order and justice means that these benefits are available to states even if they free-ride on the contribution of other states. For this reason, Suhrke claims that, in

---

2. For an analysis of international order, see, for example, Hurrell (2007); Bull (1977).

3. For an analysis of international justice and its relationship to international order, see, for example, Bull (1977); Dunne and Wheeler (1999); Reus-Smit (2001).

the absence of a binding institutional framework at the global level, refugee protection will be characterized by collective action failure. She illustrates this using the game theoretical analogy of the Prisoner's Dilemma, in which, in a two-actor model, each of two states may prefer mutual cooperation (CC) to mutual defection (DD) yet one state may be even better off when it can benefit from the unrequited cooperation of the other actor (DC). However, being the state that behaves cooperatively without a reciprocal response (CD) is the least desirable outcome. Consequently, the preference ordering of states is DC > CC > DD > CD. In a single interaction, each state will find it rational not to cooperate, and it will receive a higher payoff through defection. Consequently, even though both states have a common interest in achieving the CC outcome, acting individually, they will end up at the suboptimal DD outcome (Hasenclever, Mayer, and Rittberger 1997; see figure 1).

The Prisoner's Dilemma therefore leads to a situation in which actors are worse off when they pursue their individually rational, self-interested strategy than they would be if they cooperated. The dilemma is derived from the analogy of two prisoners who have been arrested and accused of a crime but are detained and interrogated separately from one another. Their collectively optimal strategy is for both to confess (CC) and receive short prison sentences. But their individually optimal strategy is for each to deny his or her guilt and let the other one confess (CD or DC), in which case the denier walks free and the confessor receives a long sentence. This strategy leads both of them to deny guilt, and so they both end up with moderate prison sentences and therefore in a worse situation (DD) than they would have been in had they both confessed. Examples for which this analogy applies at the international level include the mitigation of climate change, attempts by the Organization of Oil Exporting Countries (OPEC) to maintain a quota on oil production, and attempts to negotiate disarmament treaties. In these cases, the incentives of the individual states to free-ride or cheat when acting in isolation will diverge from what would be collectively optimal for the group.

One of the key challenges for IR has therefore been to identify the conditions under which the Prisoner's Dilemma can be overcome and global public goods can be provided through international cooperation. Regime theory, in particular, has attempted to identify the conditions under which international institutions may play this role. Various theoretical schools of

|  |  | Actor B | |
|---|---|---|---|
|  |  | C | D |
| Actor A | C | 3, 3 | 1, 4 |
|  | D | 4, 1 | 2, 2* |

**Figure 1.** Prisoner's Dilemma. Number left (right) of comma refers to A's (B's) preference ordering (1 = worst outcome; 4 = best outcome). * indicates the equilibrium.

IR have identified different ways in which the Prisoner's Dilemma (collective action failure) may be overcome in relation to the provision of global public goods; mainstream IR has identified two: international institutions and hegemony.

International institutions have been identified as the principal means through which collective action failure can be overcome. This is because they may enable states to take a longer-term perspective of their interests and thereby change their incentives to cooperate. The IR literature identifies three principal ways in which they can do this. First, institutions may create repeated interactions between states over time; so, instead of cooperation's being based on a one-shot interaction, as the Prisoner's Dilemma implies, institutions ensure that interaction is repeated over time (iterated). This reduces the incentives for a state to free-ride or defect because then it will forfeit potential longer-term gains. Second, institutions can provide information through surveillance that identifies free-riding states, thereby reducing the incentives to cheat. Third, institutions may play a role in reducing the transactions costs of cooperation. By institutionalizing the coordination of activities of states, cooperation becomes cheaper, and so the practical obstacles to cooperation are reduced (Axelrod 1984; Keohane 1982, 1984).

Hegemony has been suggested as a second means through which collective action failure can be overcome. According to hegemonic stability theorem (HST), the provision of a global public good depends on one state's being powerful enough and willing to either provide the good unilaterally or coerce others into doing so (Gilpin 2001, 93–100; Keohane and Nye 1989, 44; Kindleberger 1973). Andreas Hasenclever, Peter Mayer, and Volker Rittberger (1997, 88–90) describe two circumstances in which a hegemon will provide an international public good when, otherwise, there would be collective action failure: the benevolent leadership model and the coercive leadership model. The first draws on the notion of the "exploitation of the big by the small" (Olson 1965, 29). That is, if the dominant power places a higher absolute valuation on the public good than the smaller powers do, it will provide that nonexcludable good irrespective of free-riding. In other words, its valuation of the public good will be so high that it will be prepared to bear a disproportionately high cost for its provision (Olson and Zeckhauser 1966). The coercive leadership model suggests that the hegemon will coercively induce the provision of the public good by others and so ensure its provision (Calleo 1987, 104).

In Suhrke's account of the international politics of refugee protection, she is extremely skeptical about the prospects for overcoming collective action failure. For Suhrke, the absence of binding institutions relating to burden-sharing and the nonbinding nature of the global refugee regime make the prospects for overcoming collective action failure very limited. She argues that the only way in which a Prisoner's Dilemma has historically been overcome and significant international cooperation has taken place in the refugee regime has been when a hegemon provided refugee protection. She suggests that the two examples of successful multilateral cooperation—refugee resettlement in Europe after the Second World War and the re-settlement of Vietnamese refugees after 1975—had their own underlying and, implicitly, realist logic—both depended on hegemonic power. In the first case, participating states shared a sense of values and obligation to-ward the victims of the war, creating an "instrumental-communitarian" interest in resettlement (Suhrke 1998, 413). Although not explicitly stated as such, this argument can be incorporated within the notion of benevolent leadership model. The United States, for example, unilaterally established the International Refugee Organization and resettled over 30 percent of the refugees; Australia and Israel were also major contributors. This high level of commitment, Suhrke argues, stemmed from the sufficiently high valuation by states of the need to provide protection that they were pre-pared to provide resettlement outside of an institutional framework, irre-spective of the nonexcludability of the benefits. In the second case, Suhrke explicitly makes the case that coercive hegemony was required, with states' needing "to be persuaded or pressured by the hegemon," which was again the United States (1998, 413). Her argument, then, essentially reduces to the hypothesis that multilateral cooperation is possible only when either a benevolent or coercive hegemon is present (1998, 413).

Suhrke's work sheds light on certain aspects of the international politics of refugee protection. Indeed, there are nonexcludable benefits that come from the provision of refugee protection and that encourage free-riding and burden-shirking, and hegemony has at times partly explained instances of burden-sharing. But her work provides an incomplete account of the international politics of protection. In particular, it has two main weaknesses: (1) it misrepresents the source of collective action failure in the global refugee regime, and (2) it underestimates the prospects for international cooperation. Let us explore these in turn.

First, Suhrke's assumption that the refugee regime can be characterized by the Prisoner's Dilemma does not fully account for the sources of collective action failure in the refugee regime. The Prisoner's Dilemma assumes that actors have symmetrical interests and power. In the refugee regime, this assumption may apply within regions, such as within the European Union, but it certainly does not apply on a global scale. In reality, Southern states are in a far weaker position than Northern states. A better game theoretical analogy for characterizing the refugee regime is the Suasion Game; this more adequately captures the cooperation problem that arises when one of the key obstacles to international cooperation stems from the power asymmetry between the actors (Hasenclever, Mayer, and Rittberger 1997, 50; Martin 1993). Indeed, no account of the international politics of refugee protection can be complete without an analysis of the central role of North–South relations.

Second, Suhrke's work underestimates the prospects for international cooperation because it looks at the issue of refugee protection in isolation from other issue areas of world politics. The most relevant politics for refugee protection do not take place within the refugee regime but in other issue areas. Historically, Northern states have voluntarily contributed to refugee protection in the South. For example, each year donor states do make voluntary, usually earmarked, contributions to the work of UNHCR. Similarly, there have been examples of successful international cooperation. Voluntary contributions for the provision of the global public good of refugee protection are motivated by private interests in linked issue areas. When the contributions of states to refugee protection have been linked to their interests in another issue area (e.g., migration, security, trade, development, or peacebuilding), they have been prepared to contribute. It is therefore important to account for the role of the politics of other issue areas when explaining the politics of refugee protection. Linking refugee protection to the interests of Northern states in other issue areas has been a crucial element in overcoming the Suasion Game and overcoming the North–South impasse.

## The Refugee Regime as a Suasion Game

Although the Prisoner's Dilemma is the most common analogy used to describe sources of collective action failure, it is not the only one. Regime theory has identified alternative situation structures that describe a range of cooperation problems. As already mentioned, the problem with the Prisoner's Dilemma is that it assumes that the two actors in the model have symmetrical interests and power relations. In the case of the global refugee regime, this is clearly not the case. As I explain in the introduction to this book, a crucial aspect of understanding the international politics of refugee protection is North–South relations. Southern states are more likely to be close to conflict-ridden and human rights–abusing states, are more likely to have porous borders, and generally have less bargaining power in the international system. In contrast, Northern states are more likely to be further away from refugees' countries of origin, are able to control their borders to a greater extent, and are in a comparatively stronger position in international negotiations. These contrasting structural positions mean that North–South relations in the refugee regime cannot be characterized by the Prisoner's Dilemma.

The Suasion Game is one of the other situation structures (beyond Prisoner's Dilemma) that better capture the dynamics of North–South relations. In this game, in a two-actor model, one player is privileged and must be persuaded to participate and the other has little choice but to cooperate (Hasenclever, Mayer, and Rittberger 1997, 50; Martin 1993). In other words, the stronger actor has little to gain and the weaker actor little to lose, undermining the prospects for cooperation.

Because of their difference in relative power, the two actors have different interests. Formally, the situation can be represented in game theory in one of two ways. *Either* one (weaker) actor, A, has a dominant strategy to cooperate that the other (stronger) one, B, can exploit, *or* one (stronger) actor, B, has a dominant strategy to defect, and the other (weaker) actor, A, must cooperate to avoid an even worse outcome.

In either case, the weaker actor's preferred strategy is to cooperate—either because noncooperation is not practically viable or because it would lead to even greater costs. The stronger actor, however, is in a position to choose to defect and that is likely to be its preferred position. An instance of unrequited cooperation (CD) is consequently the only stable outcome of the game. Suasion Games have only a single equilibrium outcome, which satisfies only one actor and leaves the other aggrieved—the stronger actor B will always exploit the weaker actor A (see figure 2).

The weaker actor A's only alternative strategy is to move to the noncooperative position (DD), which leaves it worse off in a single-shot game. The only scenario in which this might be beneficial is if, in a repeated game, short-term noncooperation enhances actor A's bargaining power and so induces actor B to shift to box CC in the long run. But this is unlikely because it involves extremely high short-term costs for actor A.

As John Conybeare's (1984) analysis of the global trade regime illustrates, this problem is particularly likely to occur in the context of North–South relations. He uses the example of the prospects for a weak state using a retaliatory tariff against a strong state. This, he suggests, will only make the small state worse off, highlighting the extent to which a weaker actor or group of actors might be forced to either accept only very small gains or scupper the prospects for cooperation entirely. Given that the majority of world refugees are in the South, we can immediately see how the Suasion Game analogy fits the refugee regime; Southern states are frequently faced with either accepting whatever is on offer or harming themselves by rejecting a relatively small contribution from the North.

As with all game theoretical representations, the Suasion Game merely provides an analogy to a real-world situation. It should not be taken too literally. Nevertheless, it is useful because it highlights the inadequacies of the dominant conception of the cooperation problem in the global refugee regime known as Prisoner's Dilemma. Furthermore, it is an analogy that highlights the centrality of North–South relations in explaining the under-provisioning of refugee protection.

Moving beyond the game theoretical analogy of the Suasion Game, however, the source of collective action failure in the refugee regime might more generally be described as a North–South impasse. A *North–South impasse* may be defined as a situation in which a problem primarily originates in and remains relatively confined to the South while the economic and

| | | Actor B | |
|---|---|---|---|
| | | C | D |
| Actor A | C | 4, 3 | 3, 4* |
| | D | 2, 2 | 1, 1 |

**Figure 2.** Suasion Game. Number left (right) of comma refers to A's (B's) preference ordering (1 = worst outcome; 4 = best outcome). * indicates the equilibrium.

political means to address the problem are largely held by the North. Consequently, in the absence of Northern states' either having a binding legal or normative framework impelling cooperation or having a perceived interest in addressing the problem for its own sake, Southern states will have little bargaining power to induce Northern contributions. Southern states will then either have to take whatever is on offer from Northern states or risk harming themselves more by scuppering negotiations entirely. Such situations are particularly important for understanding certain areas of global governance in which collective action failure arises on a global scale because of this combination of the problem's being mainly located in and confined to the South, on the one hand, and the differential power capabilities of North versus South, on the other.

Many of these structural features apply in the case of the refugee regime. First, the proximity of Southern states to areas of conflict and human rights–abusing regimes means that that majority of world refugees come from and are in the South. Second, institutionally, there is an absence of a binding legal or normative framework relating to burden-sharing. Third, Northern states have a very low interest in contributing to refugee protection in the South for its own sake. And fourth, the bargaining power of Southern states within the regime is limited to threats that have been ineffective. Let us consider each in turn.

That Southern states generally have a greater proximity to areas of conflict and to human rights–abusing regimes means that the overwhelming majority of world refugees originate from and remain in Southern states. UNHCR estimates that in 2001 some 72 percent of world refugees were in the South (UNHCR 2002b). The majority of refugees are not permanently resettled in Northern states, nor do they move on to Northern states in what are called secondary movements. Rather, they remain in camps or settlements run by humanitarian organizations and NGOs until repatriation to their countries of origin becomes a viable option.

In addition, there is no entrenched normative or legal framework for burden-sharing in the global refugee regime. The half-complete nature of the regime means that Northern states incur binding obligations toward refugees only after they reach Northern territory. This difference in the relative importance of asylum and burden-sharing creates a perverse incentive for Northern states to allocate far more resources to refugee exclusion and deterrence policies than they do to supporting refugee protection in regions of origin. Furthermore, it means that the commitments Northern states to burden-sharing are discretionary acts, subject to their own priorities and political interests. Structurally, the obligations of states to refugees are therefore allocated in accordance with the principle of proximity: that is, how close a state is to a refugee's country of origin determines its legal and normative responsibility toward that refugee. Given that the overwhelming majority of world refugees originate from and remain in the South, this places a disproportionate responsibility on Southern states.

Also, Northern states have a very low interest in contributing to refugee protection in the South for its own sake. An analysis of the history of the political and economic contributions of Northern states to UNHCR programs highlights that, rather than being based on an altruistic concern with protection and refugee welfare, these states have supported protection only very selectively and only insofar as it has been related to other issue areas of more interest to them (Loescher 1986). The degree of selectivity and the absence of a concern with refugee welfare for its own sake is revealed by the consistently low financial commitment of states to supporting refugee protection beyond their own territory[4] and the prevalence of the use of earmarking in nearly all the contributions of donor states to the UNHCR annual budget. Statistical correlation reveals that earmarked contributions by donor states in support of protection in the South are directly related to

---

4. One indicator for this is the consistently low UNHCR annual budget, which has rarely exceeded US$1 billion. The UNHCR annual budget has varied over time; in the 1990s, for example, the funding received from donor states was high relative to any other time in UNHCR history. Nevertheless, the budget has rarely been sufficient to meet all the priorities identified by UNHCR. For an analysis of how the budget has changed over time, see Loescher (2001b).

the extent to which a given refugee problem has been perceived to have a potential spillover effect that impacts the interests of the donor Northern states (Betts 2003).

Finally, the bargaining power of Southern states within the refugee regime itself is extremely limited. The only form of implicit threat that they have available to them is to fail to meet refugees' rights in accordance with international law or to threaten to violate the principle of asylum. Yet neither of these implicit threats has been constructive in inducing a sustained Northern commitment to burden-sharing. The occasional abandonment by Southern states of the principle of first asylum when Northern states have failed to provide an adequate commitment to financial support or resettlement (i.e., moving from position CD to DD in the Suasion Game; see figure 2) has done little to change Northern behavior.[5] Hong Kong, Malaysia, Pakistan, and Tanzania, for example, are prominent examples of countries where this threat has been carried out over the last twenty-five years.[6] Yet this has rarely moved Northern states to commit to greater support for protection in the South.[7]

The refugee regime can therefore be characterized as a North–South impasse situation. The majority of refugees come from Southern states and remain in and are hosted by Southern states. In the absence of a clear binding normative framework for burden-sharing, Northern states have few obligations or incentives to contribute to refugee protection in the South. On the other side, Southern host states have only limited ability to control their borders and little bargaining power in the international system. They are therefore left in a position in which they have few options other than either to take whatever is on offer in terms of limited earmarked contributions of the North or to disengage from negotiations entirely.

---

5. The *principle of first asylum* is that the first state that a refugee reaches should be responsible for providing protection.

6. For an analysis of the relationship between burden-sharing and states' threatening not to uphold the principle of first asylum, see, for example, Milner (2009).

7. One successful example of this threat's being successful was the closure of the Macedonian border to Kosovars in 1999, which led to increased burden-sharing through resettlement. But Macedonia is notably not a Southern state, and part of the impact of its threat is attributable to the proximity of Macedonia to the European Union (Barutciski and Suhrke 2001).

## The Role of Issue Linkage

Regime theory in IR identifies a range of factors that enable international institutions to overcome collective action failure. One of the most promising, yet most neglected, of these is issue linkage, which has been identified by regime theory as a means of overcoming collective action failure, in general, and Suasion Game situations, in particular (Martin 1993). Ernst Haas defines *issue linkage* simply as "bargaining that involves more than one issue," where an issue is "a single goal that has found its way onto a decision-making agenda" (1990, 76). The issue linkage literature explores how issues are grouped into packages called issue areas that define the boundaries of a given set of interstate negotiations. The existing literature on issue linkage looks at two main questions: (1) How do issues come to be combined within formal negotiations (linkages as a dependent variable), and (2) what impact does this packaging have on international cooperation (linkages as an independent variable)? Let us explore these two lines of inquiry in turn.

The existing literature on issue linkage examines issue linkage as a dependent variable, exploring how issues come to be combined to form issue areas that represent clusters of issues that are formally negotiated alongside one another. It suggests two principal mechanisms through which this occurs: through the role of power and through the role of knowledge. In the first, tactical linkage can take place, so that two issues with no substantive relationship are combined in the same negotiations. This is the result of power insofar as certain actors have the ability to engage in agenda-setting and others do not. In the second mechanism, substantive linkage can take place, so that two issues have an empirical or ideational relationship. For example, two issues may be widely believed to be causally related to one another.

The existing literature also examines issue linkage as an independent variable. It argues that issue linkage is significant because it may enhance prospects for international cooperation; that is, adding issues to a bargaining process may serve as a means of enhancing the likelihood of mutually self-interested cooperation. This is because issue linkage increases the possibility for states to have an interest in an overall package of negotiations when they may have little interest in cooperating on just one of the issues, by itself, that is part of the wider package of negotiations. The mechanism through which issue linkage leads to international cooperation is by contributing to side-payments by creating explicit conditionality between issues. A state may not be interested in issue X, and therefore, when this issue is negotiated in isolation the state will have very little incentive to cooperate. But if issue Y, in which the same state has an interest, is introduced to the same formal negotiations, the state may be willing to cooperate, provided a return in relation to issue Y is a condition of its willingness to compromise in relation to issue X.

Issue linkage has been identified as a means of overcoming collective action failure in the provision of global public goods. As previously explained, the challenge in ensuring the provision of global public goods is that states do not derive excludable benefits by contributing to their provision. This means that there is a strong disincentive to cooperate because it is possible to simply free-ride on the provision of others. But if excludable benefits can simultaneously be derived from being the contributor to a global public good, this can create an incentive for a country to be the provider of a global public good. Todd Sandler has argued in work with different collaborators that collective action failure in relation to a public good is more likely to be overcome if contributing to that public good simultaneously yields subsidiary benefits (joint products) to the contributing state (Cornes and Sandler 1996; Sandler and Hartley 1995, 1999). Issue linkage is one way of creating such an incentive. If the contribution of a global public good by a state is made conditional on its also receiving side-payments in relation to another issue, this may create a private incentive for it to contribute to the global public good.

Lisa Martin has argued that issue linkage is particularly relevant in overcoming Suasion Game situations, claiming that "private linked benefits contribute to the supply of a public good in suasion games" (1993, 105). In a situation in which there are asymmetrical interests or power relations between actors—as in North–South relations—so that the stronger actor has little incentive to cooperate and the weaker actor has little means to induce or coerce action by the stronger actor, issue linkage may have a role to play. This is because introducing additional issues may address the underlying causes of the Suasion Game. First, it may provide the stronger actor with an incentive to cooperate. If its cooperation is linked to its derivation of side-payments in relation to another issue, this may create an interest that was previously absent. Second, this increased interest on the part of the stronger actor may, in turn, strengthen the bargaining position of the weaker actor vis-à-vis the stronger actor. Put differently, issue linkage may create an incentive for Northern states to have an interest in an issue in which they may otherwise not have an interest; this may, in turn, enhance the bargaining power of Southern states vis-à-vis the North.

Martin suggests that this creates a role for intergovernmental organizations working to overcome Suasion Game situations: "one role for multilateral organizations in suasion games is to tie together issues that have no substantive rationale for linkage" as a means to facilitate cooperation (1993, 105). By grouping together issues within multilateral negotiations, an international organization can increase the scope for side-payments across the issue areas. Furthermore, when intergovernmental organizations are responsible for overseeing a regime that exists to ensure the provision of a global public good, connecting the global public good to other issues in which states have a private interest can serve as a means of overcoming collective action failure.

A number of authors have also identified issue linkage as an opportunity for the South to enhance its bargaining power vis-à-vis the North. John Ravenhill has argued, in relation to the environmental regime, that issue linkage can empower the South: "For Southern countries, one of the major benefits to flow from increasing concern over the environment is the ability to link this with other issues in which they have a direct interest" (1990, 744). This, he suggests, can contribute to improving the prospects for North–South cooperation because it can increase the scope for mutual gain by offering inducements that are regarded as beneficial to the Southern states. Jadish Bhagwati (1984) has similarly argued that linkages represent an opportunity for Southern states. He suggests that the growing interdependence between North and South, in areas such as trade and debt, gives Southern states potentially greater leverage. This, he argues, can contribute to promoting North–South cooperation by giving the North a stake in an issue area that might otherwise be characterized by collective action failure.

The issue-linkages literature has not been applied to the analysis of the international politics of refugee protection. Nevertheless, it offers a useful starting point for exploring the subject for two reasons. First, the contributions of states to refugee protection have been shaped largely by their interests in linked issue areas. In the absence of a clear binding obligation to do so, states have rarely been interested in contributing to refugee protection for its own sake in the territories of other states. Yet states have occasionally done so insofar as they have perceived contributing to protection as a way of meeting their wider interests in other issue areas such as migration, security, development, trade, or peace-building. Second, as the issue-linkages literature predicts, these wider interests in other issue areas have been the key to overcoming the North–South impasse in the refugee regime.

One of the limitations of the existing literature on the role of issue linkage as an independent variable in international cooperation is that it examines issue linkage mainly at the level of formal instrumental bargaining. It generally explores the role of tactical linkage and assumes that two issues need to be part of the same formal negotiations and to be explicitly made conditional on one another for interests in one issue to shape action related to the other issue (Aggarwal 1998; McGinnis 1986; Stein 1980). But the emphasis in the existing literature on formal instrumental bargaining cannot fully account for the wider and arguably more fundamental role that interests in other issue areas have played in the international politics of refugee protection. Although tactical linkages have played some role in the refugee regime, the main determinant of cooperation has been the role of substantive linkages and the ability of UNHCR to create, change, or highlight the ideational, institutional, or material relationships between issue areas. To explain the conditions under which UNHCR has used substantive linkages to influence the behavior of states, I introduce a new concept—cross-issue persuasion.

## Beyond Issue Linkage: Cross-Issue Persuasion

Persuasion has been identified in IR as an important mechanism of influence in world politics (Crawford 2002; Risse 2003). *Persuasion* can be defined as influence designed to change beliefs, and it can be distinguished from other types of social influence, such as coercion, which involves the use or threat of force; bargaining, which involves offering of rewards or threats of punishment; and emulation, which involves imitation of behavior (Keohane 2003). Although persuasion is often considered to involve mainly argumentation (i.e., speech acts involving reason giving), it includes any actions that are designed to change beliefs.

Indeed, how states understand the relationship between two issue areas is subject to their beliefs about how action in one issue area will lead to consequences in another issue area. Substantive linkages—ideational, institutional, or material—are not fixed and immutable. They may be created, changed, or highlighted by an actor as a means of influencing another actor's beliefs about the relationship between action in issue area X and consequences in issue area Y. Cross-issue persuasion describes the conditions under which actor A can persuade actor B that issue area X and issue area Y are linked as a mean of inducing actor B to act in issue area X on the basis of its interest in issue area Y. The concept highlights when and how an actor can use substantive issue linkages to influence the behavior of another actor.

At times in its recent history, UNHCR has been successful in persuading states that voluntarily contributing to refugee protection is related to other issue areas in which those states have a wider interest. On other occasions, UNHCR has tried to link refugee protection to other issue areas but has failed to persuade states that their interests in other issues are linked to refugee protection. This begs the question of when and why UNHCR has been successful (or not) in persuading states to contribute to refugee protection on the basis of their wider interests in other issue areas.

For an actor to be convinced that there is a relationship between action in issue area X and consequences in issue area Y, there must, of course, be some basis for the claim. There needs to be a structural relationship between the two issue areas—a substantive linkage on an ideational, institutional, or material level. Indeed, without a structural basis, UNHCR attempts to solicit contributions to refugee protection in the South on the basis of Northern state interests have not been credible.

Identifying substantive linkages between issue areas as a condition for cooperation in the refugee regime, however, tells us only part of the story of when and why cooperation has taken place. For particular linkages to matter in the politics of protection, UNHCR has to play a crucial role. When issue linkage has been successful, UNHCR has been important for making the substantive linkages relevant. Through a combination of argumentation, provision of information, institutional design, and its epistemic role, it has been able to create, change, or simply highlight the existence of substantive linkages. In doing so, it has contributed to changing the beliefs of states about the relationship between refugee protection and other issue areas. Without UNHCR, it is unlikely that substantive linkages would have contributed to cooperation in the way that they have. The cases studies presented in this book therefore shed light on both the structural and agency conditions for cross-issue persuasion.

## Structural Conditions for Cross-Issue Persuasion

For an appeal to interests in relation to other issue areas to be effective, such an appeal must have a structural basis. UNHCR cannot simply assert that two issue areas are interrelated; this, by itself, does not induce action by states. To successfully induce a state to contribute to refugee protection on the basis of its wider interests, there needs to be an underlying structural connection between refugee protection and the other issue areas in which states have a recognized interest.

*Structure* is a challenging concept to define.[8] It can generally be understood to be the institutional, ideational, and material forces that enable or constrain the actions of an actor. In practice, however, it is methodologically almost impossible to identify exactly how two issues or issue areas were or were not materially connected at a given time in history. Furthermore, the best proxies for material interconnections are likely to be the way in which they were mediated through perception at a given time. Consequently, in this book I operationalize the concept on the basis of Alexander Wendt's (1999, 20) definition of *structure* as the institutional and ideational forces that enable or constrain the actions of an actor. Structure is important for appealing to interests in other issue areas because it is the basis for the perception by a state of the relationship between the two issue areas. In the context of a given set of international negotiations, two issues or issue areas might be conceived to be connected by institutions or by ideas.

*Institutional Linkages*     Institutions can be conceived to connect issue areas. An institution defines acceptable forms of social behavior, either through formal rules and organizations or informal norms and customs. In the case of the international politics of refugee protection, the way in which

---

8. For an overview of the relationship between structure and agency in world politics, see Carlsnaes (1992); Dessler (1989); O'Neill (2004); Wendt (1987, 1992, 1999).

refugee protection has been institutionally connected to other issue areas has depended on the institutional design of the different ad hoc burden-sharing initiatives that UNHCR has conceived. The four case studies presented in the following chapters are particularly apt for exploring the role of variation in institutional structure because each initiative was designed from scratch and had its own unique institutional design. The initiatives were conceived in ways that institutionally connected refugee protection to different degrees. The two main means of institutionally connecting refugee protection to migration, development, and security were internal connections (the way in which issue areas are connected within the initiative) and external connections (the way in which issue areas are connected by the relationship of the overall initiative to wider institutional structures). Internally, the initiatives used issue linkage to make payoffs across issues and issue areas that were formally conditional on one another. For example, in the Indochinese CPA case, the institutional design created an interlocking conditional agreement among the commitments of the main groups of states. Externally, the initiatives used nesting to embed the initiative within wider institutional structures.[9] For example, in the Central American CIREFCA case, the refugee conference was institutionally nested within the wider peace process and postconflict reconstruction initiative for the region.

The causal mechanism through which these institutional interconnections enable and constrain cross-issue persuasion is contractual. In the case of both internal issue linkage and external nesting, the interconnections make it possible for actor A (UNHCR) to credibly argue that action by actor B (a state) in issue area X (refugee protection) will lead to a payoff for actor B in relation to issue area Y (migration, security, or development) because the institutional framework makes actor B's action in issue area X conditional on another actor acting in ways that lead to a payoff for actor B in relation to issue area Y.

*Ideational Linkages*     An idea is a concept or abstraction formed in the mind of an actor. Ideas can be conceived to structurally connect issue areas because they create a perception of the causal relationship between two

---

9. *Nesting* is the way in which a given institution is part of a wider set of institutions. See Aggarwal (2006); Alter and Meunier (2009).

issue areas. For example, an idea such as human security connects issue areas such as human rights and development. Ideational interconnections emerge though learning and the development of new knowledge. They are not entirely under the control of any single actor such as UNHCR, but are nevertheless important for enabling and constraining cross-issue persuasion. They can be influenced by the work of epistemic communities (Haas 1989/1994).

Ideas that connect issue areas may be held intersubjectively or subjectively. In different eras in history, different intersubjective ideas have structurally connected refugee protection to other issue areas in different ways. At different historical junctures, different policy discourses have identified different relationships between refugee protection and other issue areas. For example, the refugee aid and development (RAD) debate emerged in the 1980s, positing a set of shared understandings about the role that development assistance could play in promoting refugees' self-sufficiency and local integration within their host states of asylum, and it was revived in the context of Convention Plus. The asylum-migration nexus emerged in the early 2000s and highlighted the way in which refugee protection is inextricably related to migration; however, the ideas present in the nexus can be traced back to the late 1980s. The security-development nexus provided a set of ideas about the relationship between state security and the access of people to opportunities and entitlements, which sometimes influenced the politics of refugee protection.

At different historical junctures, individual states or groups of states have also subjectively held ideas about the relationship between refugee protection and other issue areas. For example, during the Cold War, the United States often held a subjective set of ideas about the relationship between refugee protection in certain regions and its fight against communism, and in the post-9/11 era, a number of states hold views about the relationship between refugee camps and terrorism.

The mechanism through which these ideational interconnections enable and constrain cross-issue persuasion is causal. In the case of both intersubjective and subjective ideas, the interconnections make it possible for UNHCR to credibly argue that action in issue area X (refugee protection) will lead to a payoff in relation to issue area Y (migration, security, or development) because the institutional framework makes actor B believe that acting in relation to X will causally lead to outcomes in relation to Y.

Structural interconnections matter for cross-issue persuasion because, for an appeal to interests in other issue areas to be effective, such an appeal must have a structural basis. UNHCR cannot simply assert that two issue areas are interrelated; this, by itself, has not induced action by states. The causal mechanisms through which structural interconnections based on institutions and ideas have enabled or constrained cross-issue persuasion differ. The mechanism through which institutions have enabled or constrained cross-issue persuasion is contractual; it makes the derivation of side-payments in issue area Y conditional on action in the other issue area X. But the mechanism through which ideas have enabled or constrained cross-issue persuasion is causal; it leads to the perception that side-payments in issue area Y causally follow from action in issue area X.

In each of the four ad hoc initiatives convened by UNHCR between 1980 and 2005 and presented in this book, refugee protection was structurally connected to other issue areas in different ways through both institutions and ideas. These structural interconnections were important for the politics of each initiative because they served as a resource that enabled or constrained UNHCR in its appeal to the interests of states in relation to another issue or issue area.

## Agency Conditions for Cross-Issue Persuasion

Structural interconnections are a necessary but not sufficient condition for UNHCR to appeal to the interests of actors in other issue areas. Many substantive linkages exist, but not all of them become relevant or influential. Which linkages become relevant to the politics of protection has been significantly influenced by UNHCR. Indeed, UNHCR has played two crucial roles in this: (1) it has been able to create or change substantive linkages through its role in institutional design and its epistemic role, and (2) it has been able to recognize and effectively communicate existing linkages through argumentation or the provision of information.

UNHCR has not been a passive actor in relation to institutional linkages. Although it has had to work within the constraints of the broader institutional landscape of the UN system, it has, at times, been able to make its ad hoc initiatives part of a broader institutional framework. Because each of the four initiatives explored in the book was conceived from scratch, each had its own unique institutional design, allowing UNHCR a significant degree of autonomy to plug in its initiatives or nest them within a broader institutional context.

UNHCR has also had some influence on ideational linkages. Ideational interconnections have been even more challenging for UNHCR to influence than institutional interconnections. Nevertheless, it has occasionally been able to engage in partnerships with epistemic communities or to promote certain understandings of the causal relationship between issue areas. For example, it has played an autonomous role in shaping the RAD and asylum-migration nexus debates.

UNHCR has also played a role in cross-issue persuasion simply by recognizing and communicating the existence of substantive linkages. Often the relationship between refugee protection and other issue areas has been obscure or ambiguous. Given that refugee issues are often of low salience, few states spend significant resources monitoring the causal relationship between refugees and security, immigration, or trade. Consequently, UNHCR has sometimes been able to change the beliefs of states about the relationship between refugee protection and their wider interests by providing information or engaging in argumentation.

Successfully engaging in cross-issue persuasion through these roles has required UNHCR to have the analytical and political capacity to identify the opportunities present at different historical junctures. At times when UNHCR has had politically astute staff, it has been more able to exploit substantive linkages to persuade states that their interests in other issue areas can be met through a contribution to refugee protection. For example, in the Indochinese CPA, Sergio Vieira de Mello, widely regarded as having been one of the most talented and charismatic UN leaders, played a central role (Betts 2008; Power 2008). Table 1 illustrates the extent to which the structural and agency conditions for cross-issue persuasion were fulfilled in the four initiatives.

## Cross-Issue Persuasion and Refugee Protection

All four of the UNHCR-led initiatives explored in this book are themselves a reflection of the North–South impasse. Their very creation was the result of the absence of North–South cooperation in addressing longstanding refugee situations in the South. Northern states were unwilling

TABLE 1. Extent to which the Structural and Agency Conditions for Cross-Issue Persuasion were Fulfilled in Relation to the Four Initiatives

| Initiative | Outcome | Most relevant Issue Areas | Institutional Interconnections | | Ideational Interconnections | | Agency |
|---|---|---|---|---|---|---|---|
| | | | Internal | External | Intersubjective | Subjective | |
| ICARA | Failure | Development | No linked commitments | Not nested | RAD: contested | United States: security | Weak |
| CIREFCA | Success | Development; security | Linked commitments | Nested | RAD: accepted Refugee-security nexus: accepted | Europe: trade and human rights | Strong leadership (Leonardo Franco) |
| CPA | Success | Migration; security; development | Linked commitments | Not nested | n/a | United States: security ASEAN: migration SRV: development | Strong leadership (Sergio Vieira de Mello) |
| Convention Plus | Failure | Migration; development | No linked commitments | Not nested | RAD: contested; Asylum-migration nexus: contested | n/a | Weak |

*Notes:* ASEAN, Association of Southeast Asian Nations; CIREFCA, International Conference on Central American Refugees; CPA, Comprehensive Plan of Action for Indo-Chinese Refugees; ICARA, International Conferences on Assistance to Refugees in Africa; n/a, not available; RAD, refugee aid and development; SRV, Socialist Republic of Vietnam.

to voluntarily contribute to overcoming those refugee situations outside of an institutionalized negotiation process; this was the reason that UNHCR convened the initiatives. In each case, UNHCR created an institutional bargaining process to facilitate international cooperation and overcome the North–South impasse. As noted in the introduction to this book, two of the initiatives were successful in promoting North–South cooperation and two failed. A significant reason for the success or failure of the four initiatives was the effectiveness of UNHCR in appealing to the interests of states in other issue areas. In the two successful cases, states were prepared to cooperate because refugee protection was successfully related to a wider set of issues in other policy fields. In the two failed cases, the North–South impasse prevailed, primarily because of the absence of successful cross-issue persuasion.

The aim of the ICARA I and II (1981 and 1984) was to facilitate additional Northern donor burden-sharing to support African states in hosting and locally integrating large numbers of refugees who had fled the African liberation wars and Cold War proxy conflicts. The ICARA strategy was to channel significant additional development assistance from Northern donors to African states to simultaneously promote national development and allow refugees to be locally integrated. The two conferences were ultimately a failure, however, with Northern donors being unwilling to contribute significant additional development assistance and Southern states being unwilling to implement local integration projects for refugees. An important reason for the failure was that UNHCR failed to persuade participating states that there was a relationship between refugee protection and development. Northern states were unconvinced that making a commitment to provide additional development assistance would lead to local integration and so reduce the long-term humanitarian assistance budget. Southern states were unconvinced that if they agreed to offer local integration or self-sufficiency to refugees that this would lead to additional development assistance that would benefit their citizens. The failure to persuade both the North and South of this relationship can be found at both the level of institutions and ideas. The institutional design of ICARA created no contractual relationship between refugee protection and development; the expectation of UNHCR was that donor states would make contributions for purely altruistic reasons. It therefore designed the conferences in a technocratic way that largely addressed refugee protection in isolation from the wider interests of states. In terms of ideas, neither the Northern donors nor the African host nations found the claim of a causal relationship between development assistance and durable solutions to be credible and so remained unpersuaded that ICARA could serve their interests. The result was that there were few new donor contributions and the conferences polarized along North–South lines. ICARA therefore illustrates the archetypal North–South impasse.

The aim of CIREFCA (1989) was to provide long-term solutions for refugees displaced by civil conflicts in Central America and to improve protection standards throughout the region. It represents the single most successful example of international cooperation in the recent history of the refugee regime. UNHCR effectiveness in appealing to the interests of states in other issue areas was crucial to the success of CIREFCA. Rather than addressing refugee protection in isolation (as ICARA had done), CIREFCA was explicitly part of both the wider UN-led peace process and the postconflict reconstruction process for the region. CIREFCA therefore had an institutional connection to both regional security and development. Refugee protection was also structurally connected to development through a set of ideas—the RAD debates—that emerged in the context of CIREFCA. These structural interconnections between refugee protection and issue areas such as development, security, and peace-building created a basis on which UNHCR was able to successfully persuade states that their interests in other issue areas could be met through contributing to CIREFCA. The main donor states—mainly the European states—were willing to commit to financially support CIREFCA, not because of an interest in refugee protection per se but because of their wider commitment to peace and development in the region. The wider interests of the European Economic Community (EEC) in promoting trade links with a stable, developing, and democratic region, in turn, were the motives that underpinned this commitment. On the other side, the Central American states were persuaded to commit to CIREFCA and the adoption of new refugee protection standards because they similarly saw CIREFCA as an inextricable part of the wider security, development, and peace-building initiatives.

The aim of the Indochinese CPA (1989) was to provide a long-term solution to the mass influx of refugees fleeing mainly by boat from the Socialist Republic of Vietnam (to Southeast Asian states and Hong Kong.

Although the CPA was criticized on human rights grounds, it was a success in terms of promoting international cooperation and resolving a long-standing refugee problem. It was based on a three-way cooperative agreement. First, the refugees' country of origin, Vietnam, was willing to ensure safe return for nonrefugees. Second, the countries of first asylum in the region—the Association of Southeast Asian Nations (ASEAN) states, and Hong Kong—were willing to guarantee that they would host and not forcibly return the boat people while their asylum claims were being assessed. Third, countries outside region, led by the United States, were willing to resettle all those who were recognized as refugees. The agreement relied on issue linkage in two key ways. First, it made each of these three commitments conditional on the other two; second, the willingness of each of the three main parties to the agreement to commit to its share of the bargain was underpinned by wider interests in linked issue areas. The resettlement states—mainly the United States—saw their commitment as significantly related to the legacy of Vietnam War, regional security, and the wider Cold War context. The ASEAN states of first asylum had an interest in the overall agreement based on concerns with controlling immigration; Malaysia and Indonesia, in particular, were concerned about the mass influx of ethnic Chinese who might destabilize the ethnic balance in their countries. Finally, the Vietnamese motivation for the agreement came not from a concern for refugee protection per se but from a desire to attract development assistance and to rehabilitate itself in the eyes of the international community in the aftermath of the collapse of the Soviet Union. In each case, UNHCR was able to persuade the states that their wider interests could be met through refugee protection, that is, that refugee protection was structurally interconnected with these wider issue areas through the ideas subjectively held by the relevant actors. UNHCR was therefore able to draw on the structural relationships between the issue areas and to connect them within the negotiation of the CPA.

The Convention Plus initiative (2003–2005) attempted to create a normative framework for burden-sharing that could then be applied to overcome specific long-standing refugee situations in the South. Ultimately, the initiative was characterized by North–South polarization and failed. The basis of the project was to persuade both the North and South to agree to a set of differentiated but complementary commitments. Northern states were to make financial and resettlement commitments; in return,

Southern states were to commit to enhance their refugee protection capacity and make local integration and self-sufficiency available to refugees. The initiative was explicitly premised on issue linkage in two ways: (1) it attempted to connect these two broad commitments together by making one conditional on the other, and (2) it appealed to the North and South to fulfill these commitments on the basis of their wider interests. UNHCR appealed to Northern states on the basis of their security and migration concerns, arguing that burden-sharing and addressing protracted refugee situations could serve as a means of achieving these wider goals. UNHCR appealed to Southern states to commit to enhancing refugees' access to protection as a means of attracting development assistance that could simultaneously benefit the local population. Unfortunately, the UNHCR attempt to appeal to the interests of the states in other issue areas was not perceived as credible by the states. This is because there was little structural basis on which to connect refugee protection to migration and development. The North–South impasse therefore prevailed, and the initiative did not lead to an agreement on a normative framework for burden-sharing.

The case studies presented in this book highlight the conditions under which international cooperation in refugee protection can take place. In each case, states were not concerned with refugee protection per se; however, they were motivated to engage in burden-sharing insofar as they believed or were persuaded that the other issue areas in which they had an interest were related to refugee protection. By formally or informally adding other issues to the negotiations on refugee protection or simply appealing to the wider interests of states in other issue areas, UNHCR was able to motivate states to voluntarily contribute to refugee protection. But its being able to persuade states that two issue areas were linked relied on there being a structural basis for persuasion and also on UNHCR's effectively drawing on and using these structural interconnections.

In summary, one of the defining characteristics of refugee protection is that it can be conceived to be a global public good. The main benefits that it confers to states—order and justice—are at least partly nonexcludable and available to states irrespective of whether they contribute to the global availability of refugee protection. The nonexcludable nature of these benefits encourages states to free-ride on the contribution of other states, leading to the underprovision of refugee protection. In addition, one

of the greatest obstacles to developing the type of international cooperation that could ensure that states contribute equitably to the global provision of refugee protection is the North–South impasse, characterized by
the game theoretical analogy of a Suasion Game. The majority of world
refugees originate from and remain in the South; Northern states have no
obligation to contribute to support refugee protection in the South and are
therefore in a position to free-ride on the contribution of Southern states.
Given this structural inequality, Southern states have been faced with the
stark choice to take whatever is on offer or hurt themselves more by refusing to cooperate.

Yet, as regime theory predicts, the Suasion Game has at times been
overcome through a form of issue linkage. Historically, Northern states
have seldom been willing to contribute to refugee protection in the South
for altruistic reasons, but they have done so when they have believed that
contributing is linked to their own interests in other issue areas, such as security, migration, and trade. Linking issue areas has also offered Southern
states an additional incentive to go beyond their most basic obligations and
consider, for example, providing local integration or self-sufficiency to refugees. Persuading Northern and Southern states that refugee protection is
contractually or causally related to their wider interests in other issue areas
has thereby been the key to overcoming the North–South impasse.

For UNHCR, as the international organization responsible for refugee
protection, to effectively persuade states that two issue areas are connected,
two principal conditions have to exist. First, there has to be a structural
basis for claiming that two issues or issue areas are linked (the structural
conditions); only when issues have been structurally connected in some
way has UNHCR been able to persuade states to contribute to refugee
protection on the basis of their interests in wider issues. Second, UNHCR
has had to demonstrate the leadership to create, change, or communicate
the substantive linkages. When these two conditions have been fulfilled,
the North–South impasse has been overcome; when they have not, the impasse has prevailed. I now turn to the four empirical case studies to demonstrate how cross-issue persuasion has influenced the success or failure
of the UNHCR attempts to overcome the North–South impasse.

2

# The International Conferences on Assistance to Refugees in Africa (1981 and 1984)

By the end of the 1970s, around 3–4 million refugees were living in rural areas in Africa, generally in large, spontaneously created settlements. During the 1960s and 1970s, African host states had been relatively tolerant about hosting refugees on their territory. There had been a widely held assumption that the African refugees mainly emanated from colonial liberation wars and, as such, would return home as soon as independence was achieved. But by 1979 it was clear that the majority of the African refugees had been displaced not by the liberation wars but by increasingly intractable civil conflicts that had become Cold War proxy conflicts. Many of these refugees had been living in exile for a number of years after having fled violence in states such as Burundi, Chad, Ethiopia, Angola, Uganda, and Zaire. Whereas the liberation wars had been assumed to result in the refugees' imminent repatriation, for these intractable conflicts there appeared little immediate prospect of return for those who had fled. Neighboring states such as Lesotho, Mozambique, Somalia, Sudan, Tanzania, and Zambia therefore hosted significant numbers of refugees alongside their own citizens, supported by the infrastructures and resources of the country and with little support from the international community.

The increasingly protracted situation of African refugees led a number of African states to argue the African commitment to hosting refugees had become what one author describes as an "open-ended burden" (Stein 1987, 50). In many cases, these spontaneously settled refugees were using the same agricultural land, natural resources, and social services as the people in the host communities. The African states argued that this placed an unreasonable strain on their resources, for which they were inadequately compensated by the international community. This recognition led the OAU to convene the Arusha Conference on the Situation of Refugees in Africa (May 7–17, 1979) on behalf of Africa's refugee-hosting states to discuss the challenges faced by these states. The conference explored how African states could equitably share the burden among themselves and how African states might attract greater support and burden-sharing from the international community, both to compensate them for the infrastructural and economic costs of past hosting and to share the costs of refugee protection in the future.

As well as reaffirming the commitment of African states to providing refugee protection, Arusha highlighted the disproportionate burden of refugee hosting that these states carried compared to the rest of the international community. The conference therefore called on donor states to commit to share a greater proportion of the social and economic infrastructural costs of refugee settlement. Among its recommendations, the Arusha Conference sought a new form of burden-sharing in which international support for development projects would target both refugees and host communities. The hope was that such targeted development assistance would contribute to promoting the self-reliance of refugees pending their eventual repatriation (UNHCR 1984). To realize these goals, the Arusha Conference called for an international conference to explore how the international community could compensate the host states for the developmental costs of long-term hosting.

This call led UNHCR and the African states to convene the International Conferences on Assistance to Refugees in Africa (ICARA I) in 1981 and then a second such conference in 1984 (ICARA II). These were two one-off donor conferences, held in Geneva. At these conferences, the

African states submitted a range of development projects and programs to prospective donor states, which had been jointly compiled by UNHCR, UNDP, and the host states in the region. The aim of the African states was to attract greater development assistance from donors that would support both the refugees and host communities simultaneously. To achieve this goal, the ICARA conferences advanced a new concept—refugee aid and development (RAD)—an integrated development approach that would both improve refugees' access to natural resources and social services in order to promote their self-reliance and local integration and simultaneously benefit the host states and hosting communities through funding to support infrastructure and social service provision.

Ultimately, however, the conferences failed to achieve their stated aims. Neither ICARA I nor ICARA II led to significant new sources of development assistance for African states, nor did they lead to the improved access to local integration or self-sufficiency for refugees. Although the first conference raised significant funds, these were selectively applied in accordance with the Cold War interests of donors and were generally earmarked for short-term relief projects that did little to alleviate the long-term burden of hosting. The second conference, despite attempts to address the shortcomings of the first conference, led to few additional financial commitments from Northern donors and similarly culminated in North–South polarization.

In this chapter, I unpack the reasons for the failure of ICARA I and II to lead to successful North–South cooperation. I begin by explaining the content, process, and outcome of the two ICARA conferences and then examine the role of cross-issue persuasion as a factor in explaining the outcome. I argue that a significant element of the ICARA failure lies in the inability of UNHCR to use cross-issue persuasion to convince both Northern and Southern states that they could meet their wider interests through a commitment to ICARA. ICARA was premised on UNHCR's persuading states that there was a relationship between refugees and development. It relied on persuading Northern states that a commitment to providing development assistance would lead to African refugees' having access to durable solutions and that this would lead to a reduction in the long-term humanitarian assistance budget. It also relied on persuading Southern states that a commitment to providing local integration for refugees would yield additional development assistance. But, in this case, Northern states remained unconvinced that contributing additional development assistance would serve their interests in reducing their long-term humanitarian responsibilities; and Southern states remained unconvinced that offering local integration would contribute to national development. The conferences left little legacy, but they serve to illustrate the archetypal North–South impasse described in chapter 1.

## The First Conference

ICARA I was an initiative called for by the OAU in which the relatively newly independent African states came to the international community in a spirit of pan-Africanism to call for new burden-sharing. The conference, held April 9–10, 1981, had three stated objectives: (1) to "focus attention on the plight of refugees in Africa," (2) to "mobilize additional resources to assist both refugees and returnees," and (3) to "aid countries of asylum in bearing the burden imposed upon them by the large number of refugees" (UN General Assembly Resolution 35/42, November 25, 1980). Its focus was largely on burden-sharing, and it was primarily a pledging conference, setting out few ideas, principles, or guidelines.

The African states were invited by UNHCR to compile project proposals with the technical assistance of UNHCR, which would then be submitted to the conference. The intention was that the projects would focus on supporting long-term infrastructural development that could simultaneously compensate host communities while improving refugee protection and the prospects for durable solutions. Bearing in mind the neglect of the increasingly protracted rural and border settlements, much of the focus was on meeting basic needs such as food provision. For example, the UNHCR chief of West and Central African operations argued that the priority for the funds falling within the UNHCR mandate should focus on "immediate needs" such as shelter, clothing, and blankets;[1] meanwhile, $175 million of the $560 million initially pledged at the conference was earmarked for

---

1. Bwakiri to Asomani, "Note on Selecting Priority Projects, Falling within/outside UNHCR's Mandate," Memorandum SACO/1153, 27 July 1981. UNHCR Fonds 11, 391.62/374, UNHCR Archives.

food aid.[2] Kurt Waldheim, the UN secretary-general, proclaimed in his concluding statement that the conference had been a success. He claimed, in relation to the conference objectives: "We have made major strides on all three fronts." In commenting on the $560 million in conference pledges, he continued, "one may conclude, therefore, that the immediate priority requirements will be met and that a solid base has been laid for the development of the necessary support to accommodate the long-term needs involved."[3] In the immediate aftermath, numerous African representatives wrote from their capitals to congratulate the high commissioner on the initiative. The foreign minister of Cameroon, for example, wrote that the $560 million pledged represented "a first sign of significant international solidarity."[4]

It was only later that the extent to which these pledges had been earmarked by donor states became increasingly apparent. By September 1981, the Steering Committee in charge of post-ICARA coordination noted that further specifications by donors left only $144 million not earmarked, leaving UNHCR with an estimated $40 million available for the high-priority projects that did not fall under its regular or specific programs. Consequently, a ceiling of $2 million per country was fixed, and this was focused on humanitarian assistance needs such as food, water, shelter, and the delivery of medical services.[5] In Gil Loescher's (2001b, 227) words, "almost all of the $560m offered by donor states was earmarked for projects and allocated to most favoured nations. Very few funds went to especially hard hit nations like Ethiopia and other countries in the Horn of Africa." Consequently, when the UN General Assembly reflected on the achievements of ICARA I, it regretted "that, in spite of efforts made, the assistance provided to an increasing number of African refugees is still very inadequate"

---

2. UN Middle East Information Centre, ICARA: Press Release 66/1981, 28 April 1981, UNHCR Fonds 11, 391.62/306A, UNHCR Archives.

3. Kurt Waldheim, "Concluding Statement by the Secretary-General to ICARA, 10/4/81," Report to the UN on ICARA, 21 April 1981, UNHCR Fonds 11 391.62/300A, UNHCR Archives.

4. Foreign Minister of Cameroon, to High Commissioner, Correspondence, 11 May 1981, UNHCR Fonds 11, 391.62/318A, UNHCR Archives.

5. Post-ICARA Steering Committee, "3rd Draft of Steering Committee of Post-ICARA Coordination Meeting," HCR/NY/572, 15 September 1981, New York, UNHCR Fonds 11, 391.62/460, UNHCR Archives.

(UN General Assembly Resolution 36/124 of 14 December 1981, quoted in Milner 2004).

ICARA I therefore failed to satisfy host states in Africa because the financial contributions of the donors did not meet their expectations. In the words of Ambassador Skalli of Morocco (the chair of the Geneva African Group), "Although ICARA I had succeeded in certain respects, it had not raised the additional resources hoped for."[6] This brought calls for "additionality," by Egypt, among others, which, concerned that other development resources destined for the citizens of host states might been diverted into refugee protection, stressed "the need to increase the developmental assistance to asylum countries."[7] Equally, the legacy of ICARA I failed to satisfy Northern donor states, particularly the United States, which, after observing that no greater access to durable solutions for refugees had resulted from its $285 million pledge, remained on the fringes of ICARA II. The concerns of Northern donors were largely that financial commitments had not translated into durable solutions for refugees but had either been squandered on short-term assistance or had been used by African states simply to fund outdated development projects that offered little benefit to refugees.[8] Robert Gorman (1993, 63) diagnoses the failure of ICARA I to ultimately meet its third goal of addressing refugee-related development needs as a consequence of its failure to systematically involve UN development agencies in the conference-planning and project-proposal preparations.

ICARA I did, however, have an intellectual legacy. Although its focus had mainly been on basic needs, much the rhetoric of the conference and many of the projects submitted by states focused on building infrastructural capacity in order to facilitate the hosting of refugee populations. This represented the starting point for the UNHCR RAD strategy. For example, the General Assembly resolution establishing ICARA I identifies the need "to strengthen the capacity of countries of asylum to provide

---

6. Meeting on ICARA II with African Missions, HCR/ETH/610, 5 October 1983, UNHCR Fonds 11, 391.78/373, UNHCR Archives.

7. Ibid.

8. This was evident from the comments of the representatives of the European states at the informal meetings of ExCom. See, for example, European States' Comments, informal meetings of ExCom representatives, multiple documents, including "Note for the File: Summary of Statements Relating to ICARA II," 27 May 1983, UNHCR Fonds 11, 391.78/215, UNHCR Archives.

adequately for the refugees while they remain in their countries, as well as to assist the countries of origin in the rehabilitation of genuine voluntary returnees" (UN General Assembly Resolution 35/42 of 25 November 1980, Preamble, para. 8). A number of project submissions focused on this kind of capacity building with a view to facilitating self-sufficiency and local integration. In the case of Lesotho, the submission prepared for the conference notes, "The Lesotho Government Policy...is to integrate them into the community as soon as possible. Integration in this case means that the relief for the people should not be handled separately from the national development objectives; therefore the Government has considered the creation of conditions where self-development is possible."[9] The submission goes on to propose credit schemes, workshop facilities, and the expansion of education facilities at the National University of Lesotho.[10]

In reviewing the government submissions, David Lambo, head of the UNHCR Southern African Regional Section, similarly placed emphasis on capacity building as part of a shift toward local integration and self-help, as opposed to the dependency of many rural settlements. He drew attention to the need to support, for example, educational and agricultural projects to benefit the Barundi refugees in Tanzania.[11] Self-sufficiency through capacity building was also a major theme in the conference speeches. For example, the secretary-general emphasized the need to "promote self-sufficiency of refugees through various local integration programmes."[12] Meanwhile, Siaka Stevens, as chair of the OAU, claimed: "The assistance of the world community...should aim at helping them [refugees] to help themselves, particularly in cases where repatriation could no longer be envisaged. Refugees should not be assisted in ways which would create overdependence. Rather, they should be guided and enabled to become self-supporting as quickly as possible."[13]

---

9. Government of Lesotho, "Lesotho Government Assistance Proposals for Submission to the Conference," 19 December 1980, UNHCR Fonds 11, 391.62/113, UNHCR Archives.

10. Ibid.

11. David Lambo (Chief, Southern African Regional Section) to the Deputy High Commissioner, letter, 19 December 1980, UNHCR Fonds 11, 391.62/154A, UNHCR Archives.

12. Waldheim, "Concluding Statement by the Secretary-General."

13. Siaka Stevens, Statement to ICARA I, 9 April 1981, UNHCR Fonds 11, 391.62/316, UNHCR Archives.

## The Second Conference

Addressing the limitations of ICARA I, ICARA II drew on many of the underdeveloped ideas that had been implicit in the first conference. ICARA II was seen by donor states as needing to be, in the words of the Austrian ambassador, more of a "think tank" than a "pledging conference."[14] The second conference (held in Geneva, July 9–11, 1984) benefited from having a far greater planning time than its predecessor. Soren Jessen-Petersen was appointed the head of an ICARA Unit, which coordinated the Steering Committee and Technical Teams from 1983. He noted that the need for the second conference was due to the failure of the first in terms of capacity building: "It fell short of meeting the expectations of the African Governments for support towards strengthening their institutional capacity to receive refugees.... Hence, resolution 37/197 calling for the convening of ICARA II."[15] The objectives of the conference were to (1) "thoroughly review the results of ICARA I and the state of progress of projects submitted to it"; (2) "consider the continuing need for assistance with a view to providing, as necessary, additional assistance to refugees/returnees in Africa for the implementation of programmes for their relief, rehabilitation and resettlement"; and (3) "consider the impact imposed on national economies of the African countries concerned and to provide them with required assistance to strengthen their social and economic infrastructure to cope with the burden of dealing with large numbers of refugees and returnees" (UN General Assembly Resolution 37/197, 18 December 1982, operational para. 5a–c).

The central theme was Time for Solutions, which the high commissioner explained represented "a joint responsibility for all participants.... I am thinking particularly of the relationship between relief and development aid, and the primacy of durable solutions."[16] This reflected the 1983

---

14. Informal ExCom Meeting, "Note for the File: Summary of Statements Relating to ICARA II Made at Informal Meetings of ExCom Representatives," 27 May 1983, UNHCR Fonds 11, 391.78/215, UNHCR Archives.

15. Jessen-Petersen to Moussalli, "Talking Points on ICARA II," 23 November 1983, UNHCR Fonds 11, 391.78/399, UNHCR Archives.

16. Poul Hartling, "High Commissioner's Opening Remarks at the 3rd Steering Committee Meeting on ICARA II," Jessen-Petersen's summary of the debate, 14 November 1983, UNHCR Fonds 11, 391.78/398A, UNHCR Archives.

UNHCR ExCom resolution on durable solutions, which "recognized the importance and timeliness of ICARA II in connection with the pursuit of durable solutions to refugee problems in Africa."[17]

Consequently, whereas ICARA I had ultimately focused on short-term relief, ICARA II was intended to direct funds toward durable solutions and acknowledged that this would require a greater developmental emphasis. ExCom noted that "Given the economic and social fragility of those African countries receiving refugees, UNHCR's work needs to be complemented by efforts of a more developmental nature."[18] This acknowledgement led UNHCR to attempt to build partnerships with development agencies. For example, the Steering Committee for ICARA II included UNDP "because of the development aspect."[19] This reflected a growing awareness of the need to address the now famous transition gap between relief and development.[20] The United Nations International Children's Emergency Fund (UNICEF) report in the aftermath of ICARA I, for example, noted that "It was also apparent that during the first emergency phase, donors wished to see their commitments applied for humanitarian purposes only. A number expressed the view that the longer-term aspects of the refugee problem and the strengthening of infrastructure should be considered as part of the international agencies involved with development in co-operation with the Governments concerned."[21]

By mid-1983, consideration of the gap was emerging in UNHCR thinking. In representing the organization at a Symposium on African Refugees in Tokyo, Dessalegne Chefeke, UNHCR representative, noted that, although the "most ideal solution" for refugees was voluntary repatriation,

---

17. See Executive Committee on International Protection of Refugees, "Conclusions Adopted by the Executive Committee on International Protection of Refugees," ExCom Conclusion no. 29 (XXXIX) of 1983, para. (l), Geneva.

18. "For the Information of ExCom: ICARA II," 21–23 May 1984, Geneva, UNHCR Fonds 11, 391.78/307, UNHCR Archives.

19. Jessen-Petersen to Moussalli, "Talking Points on ICARA II," memorandum, 23 November 1983, UNHCR Fonds 11, 391.78/399, UNHCR Archives.

20. The *relief-to-development gap* is the long-standing separation of humanitarianism and development in global governance. It has been suggested that this gap has negative practical implications because in complex humanitarian emergencies there is often inadequate institutional collaboration to ensure the smooth transition in responsibility from humanitarian agencies to development agencies.

21. UNICEF document for Executive Board on Cooperation with African Countries. E/ICFF/P/L.2094, UNHCR Fonds 11, 391.62/319, para. 29, UNHCR Archives.

"there are, unfortunately, also situations where voluntary repatriation is most unlikely" and these require "local integration" and "self-sufficiency." He argued that "ICARA II will try to bridge the gap between the humanitarian aid to refugees and development aid to the countries concerned, claiming "the process leading to refugee integration is not simply a succession of phases i.e. relief, self-reliance and development. These phases overlap."[22]

In preparation for the conference, the ICARA Unit invited submissions from African states under the heading Proposals for Development Assistance to Areas with Refugee Concentrations, in which states were to focus on (1) government policy in regard to refugees (including efforts to reach durable solutions), (2) the impact of refugees on the national economy, and (3) overall plans designed to deal with refugee problems particularly through development projects. In outlining the "additional resources sought," they were required to provide a "statement of refugee-related development projects which are already underway."[23]

During this process, the Tanzanian prior experience of incorporating refugees into national development projects as a means of achieving self-sufficiency and local integration was championed as the pioneering example of success.[24] The Tanzanian model was used particularly as a means of encouraging involvement from UNDP. For example, in a letter from the UNHCR representative in Dar es Salaam to the UNDP resident representative, an enclosed background paper set out some key illustrations of the success of local integration through self-sufficiency. It looked at the self-sufficiency achieved by Barundi refugees in Katumba, Ulyankula, and Mishamo and by self-settled Zaireans in Kigoma, showing how "with the assistance of settlement and project personnel the refugees themselves are

---

22. Dessalegne Chefeke, "Keynote Address to Symposium on African Refugees," 24 May 1983, Tokyo, UNHCR Fonds 11, 391.68/234, UNHCR Archives.

23. "ICARA II: Guidelines for Country Submissions on the Impact of Refugee Problems on National Economies and Possible Development Assistance Required to Alleviate These Problems," YZF 306–03, 15 March 1983, UNHCR Fonds 11, 391.78/91, UNHCR Archives.

24. For example, the UN Technical Team for ICARA II noted "The deep-rooted and internationally well-known humanitarian concern of the Government of the United Republic of Tanzania towards refugees." "Report of the UN Technical Team for ICARA II on Tanzania," note, "The Deep-Rooted and Internationally Well-Known Humanitarian Concern of the Government of the United Republic of Tanzania towards Refugees," 29 August 1983, UNHCR Fonds 11, 391.78/45, paras. 12 and 13, UNHCR Archives.

responsible for land clearance and for building their own homes, as well as for various community projects designed to foster a community spirit of self-reliance and cooperation." It argued that government encouragement of refugee agriculture and the construction of infrastructure such as roads, water systems, education, and health facilities had promoted this integration, and it called on UNDP to contribute through ICARA II to strengthening the process.[25]

After receiving project submissions from states, the UN Technical Team for ICARA II conducted a series of visits to the fourteen states concerned. The team's aim was to compile reports on the infrastructural burden of states' dealing with large numbers of refugees and to assess and prioritize project submissions "that would enhance the capacity of the country to support refugees." All the visits lasted between three and ten days; involved meetings among UNHCR, UNDP, donor countries, host states, and NGOs; and reviewed the current situation and policy while describing and prioritizing projects. The projects in the report all focused on infrastructural development initiatives planned and owned by the host governments, with the explicit intention of providing development facilities such as health, education, road access, agricultural training and equipment, and other forms of vocational training that would better provide a social and economic link between the refugee populations and the citizens of the states.[26]

When the conference met in July 1984, its aim was to raise $392 million to meet 128 aid schemes in the fourteen African states over a period of three years and Leo Tindemans, the chair, proclaimed the event a success.[27] Although only $81 million was pledged at the conference, the consensus reached in Geneva was seen as a starting point and not an "end unto itself" (Gorman 1987, 40). In particular, there was optimism that the Final Declaration and Program of Action set out generic principles that could be built on. These included (1) the need for ongoing assistance, (2) acknowledgment of the disproportionate refugee burden of African nations, (3) the

25. Abdellah Saied (UNHCR representative to Dar es Salaam), to Mr D. Outtara (resident representative of UNDP), Re: proposed development assistance projects for ICARA II, letter, 7 June 1983, UNHCR Fonds 11, 391.78/227A, UNHCR Archives.

26. "Reports of the UN Technical Team."

27. Press Clippings on ICARA II, 26 July 1984, UNHCR Fonds 11, 391.78/1019C, UNHCR Archives.

desirability of additionality, and (4) the need to institutionally mainstream the process within development planning (Gorman 1987).

The cause of the failure of ICARA II was once again primarily a North–South polarization in expectations and interests, and a lack of commitment on the part of both donors and recipient states. Barry Stein (1997) suggests that there was a North–South division in the understanding of the purpose of the conference. Whereas the African states wished to focus on burden-sharing, the donor states wished to focus on the durable solutions theme reflected by the conference title, "A Time for Solutions." Stein suggests that, although donors did not reject the notion of expanded burden-sharing per se, they felt that an increased economic commitment should be directly linked to expanded access to durable solutions other than voluntary repatriation. In other words, they wanted "results" rather than "an open-ended claim on their resources" (Stein 1997).

Most donors had regarded ICARA I as a major commitment and were highly suspicious of African motives for convening a second conference (Gorman 1987, 67). Donors were therefore no longer prepared to commit to providing significant funding unless the projects were clearly linked to durable solutions. With the exception of those states that had already been relative champions of local integration, such as Tanzania, there was a lack of additional willingness on the part of African states to provide local integration. Most African states emphasized voluntary repatriation, which was the ideal durable solution throughout the conference. If there were no significant benefits in terms of additional development assistance, it suited African states to leave refugees in camps and settlements rather than to offer them the same opportunities as their citizens to use their infrastructure and services. Later, a UNHCR evaluation revealed that "the African countries tried to win funds for development projects under the guise of refugee emergency relief. They were more interested in being compensated for the burden of hosting refugees than they were in using these funds to promote local integration" (Loescher 2001b, 228).

In summary, the ICARA process resulted in North–South polarization because African host states wanted additional development assistance while Northern states were unwilling to provide significant nonearmarked assistance without a guarantee that this would translate into an African commitment to local integration. In the absence of a firm donor commitment to provide additional development assistance, the African states were even more reluctant to consider local integration or self-sufficiency for refugees. Given this polarization, as soon as donor attention shifted to the Ethiopian famine in 1984, ICARA dropped off the radar of international attention.

The ICARA process was characterized by an archetypal North–South impasse. Donor states had little incentive to offer funding to programmatic areas that fell outside the scope of their own strategic interests. On the other side, African states had little bargaining power other than to take whatever was on offer or to scupper negotiations entirely. The reasons for the failure of ICARA to promote North–South cooperation can be traced back to the failure to persuade states on both sides that the initiative could serve their wider interests. Northern states were not convinced that a commitment to provide additional development assistance would translate into durable solutions and so reduce their long-term humanitarian assistance obligations. Southern states were not convinced that a commitment to offering local integration or self-sufficiency to refugees would contribute to national development.

To explain the failure to convince Northern and Southern states that their wider interests could be served by ICARA, I now return to the conceptual framework developed in chapter 1. That is, the failure of UNHCR to persuade Northern and Southern states that ICARA was in their interests can be attributed to both the structural relationship between refugee protection and development and to the role of UNHCR.

## The Role of Cross-Issue Persuasion

ICARA I and II were a failure because of the absence of effective cross-issue persuasion. UNHCR implicitly assumed that Northern states would altruistically pledge money to support refugee protection in Africa for its own sake. The pledging conferences addressed refugee protection in isolation, creating no basis for political dialogue within which refugee protection could be discussed or debated within its broader context. But Northern states had little interest in voluntarily contributing to refugee protection in Africa for its own sake. The only significant donor contributions made were done on the basis of wider strategic and foreign policy interests. The heavily earmarked U.S. contributions in ICARA I, for example, were channeled almost exclusively toward its strategic allies in African Cold War proxy conflicts.

UNHCR was unable to successfully persuade Northern donors that contributing additional development assistance would lead to local integration and so reduce the long-term humanitarian aid burden. Nor was it able to persuade African host states that offering local integration would be a means of facilitating development.

The existing literature offers some alternative explanations for the limited legacy of ICARA. These include the lack of effective partnership between UNHCR and UNDP, the role of the 1984 drought and famine in sub-Saharan Africa in diverting international attention from ICARA, and the unwillingness of Northern donors to provide additionality (Gorman 1986, 1987, 1993; Stein 1987, 1997). But each of these mattered only insofar as it contributed to, or was a manifestation of, the failure of cross-issue persuasion. The reason why Northern donors were unwilling to provide additional assistance was because they were not convinced that they had an interest in doing so. The reason why the 1984 drought and famine diverted international priorities was because donor states had no strong self-interested commitment to protecting African refugees. And the reason why the limited partnership between UNDP and UNHCR mattered was because it undermined the institutional basis for linking refugee protection to development.

The UNHCR inability to use cross-issue persuasion to appeal to and channel these wider interests into a commitment to refugee protection is attributable to the absence of either the structural or agency conditions required for cross-issue persuasion. On a structural level, the design of the initiative meant that the institutional connections between refugee protection and development were weak; the prevailing ideas relating refugee aid and development were highly contested and not widely accepted. On an agency level, UNHCR failed to create the type of institutional design that could have facilitated cross-issue persuasion.

## Structural Conditions

The central problem with ICARA I and II was the limited degree to which refugee protection was structurally connected to development in the initiative. The conferences were conceived in a manner that addressed the

**TABLE 2.** Structural Interconnections of ICARA

| Type of Structural Interconnection | Subtype of Structural Interconnection | Refugees-Development | Refugees-Security |
|---|---|---|---|
| Institutions | Internal linkages | No clear conditionality between development and durable solutions | — |
| | External nesting | Lack of effective partnership between UNHCR and UNDP | — |
| Ideas | Intersubjective | RAD: contested | — |
| | Subjective | — | **United States: Cold War proxy conflicts** |

*Notes:* Bold represents structural interconnections that enabled cross-issue persuasion. ICARA, International Conferences on Assistance to Refugees in Africa; RAD, refugee aid and development; UNHCR, United Nations High Commissioner for Refugees; UNDP, United Nations Devolpment Programme.

refugee issue largely in isolation from other issue areas. Indeed, the process ultimately amounted to two one-off pledging conferences in which African states were invited to submit a range of programs and projects to donor states. The underlying assumption was that the donors would provide funding purely because of an altruistic commitment to refugee protection. The way in which refugee protection was structurally connected to other issue areas in the context of ICARA I and II is illustrated in table 2.

In conceiving the initiative, UNHCR did attempt to connect refugee protection to development on institutional and ideational levels. The relationship to development was important because the conferences were an attempt to move beyond short-term relief and emergency assistance to the long-term development of the infrastructure and social services of the host states. In practice, however, the structural connections between refugee protection and development were tenuous and left few opportunities for cross-issue persuasion. Let us explore the extent to which refugee protection was structurally connected to other issue areas through institutions and ideas, and the reasons why these structural interconnections were so tenuous.

## Institutional Linkages

The premise of ICARA I and II was that Northern states would provide development assistance and, in exchange, Southern states would offer refugees local integration and self-sufficiency. On the surface, this suggests that North–South cooperation could have been mutually beneficial if development assistance and durable solutions had been made conditional on one another. In their institutional design, however, neither ICARA I nor ICARA II created a clear contractual relationship between development and durable solutions.

Instead the ICARA institutional design served to separate these two elements. Nowhere in the initiative was an unambiguous contractual relationship between the commitments of donor states and African states established. Indeed, the approach of the conferences as technocratic, one-off pledging conferences reduced the scope for political dialogue in which North–South agreement could have been negotiated. The implicit assumption of UNHCR was that the North and South would simply fulfill their ends of the bargain in the spirit of solidarity and burden-sharing.

The General Assembly Resolution that convened ICARA II further illustrates the degree of institutional separation between development assistance and durable solutions. Rather than creating a contractual relationship between the obligations of North and South, it institutionally divided development assistance and durable solutions, according responsibility for the former to UNDP and the latter to UNHCR.

In General Assembly Resolution 37/197, UNHCR took responsibility for "relief, rehabilitation and local settlement, and durable solutions" (para. 5b), whereas UNDP took responsibility for "strengthening host infrastructure" (para. 5c) (Gorman 1993). This division of labor between UNDP and UNHCR contributed to a separation between durable solutions, for which UNHCR took responsibility, and infrastructural development, for which UNDP took responsibility. This institutional division serves to illustrate how, instead of creating a contractual or conditional relationship between the Northern commitment to development assistance and the Southern commitment to local integration, the two areas were addressed in isolation from one another.

One of the wider structural constraints that UNHCR faced in trying to more fully integrate development and durable solutions in the ICARA institutional design came from the wider UN system. Given that UNHCR had no mandate or expertise in development, UNDP was included in the ICARA II Steering Committee alongside UNHCR, the Secretary-General's Office, and the OAU, with personnel from all four agencies participating in the evaluation of host country project submissions by the technical team. UNDP was a reluctant partner in ICARA II because it was "struggling at the time with 'an unparalleled reduction' in its own resources"; it "was a hesitant, reluctant and uninterested participant" (Stein 1987, 58). It, therefore, had to be cajoled into being involved by the secretary-general. This had implications for ICARA II because it meant that, even though UNDP played a significant technical role, its willingness to engage in advocacy to change donor or host state practices was limited. For example, despite UNDP active involvement in the negotiations, their representative, Orlando Olcese, made it clear that the role of the organization was limited by the level of commitment by states: "present UNDP resources do not allow for any additionality. Host governments are not willing to allow use of present UNDP resources for refugees."[28] The difficulty was that, as previously noted, UNDP was reluctant to be involved because it was going through a funding crisis with declining state contributions in the early 1980s and because refugees were not a priority for the agency (Stein 1987, 52). Therefore, the UNDP technocratic role in ICARA II was limited and did nothing to ensure that the institutional design created an unambiguous linkage between development assistance and durable solutions.

## Ideational Linkages

The dominant discourse in the context of the ICARA process was the notion of RAD, which causally connected development and refugee protection. The discourse had emerged in an academic context in the 1970s, particularly among British academics working on integrated rural development in Africa (Betts 1981, 1984; Chambers 1979). It highlighted the impact of refugee hosting on development and argued that refugee problems should be addressed in the context of development. Given the growing number of long-standing refugee situations in which voluntary repatriation was not immediately possible, RAD pointed to the possibility of moving beyond the dependency created by relief and emergency assistance and instead promoting the self-sufficiency of refugees or even their

---

28. ICARA II briefing, Refugee Policy Group Meeting of OAU Secretariat and voluntary agencies on assistance to refugees in Africa, 22 March 1983. UNHCR Fonds 11, 391.78/200B, UNHCR Archives.

local integration through a developmental approach (Rogge 1987, 86; Stein 1987). Gorman (1993) highlights how the RAD discourse had a number of features: (1) it had a development orientation, (2) it attempted to move refugees toward self-reliance and self-sufficiency, (3) its normative focus was on helping less-developed countries to cope with the impact of refugees on their infrastructure, (4) its approach sought to include the local population as the beneficiaries of projects alongside the refugees, and (5) it was consistent with national development plans. However, one of the weaknesses of RAD was that its definition remained extremely vague and contested during the 1980s (Gorman 1987, 68).

The RAD debate moved beyond academia to become an influential discourse within policy circles (Gorman 1986; Keeley 1981). Poul Hartling adopted RAD as the dominant theme of his term as high commissioner, and in August 1983 a Meeting of Experts on Refugee Aid and Development was convened by UNHCR, bringing together many of the academics who had contributed to the RAD debate. This meeting led to the UNHCR "Refugee Aid and Development Report," which was submitted to ExCom in 1983. The report developed the idea of self-sufficiency as an alternative to local integration and voluntary repatriation and noted, for example, that "it is essential to seek ways of channelling the abilities and energies of the refugees into constructive activities, rather than allowing them to languish in indefinite dependence on care and maintenance." After further consultations with NGOs and other stakeholders, UNHCR then incorporated the report within its *Principles for Action in Developing Countries,* adopted by ExCom in 1984 (Clark and Stein 1985, 37).

RAD clearly structurally connected refugee protection with the development concerns of host states. But, in practice, these ideas offered little to empower the African states or UNHCR vis-à-vis the donor community. First, RAD was not based on consensus. In many ways, it was still an emerging discourse that only fully developed in the aftermath of the ICARA experience. In the early 1980s, it remained a contested concept that had little Northern buy-in. Its relationship to durable solutions was contested because this entailed a number of ambiguities. In particular, although the concept promoted the synonymous concepts of self-reliance, self-help, and self-sufficiency for refugees, it was unclear what relationship, if any, these had to either permanent local integration or voluntary repatriation. Consequently, there was a degree of disconnect between the

concept and potential donor interests in using RAD to facilitate durable solutions and, hence, reduce the long-term commitment of the international
community to emergency relief and to care and maintenance.

Another important structural connection between refugee protection
with other issue areas was the relationship between refugees and security
in the context of the Cold War. The ICARA process must be seen within
its Cold War context, in which refugees were perceived as a tool of the
East-West superpower rivalry. Indeed, as we have noted, many of the self-
settled rural refugees whose situation ICARA attempted to address had
been displaced not by national liberation wars but by proxy conflicts associated with the Cold War. This was particularly the case in southern
Africa and the Horn of Africa. For example, the civil conflicts in, and the
resulting refugees from or in, Ethiopia, Sudan, Angola, and Mozambique
were seen very much in the context of the Cold War (Zolberg, Suhrke, and
Aguayo 1989, 37–102). Viewed in security terms and as possible refugee
warriors, these refugees were selectively supported. Hence, the position of
the major UNHCR contributor to ICARA, the United States, as anticommunist structurally connected the issue of refugee protection to its broader
foreign policy concerns (Loescher 1993, 14–15).

The Cold War ideas that connected refugee protection to security represented one of the few structural opportunities available for UNHCR
and African states to appeal to the interests of donor states in other issue
areas. The United States, in particular, identified the refugee issue within
the context of its policy of supporting exiled guerrilla movements in the
proxy wars in Africa. This created an opportunity for UNHCR to appeal
to these wider interests to attract additional funding. Unfortunately, this
approach had an extremely limited scope for appealing to linked interests
because of the selectivity that it led to, with anticommunist groups and
host states receiving the bulk of the earmarked U.S. contributions.

## Agency Conditions

Even at the time of ICARA, there was a recognition that the success of
the process would rely on creating a structural interconnection between
the refugee issue and development. Northern donors and African states
had divergent interests that related to opposite sides of this relationship.

The African states wanted additional development assistance to compensate for past hosting; the Northern donors wanted to promote local integration for refugees as a durable solution that would remove the need for a long-term financial commitment to refugee protection in Africa. Both aims were reflected in the "two-sided nature" of the ICARA II theme, emphasizing the Southern concerns with burden-sharing and the Northern concern with durable solutions (Stein 1987, 49). Ultimately, ICARA failed to create a credible linkage between the interests of Northern states in sustainable local integration for refugees (durable solutions) and the interests of Southern states in attracting additional development assistance (burden-sharing). Stein highlights this polarization:

> To the African countries of asylum, ICARA II was to be a burden-sharing conference to provide assistance to strengthen their social and economic infrastructure. To the donors, however, the conference provided a chance to achieve durable solutions to prevent future refugee problems and lead to the voluntary repatriation or permanent integration of refugees. Such durable solutions would ease the burden of funding care and maintenance on the international community. (1987, 49)

One of the central limitations on achieving cross-issue persuasion was that ICARA was conceived as a technocratic process. In contrast to CIREFCA and the Indochinese CPA, it was not intended to be a political process. The absence of sustained interstate dialogue or political facilitation by UNHCR meant that there was little opportunity for African states and prospective donors to debate the issue of refugee protection alongside other issue areas. Because the conferences were conceived largely as one-off pledging conferences, they were structurally isolated from other issue areas in a way that greatly reduced the opportunities for Southern states and UNHCR to engage in cross-issue persuasion. In addition, the institutional and ideational links between the refugee issue and development were not sufficiently strong to enable Southern states to use them to be a basis for cross-issue persuasion. This meant that there were few side-payments available to Northern states and little basis for them to overcome the North–South impasse.

The structural relationship of UNHCR to UNDP might have represented an opportunity for the African states to create a linkage between refugee protection, on the one hand, and compensatory development assistance, on the other. The UNDP responsibility for managing the third goal of the conference—"strengthening host infrastructure" (para. 5c)—led to the creation of the "Guidelines for Country Submissions on the Impact of Refugee Problems on National Economies and Possible Development Assistance Required to Alleviate These Problems" (Gorman 1993). This gave African states the opportunity to submit fairly mainstream development projects for assessment by the technical team and then submission to the conference. These Guidelines set out a fairly broad definition for eligible projects to "strengthen existing services, facilities and infrastructure" in a range of areas in which a host country's development was affected by the burden of hosting refugees (Gorman 1987, 177–81). The project submissions, which could be prepared with the support of Resident Representative of UNDP and the local representative of UNHCR, could include almost any development project designed to assist refugees, returnees and host countries.

The Guidelines set out a vast range of possible projects—including infrastructural development, food and basic needs, budgetary support, employment, and even a reference to balance of payments problems (Gorman 1987, 179–80). This gave the African countries an opportunity to prioritize areas of national concern. General Assembly Resolution 37/197 (para. 5c) therefore created a structural opportunity for African states to link their own very broad developmental goals to ICARA II. Unsurprisingly, the majority of the project submissions focused on infrastructure projects to be primarily administered by UNDP which host states believed could provide long-term benefits to their own citizens.

But, when it came to the Conference and its aftermath, this potential source of linkage between refugee protection and development assistance failed to induce greater donor commitment to fund such projects. This was partly due to the divergence in expectations between the North and South, with Northern states refusing to fund projects that had no clear link to durable solutions. The failure was also significantly due to the formalized separation of the UNHCR mandate for durable solutions (under para. 5b) and the UNDP mandate for infrastructural development projects (under para. 5c), so that there was little structural basis on which to connect country submissions to durable solutions and hence to the stated interests of donor states.

The only successful cross-issue persuasion in the context of ICARA was based on the Cold War foreign policy concerns of the Northern donors. As the capitalist superpower, the United States believed that its concern with the containment of communism was related to the protection of African refugees. This provided an ideational basis for cross-issue persuasion. Some African states succeeded in attracting contributions from the United States on the basis of this structural connection. In ICARA I, the most significant contributions went to supporting refugees who were strategically positioned in the proxy conflicts of the Cold War; for example, significant U.S. funding went to addressing the situation of Angolan refugees implicated in the Frente Nacional de Libertação de Angola–União Nacional para a Independência Total de Angola (FNLA-UNITA) struggle against the Movimento Popular de Libertação de Angola (MPLA) and to supporting the Sudan of Colonel Jaafar an Nimeiri. In contrast, very little funding went to support the refugees hosted by Ethiopia because of the links of the Mengistu Haile Mariam regime to Cuba and the Union of Soviet Socialist Republics (USSR), despite the great humanitarian need. The United States and other donors, implicitly linking their earmarked contributions to U.S. alignment in the Cold War, used support for refugees as a strategic tool to support anticommunist guerrilla movements in exile.

Donor states' being able to earmark their contributions in accordance with their interests led to a degree of funding based on these linked interests that may not have been possible had all contributions been commonly pooled and then shared equally.[29] Clearly, however, the disadvantage of this practice was that funding was not allocated on the basis of need but on the basis of extremely selective interests. In the context of the OAU collective bargaining position, the selectivity of donors served to undermine its trust in the process and contributed the lack of confidence in ICARA II by African states.

In CIREFCA and the Indochinese CPA (see chapters 3 and 4), regionalism played a role in enhancing UNHCR agency in the use of cross-issue persuasion in its bargaining. In ICARA, OAU played a strong role in convening the conferences and collectively representing the African states. ICARA had an indirect link to the OAU Refugee Convention, which was

---

29. For a conceptual distinction between *common pooling* and *bilateral allocation* (earmarking), see Kanbur, Sandler, and Morrison (1999).

widely acknowledged as having normative significance within and beyond the continent. The Arusha Conference was a pan-African conference at which African states explicitly reasserted their commitment to the 1969 Convention. This offered the basis for their collective commitment to refugee protection and their collective position with respect to approaching the international community to engage in the ICARA process. What is notable about ICARA is that even in spite of the OAU role in enhancing collective bargaining power, the conferences attracted relatively little international commitment. This illustrates how even strong regional solidarity contributes little to overcoming the North–South impasse in the absence of structural opportunities to appeal to linked interests.

One reflection of the absence of opportunities for cross-issue persuasion was the persistent normative appeal of the Southern states to the principle of burden-sharing throughout the two conferences. Throughout the ICARA process, the African host states and UNHCR attempted to mobilize the concept of burden-sharing to establish that Northern states had an obligation to contribute more equitably and to share financial responsibility for supporting African refugees. In just about every statement by the OAU or individual African states, burden-sharing was invoked to appeal to the general normative obligation of the North to support refugees in the South. At the Arusha Conference, burden-sharing was used by the OAU and the main host states to establish a principle of equitable responsibility and collective solidarity among the African states; in the ICARA conference, it was used as a form of moral and normative persuasion vis-à-vis the international community. But this attempt by Southern states to link ICARA to the wider principle of burden-sharing was not accepted by Northern states and appears to have added very little. Although Northern states did not contest the language and rhetoric of the principle, they simply disengaged from seeing ICARA in those terms, invoking the concept far less commonly. This further highlights the relative futility of appealing to moral obligation rather than trying to create linkages between refugee protection and issue areas in which the North has an interest.

ICARA was premised on persuading states that refugee protection and development were interconnected. It relied on convincing Northern states that committing to additional development assistance would lead to durable solutions for refugees and that this, in turn, would reduce the long-term humanitarian assistance budget. It also relied on convincing Southern states that a commitment to durable solutions in terms of allowing refugees access to local integration would contribute to national development. Ultimately, neither Northern donors nor African host states were persuaded that contributing to ICARA would lead to a payoff in terms of their own interests.

The reason for the failure of cross-issue persuasion can be mainly found in the ICARA institutional design. UNHCR designed ICARA I and II as technocratic pledging conferences in which it was assumed that donors would voluntarily pledge additional resources on the basis of an altruistic commitment to refugee protection. The institutional design of ICARA failed to establish any kind of formal linkage between development and durable solutions; nowhere in the initiative were a Northern commitment to development assistance and a Southern commitment to durable solutions made conditional on one another. Instead, development and durable solutions were institutionally separated from one another in ICARA II, with UNDP taking responsibility for the former and UNHCR for the latter. This institutional design is partly attributable to the decision by UNHCR to conceive ICARA as technocratic pledging conferences rather than as politically engaged dialogues; it is also attributable to the deeper structural constraints posed by the wider UN system and, in particular, the reluctant involvement by UNDP in ICARA II.

Furthermore, on an ideational level, although the RAD debates were emerging, there was no consensus on the causal relationship between development assistance and refugee protection; both donors and hosts were skeptical about the relationship between additional development assistance and durable solutions. The only exception to this absence of structural interconnections in ICARA was the way in which ideas held by the United States about the relationship between refugees and Cold War security connected the refugee issue to wider foreign policy concerns. This created a structural opportunity for a minority of African states to attract additional financial support on the basis of their strategic relevance to Cold War proxy conflicts.

UNHCR therefore had few possibilities to appeal to the interests of states in other issue areas while bargaining. Its capacity to use cross-issue persuasion was greatly diminished by the institutional design and ideational context of the initiative. This meant that the conferences reverted to the type of North–South impasse described in the Introduction. Without significant connected interests, Northern commitment to refugee protection in Africa remained limited. Once other humanitarian priorities such as the sub-Saharan African famine emerged, there was no remaining donor commitment to ICARA, and it faded from political attention with little lasting material legacy.

The ICARA process serves to illustrate the archetypal North–South impasse. With few Northern interests in supporting the hosting of refugees in the South and little Southern power to induce additional Northern support, the African states simply had to take whatever was on offer. The ICARA experience highlights that a significant part of the failure to overcome the impasse was attributable to the way in which UNHCR conceived ICARA, which created only weak structural interconnections between development and refugee protection. In the absence of such structural interconnections, UNHCR was unable to successfully appeal to Northern interest in reducing the long-term humanitarian assistance budget and Southern interest in attracting additional development assistance and to connect the two within multilateral negotiations.

# 3

# The International Conference on Central American Refugees (1987–1995)

During the 1970s and 1980s, the civil conflicts in Central America led to significant levels of human displacement in the region. Of a total displaced population in the region of around 2 million at the end of the 1980s, some 150,000 were recognized as refugees and were therefore of direct concern to UNHCR. Toward the end of the Cold War, the prospect of a regional peace deal opened up possibilities for refugees to receive access to the durable solutions of either returning home or being locally integrated. The possibility of peace brought with it hope of a renewed commitment to refugee protection, with states moving beyond the widely held perception that refugees constituted an inevitable security threat to the state or were guerrillas fighting on behalf of one or other of the Cold War superpowers.

To take advantage of the new opportunities for refugee protection available within the region, UNHCR conceived the Conferencica Internacional sobre los Refugiados Centroamericanos (International Conference on Central American Refugees; CIREFCA). CIREFCA had some similarities with the African ICARA conferences explored in the previous chapter insofar as it was a regional conference intended to enhance refugees' access to protection and resolve a long-standing refugee situation. It was also similar inasmuch as it was based on the notion of RAD; that is, it attempted to use development assistance as a means of enhancing refugees' access to durable solutions. Aside from these superficial similarities, the contrast between ICARA and CIREFCA could hardly be greater. Whereas the African conferences had addressed refugee protection largely in isolation, the Central American conference was part of a much wider process, being an explicit element of both the wider regional peace process and its related postconflict reconstruction and development initiative. Furthermore, whereas ICARA had been conceived as a technocratic initiative based around two one-off pledging conferences, CIREFCA was a political process that ran over a number of years.

In contrast to ICARA, CIREFCA was highly successful in leading to North–South cooperation and enhancing refugees' access to both legal protection and durable solutions within the region. It also made an indirect contribution to peace in the region. The projects and programs compiled by UNHCR and submitted to the main 1989 CIREFCA conference were almost fully funded, mainly by European donor states, and the Central American states cooperated in the implementation of most aspects of CIREFCA. What is notable about CIREFCA is that its success can be significantly attributed to cross-issue persuasion. Neither the European donors nor the Central American states were interested in promoting enhanced refugee protection for its own sake; nevertheless, both groups of states were persuaded that their wider interests could be met by cooperating in refugee protection. In particular, both groups of states regarded refugee protection to be an important component of peace, security, and development in the region.

What was crucial to the CIREFCA success was the way in which it was institutionally designed by UNHCR. Rather than addressing refugee protection in isolation, CIREFCA was conceived to be nested within a wider set of institutions, including the Esquipulas II Peace process for the region and the Special Programme of Economic Cooperation for Central America (PEC). CIREFCA therefore came to be seen as a central part of these wider structures, which were valued by both the Central American states and the European donors. UNHCR consciously used these and other interconnections as a means to channel the wider interests of states into refugee protection.

I begin this chapter by explaining the context, process, and outcome of the initiative, how CIREFCA was conceived and its contribution to legal protection and durable solutions. I then highlight the crucial role that cross-issue persuasion played in UNHCR's successfully overcoming the North–South impasse and the conditions that enabled cross-issue persuasion to take place. As I show, CIREFCA represents the single most successful example of North–South cooperation in the history of the global refugee regime because it met the preconditions for successful cross-issue persuasion.

## The CIREFCA Process

At the end of a decade of civil conflict in which around 160,000 people were killed, around 2 million people were estimated to have been displaced in Central America. Of these, approximately 150,000 were recognized as refugees, approximately 900,000 were undocumented externally displaced, and approximately 900,000 were IDPs. With the rapprochement at the end of the Cold War, the prospects for regional peace improved. The Contadora Act for Peace and Cooperation in 1986 and the subsequent Arias Peace Plan[1] ultimately led to the Esquipulas II Peace Accords in August 1987, which provided an enduring peace deal for the region. Until the Esquipulas II peace deal, the displaced had been selectively supported or vilified depending on whether they were perceived as a source of instability for governments of the left or right. The peace process therefore created new opportunities and incentives for addressing displacement by changing the perceived relationship between refugees and national security.

In the context of this peace process, renewed prospects for durable solutions for the displaced started to emerge. The viability of refugee repatriation began with the Tripartite Agreements for the return of Nicaraguan and Guatemalan refugees. These were concluded among Mexico, Guatemala, and UNHCR, and among El Salvador, Nicaragua, and UNHCR.

---

1. This process was led by Oscar Arias, the Costa Rican president. He was later awarded the Nobel Peace Prize for his part in facilitating the Esquipulas II agreement.

Meanwhile, a renewed commitment to regional economic development under the UNDP PEC opened the possibility for UNHCR and UNDP to begin to collaborate on ways in which this program might benefit the displaced.

UNHCR had been active in Central America states since the late 1970s. The 1984 Cartagena Declaration, although not legally binding, recommended minimum standards for refugee treatment in the region and provided a definition of *refugee* tailored to the particularities of displacement in Latin America. In this context, and with the growing prospects for peace in the region and the recognition of the need for durable solutions, a Consultative Working Group on Possible Solutions to Refugee Problems in Central America was convened by UNHCR in May 1987 to consider the possibility of a conference to build on the legacy of Cartagena. In the words of the UNHCR Mexican representative, this initial group was "conceived as a pragmatic followup to Cartagena in the search for political consensus and viable solutions."[2] Its work eventually led to the elaboration of CIREFCA.

## Conceiving CIREFCA

From early in its planning, CIREFCA was "conceived not only as an event, but, perhaps even more significantly, as a process."[3] Rather than being a one-off conference, its work ran from 1987 until 1994. Beginning with two Consultative Working Group sessions in 1987 and drawing on the input of experts from the region, CIREFCA was conceived as a followup to the 1984 Cartagena Declaration but received new impetus as a result of the peace deal (Esquipulas II) agreed on by the regional heads of state in August 1987. This allowed UNHCR to draw on the commitment to peace and development of the countries in the region and of donors, and to channel this into a commitment to finding solutions for the displaced. CIREFCA received much of its legitimacy from Article 8 of Esquipulas II and its reference to displacement, and the CIREFCA Concerted Plan

2. Santistevan to Franco and Muller, memo, August 1987, UNHCR Fonds 11, Series 3, 391.86C Mex/HCR/0556, UNHCR Archives.

3. Deljoo to Asomani, "International Conference on Central American Refugees, Guatemala City, May 1989: Preliminary Information," memo, 5 December 1988, UNHCR Fonds 11, Series 3, 391.86, HCR/NYC/1466, UNHCR Archives

of Action itself was incorporated as the chapter on displacement in the UNDP wider postconflict reconstruction initiative, PEC.

The underlying ethos of CIREFCA was to find durable solutions for displacement through an integrated development approach, closing the gap between relief and development. This meant that collaboration between UNHCR and UNDP was a central feature of CIREFCA. They jointly ran a permanent secretariat for the initiative, the Joint Support Unit (JSU), based in San José, Cost Rica. Both organizations provided the seven regional states with technical support in developing their own priority projects, both for initial submission to CIREFCA and for submission to the International Follow-Up Conferences. Integrated development was seen as a means to simultaneously address the needs of refugees, returnees, and the internally displaced while also benefiting local communities (UNHCR 1994a).

The Guatemala City Conference adopted a Declaration and a Concerted Plan of Action. The Concerted Plan of Action provided an initial portfolio of thirty-six projects, requiring US$375 million over a three-year period, which was later added to. The initial project submissions were compiled by states with the support of a five-week UNHCR mission to the region in mid-1988. The Concerted Plan of Action also provided a set of Principles and Criteria for Protection and Assistance. Implicitly, the adoption of policies, standards, and legal norms was posited by UNHCR as a condition for states to receive financial support through CIREFCA. In practice, however, the availability of relatively large amounts of unconditional funding from UNDP and the simultaneous Italian government Programa para los Desplazados (Development Programme for Displaced Persons, Refugees and Returnees in Central America; PRODERE) project, which principally targeted IDPs rather than refugees, undermined the credibility of this implicit conditionality.[4]

Significantly, and in contrast to ICARA, the Guatemala City Conference, the focal point of CIREFCA, was explicitly *not* conceived as a pledging conference. Instead, its primary aim was to establish a political consensus on which UNHCR could build a multiyear process. The strategy for how to develop political support and then translate this into the mobilization of

---

4. Interview with José Riera, programme officer to the JSU during CIREFCA, UNHCR, October 24, 2005.

resources was clearly elaborated from an early stage in the preparations.[5] A tactical proposal divided the promotion of funding into four phases, going from the lead-up phase (prior to the final preparatory conference) to the postconference followup. The initial stages of the strategy explicitly shunned a financial emphasis in favor of fostering political support. It noted of the lead-up phase: "The top priority must be promotion of policy/political/diplomatic support for the Conference as such and for the strategies it represents. In this perspective, fund-raising of any active or specific kind is dangerous. Too much pressure on the fund-raising issue now could even affect the yet-to-be determined level and quality of political/policy support for the Conference."[6]

Instead of encouraging pledging, support for the process, high-level participation at the conference, and "mention[ing] discretely that it is... the hope of UNHCR that policy support would be translated at a later date into a financial contribution/commitment" were highlighted as preconference priorities, and CIREFCA itself was seen primarily as a political event, with the Declaration and Concerted Plan of Action being an interstate consensus rather than a programmatic list intended to attract money.[7] This approach contrasted significantly with that of ICARA. The tactical plan for funding envisaged that the financial issue would be raised informally, at least until political will had been mobilized and consolidated. A meeting for ExCom members in Geneva in May was the first time that the financial issue was raised directly with donors, and this was simply to forewarn delegations that, at the Guatemala Conference, "UNHCR would like to meet each donor delegation informally outside the plenary session to discuss with them possible contribution levels."[8]

At the conference itself, when the issue of contributions was broached in bilateral consultations, the UNHCR strategy emphasized flexibility and

---

5. "Procedures for the Preparatory Activities of the Conference Itself and the Establishment of Follow-Up Mechanisms," proposal submitted to the Organizing Committee Meeting, 24 January 1989, Guatemala, UNHCR Fonds 11, Series 3, 391.86.3 HCR/NYC/0102, UNHCR Archives.

6. Kevin Lyonette to Leonardo Franco, "Tactical Proposal for Promotion of Funding of CIREFCA Projects," memo, 19 April 1989, UNHCR Fonds 11, Series 3, 391.86.3, UNHCR Archives.

7. Ibid.

8. Ibid.

informality, arguing that "The informality will encourage donor frank-
ness plus emphasise the flexibility and dynamism of the UNHCR approach
without prejudicing the status of the Conference as *not* being a pledging
conference." Once the tentative indications of areas of donor support were
made in the aftermath of the conference, the tactical plan foresaw that
these would be entered into a master chart to be shared with donor representatives, allowing the political momentum to snowball.[9] Unlike with the
earlier ICARA II experience, the process was therefore based on a clear
strategy to generate and build political impetus toward and beyond the
main conference, rather than focusing exclusively on a one-off, financially
focused pledging conference (Betts 2008). Ironically, this strategy brought
fairly immediate expressions of financial interest.[10]

The project proposals varied from country to country depending notably on whether the state was primarily a country of origin or one of
asylum and, in the latter case, how tolerant or restrictive that country
was toward freedom of movement and the socioeconomic integration of
refugees.

- In Guatemala, the projects focused on facilitating the reintegration for returnees in Huehuetenango and El Quiche by strengthening health, education, and sanitation services and by improving basic infrastructure.
- In Costa Rica, the projects aimed primarily at promoting labor market integration to allow refugees and another 250,000 externally displaced people from El Salvador and Nicaragua to socially and economically integrate
  through, for example, improved access to the jobs market and health care.
- In Mexico, the projects focused on self-reliance for Guatemalan refugees,
  notably through agricultural projects in Chiapas and the rural resettlement
  projects in Campeche and Quintana Roo.
- In Nicaragua, the projects focused on rehabilitation and reintegration activities for returnees mainly from Honduras.
- In Honduras, given the restrictions on freedom of movement there, the projects paid attention to strengthening UNHCR assistance in camps, pending
  the refugees' return to Guatemala and Nicaragua.

---

9. Ibid.

10. Kevin Lyonette to High Commissioner, "Note on Potential Donor Attitudes to the
CIREFCA Project Proposals," 13 June 1989, UNHCR Fonds 11, Series 3, 391.86.3, UNHCR
Archives.

- In Belize, the projects focused on improving self-reliance and local integration opportunities for refugees, mainly through strengthening the existing integrated rural development project at the Valley of Peace and improving infrastructure in the Northern Orange Walk and Western Cayo districts.
- In El Salvador, aside from nominal support for Nicaraguan refugees and returnees, PRODERE, in particular, envisaged meeting the basic needs of the IDPs in the country.

The process evolved as it went along to integrate new approaches and enlarge its portfolio of projects. In particular, the Italian government decided to allocate its US$115 million budget surplus to a development project in Central America, expanding the embryonic PRODERE territorial development project already underway in El Salvador under the auspices of UNDP. Then, late in the process, UNHCR also developed complementary initiatives such as its Quick Impact Projects (QIPs) to support the immediate developmental needs of returnee integration, and the First Regional Forum on Gender Focus in Working with Refugee, Returnee and Displaced Women (Forefem), which created a forum for mainstreaming a gendered approach to protection and solutions. A crucial component of the CIREFCA political momentum was also its followup mechanisms, coordinated by the JSU. The National Coordinating Committees facilitated the ongoing formulation of projects and solicited financial support for them. Perhaps most significantly, however, the JSU contributed to convening International Follow-Up Meetings in New York in June 1990 and San Salvador in April 1992. These meetings, unlike the 1989 conference, were explicitly conceived as pledging conferences and allowed CIREFCA to maintain an ongoing donor focus.[11]

In total, CIREFCA is estimated to have channeled US$422.3 million in additional resources to the region, and the process has been widely credited with helping to consolidate peace in Central America. This financial support emerged gradually as the process evolved. The First International Follow-Up Meeting in New York in June 1990 pledged US$245 million, and the Second Follow-Up in El Salvador in April 1992 pledged a further

---

11. Pablo Mateu (JSU) to K. Asomani (RBLAC), "From Conflict to Peace and Development: Note on Implementation of the Concerted Plan of Action of CIREFCA,"17 March 1992, UNHCR Fonds 11, Series 3, 361.86.5, UNHCR Archives.

US$81 million. Of the initial pledges, the commitment by the Italian government of US$115 million to fund PRODERE was by far the largest. Throughout the process, the most significant group of donors was the European states, both bilaterally and through the EEC.

In its immediate aftermath, CIREFCA was generally seen as a success in terms of enhancing refugees' access to protection and durable solutions (UNHCR 1994b). Although there has been little formal monitoring of the projects implemented under CIREFCA, the extent to which it raised a significant proportion of its required funding clearly distinguishes it from the limited legacy of ICARA I and II. A General Assembly Resolution on CIREFCA passed at the Eighty-Fifth Session in late 1993 expressed "its conviction that the work carried out through the integrated conference process could serve as *a valuable lesson to be applied to other regions of the world.*"[12] Furthermore, over time, UNHCR has increasingly highlighted CIREFCA as a model because many of its achievements in facilitating access to durable solutions.[13] The initiative is seen as an example of successful international cooperation between regional host states and countries of origin, on the one hand, and donor states beyond the region, on the other, for improving access to durable solutions, enhancing protection within the region, and addressing the root causes of displacement through peacebuilding. Let us highlight the way in which CIREFCA contributed to each of these in turn.

## Contribution to Refugee Protection

The most obvious contribution of CIREFCA was the projects that it developed, implemented, and financed. Although the total amount of additional funding attracted by CIREFCA is difficult to estimate accurately because of difficulties in tracking bilaterally funded NGO projects implemented in the framework of CIREFCA, a total of US$422.3 million was recorded by the CIREFCA JSU by 1994, which amounts to an estimated

---

12. "International Conference on Central American Refugees," UN General Assembly Resolution A/RES/48/117, 85th Plenary Session, 20 December 1993, New York, UNHCR Fonds 11, Series 3, 391.86.5, UNHCR Archives.

13. For an account of some of the difficulties that UNHCR has had in replicating the success of CIREFCA, see UN High Commissioner for Refugees ([UNHCR] 2006), chaps. 5 and 6.

86 percent of the total project requirements. Of this, 32 percent was channeled via UNDP, 24 percent via NGOs, 19 percent via UNHCR, and 17 percent directly to governments.[14] By 1993, this funding had provided full or partial financing for seventy-two priority projects in the seven countries and US$240 million of the US$345 million pledged up to that point had been disbursed (UNHCR 1993). The projects focused on a range of areas, including immediate assistance, rehabilitation, economic development, and institution-building. The underlying ethos of all of the projects, however, was to develop an integrated approach that would span the relief-to-development continuum and support integration or reintegration. Although the intention was to incorporate externally and internally displaced people as "beneficiaries of multi-sectoral development projects," the reality was that refugees and returnees ultimately represented the principal beneficiaries, despite constituting only a small proportion of the total displaced population. UNHCR later recognized that in focusing mainly on refugees, the projects addressed only "the tip of the iceberg."[15] One of the criticisms made in the UNHCR independent review of CIREFCA was that it "did not establish appropriate mechanisms at the start to track funding and monitor projects" (UNHCR 1994b). This shortcoming makes retrospective assessment of the projects extremely sketchy.

In terms of durable solutions, CIREFCA contributed to voluntary repatriation through the protection principles it elaborated in the Plan of Action, through both the resources it allocated to support reintegration and notably through political dialogue in relation to the Tripartite Agreements. This work allowed the repatriation of some 27,000 Salvadorans and 62,000 Nicaraguans, and the return of 45,000 Guatemalans from Mexico.[16] These returns were supported by what might be considered the precursor of the UNHCR 4Rs (repatriation, reintegration, rehabilitation, and reconstruction) framework (UNHCR 2003b). Indeed, the PRODERE approach to integrated development linked assistance for local communities with that for returnees by developing social services and infrastructure in border

14. D. Chefeke to all SMC members, "CIREFCA Process: External Evaluation," memo, 21 September 1994, UNHCR Fonds 11, Series 3, 391.86.5, UNHCR Archives.

15. Jenifer Otsea to Von Arnim, "CIREFCA: A Strategy for Solution," memo, 8 February 1993, UNHCR Fonds 11, Series 3, 361.86.5, UNHCR Archives.

16. For an evaluation of the UNHCR repatriation reintegration programs in Guatemala, see UNHCR (1999).

regions (UNHCR 1993). Within the framework of CIREFCA, UNHCR and UNDP also developed QIPs, which supported basic needs and short-term productive infrastructure for 70,000 returnees in Nicaragua (Crisp and Martin 1992).

The CIREFCA projects were also notable for the extent to which they facilitated self-sufficiency and local integration. The most obvious case study for successful self-sufficiency was in Mexico in Campeche and Quintana Roo in the Yucatan Peninsula, where consolidation of the local agricultural settlements and the development of integrated service provision benefited both the 18,800 refugees and the host communities. In Chiapas, self-sufficiency was also encouraged, but a shortage of land was an obstacle to allowing refugees to become equally engaged in agricultural activities. In the Campeche and Quintana Roo, local integration and repatriation were promoted simultaneously from 1996, whereas in Chiapas local integration *followed* repatriation from 1998 onward. The self-sufficiency and local integration projects ultimately provided education, health services, access to markets, and sustainable livelihoods. For the Mexican government the projects were seen as an attractive means of developing the poorest areas of the country, particularly in the Yucatan Peninsula.[17]

CIREFCA also provided local integration for Salvadoran refugees in Belize, particularly through the Valley of Peace project. Although the project had begun in 1983 and had been widely criticized for relocating refugees to a jungle area with poor roads and poor-quality land, CIREFCA helped to resurrect the Valley of Peace project.[18] By 2003, some three hundred families remained and were integrated alongside the Belizeans of predominantly Maya Quechi ethnicity. Initially supported with food aid, a fund to build housing and provide tools and seeds, many of the Salvadorans now work in the tourism industry or in local employment, receiving social services alongside the Belizean community (*El Diario de Hoy,* "From Conflict to the Valley of Peace," October 18, 2005).

There was also a degree of local integration in Costa Rica. This took place on a smaller scale and was mainly for Salvadoran refugees in urban

---

17. Interview with Ana Low, UNHCR intern researching self-sufficiency and local integration in southern Mexico, UNHCR, October 25, 2005.

18. Interview with Pablo Mateu, former programme officer (JSU), UNHCR, October 18, 2005.

areas, who were few in number and were perceived to be hard-working. This contrasted with the Costa Rican approach to the Nicaraguan refugees, who, although they were given a degree of self-sufficiency in agricultural production, had been largely confined to camps and were not given the same level of opportunities to integrate.[19]

In addition to facilitating access to durable solutions for refugees, the development of international protection norms within the region was one of the most significant outcomes of the process. CIREFCA was explicitly conceived as a followup to the Cartagena Declaration, and a major part of the UNHCR contribution to the initiative was the drafting of legal standards for adoption by the countries in the region. As part of the CPA, a document was prepared, entitled "Principles and Criteria for the Protection of and Assistance to Central American Refugees, Returnees and Displaced Persons in Latin America," which summarized and offered guidance on issues relating to protection standards. Indeed, UNHCR concluded that "Throughout CIREFCA, international protection has undoubtedly been strengthened in the region through the reaffirmation of the fundamental principle of *non-refoulement* and the notion that refugees should not be the objects of discriminatory treatment."[20] For example, Belize acceded to the 1951 Convention and passed a 1991 Refugee Act, which included the incorporation of refugees in national development plans; Honduras acceded to the 1951 Convention and 1967 Protocol; Mexico introduced the refugee concept into its national legislation even though it did not accede to the 1951 Convention until later; and Costa Rica passed a one-year amnesty for all externally displaced people, allowing them to regularize and locally integrate.[21]

Another significant element of the dissemination of protection norms concerned the work of Forefem, which was convened toward the end of the CIREFCA process.

CIREFCA also contributed to the dissemination of protection norms through promoting the role of NGOs in the region. A UNHCR representative reflecting on CIREFCA noted that "The formal recognition of the significant potential contribution of NGOs has proven to be one of the

---

19. Ibid.
20. Mateu to Asomani, "From Conflict to Peace and Development."
21. Ibid.

most significant achievements of CIREFCA."[22] In a region where states had been reluctant to acknowledge the role of civil society, CIREFCA allowed a growing acceptance of their role within the humanitarian sphere. For example, Nicaragua included NGOs in its own CIREFCA Working Group, El Salvador drafted its official documentation for the Second International Follow-Up Committee Meeting in full consultation with NGOs, and Guatemala negotiated with NGOs in its implementation of returnee assistance programs.[23] NGOs ultimately served as implementation partners for around 60 percent of the CIREFCA projects,[24] with 38 percent of funding being channeled directly to NGOs.[25] Aside from implementation, NGOs also played a growing role in the multilateral negotiations on CIREFCA. For example, the Swedish Refugee Council appears to have played a particularly important role in enlisting the support of other international NGOs for the CIREFCA process. The Swedish Refugee Council was particularly highly regarded in El Salvador, which had been identified as one of the key CIREFCA countries for UNHCR.[26]

Throughout the process, NGOs from the region seized the opportunity to mobilize and establish wider networks. In particular, the First International Conference of NGOs on Central American Refugees, Displaced Persons and Returnees was held in Mexico City for three days in March 1989 and was led and coordinated by the main NGOs from the region.[27] The conference was significant because it led to the formation of a regional association, which held a constituent assembly in March 1990 in Guatemala City; this led to the Second International Consultation of NGOs in Managua in July 1991.[28] Therefore, not only did NGOs contribute to CIREFCA, but the development of civil society within the region was itself a successful outcome of CIREFCA.

---

22. Ibid.

23. Ibid.

24. "UNHCR Report on General Assembly Resolution," no. 46/107 (CIREFCA), 28 June 1992, UNHCR Fonds 11, Series 3, 391.86.5, UNHCR Archives.

25. Otsea to Von Arnim, "CIREFCA."

26. Information obtained through informal discussions with UNHCR staff.

27. Claus Van der Vaeren (EEC), "Report on the Preparatory Meeting for CIREFCA, Antigua, Guatemala, 28–30 February 1989," UNHCR Fonds 11, Series 3, 391.86.1, UNHCR Archives.

28. Mateu to Asomani, "From Conflict to Peace and Development."

## The Role of Cross-Issue Persuasion

The success of CIREFCA relied on the commitment of the European Community (EC) as the main group of donor states and of the Central American host states and countries of origin. Without their willingness to cooperate, CIREFCA would not have been able to overcome the long-standing regional refugee crisis. Yet, on both sides, the motives underlying a willingness to contribute were based on a belief that contributing to refugee protection was a means of meeting their wider interests in a combination of peace and security or development. For both sets of actors, UNHCR played an important role in persuading them that these wider interests in security, peace-building, and development could be achieved through a commitment to CIREFCA. As High Commissioner Sadako Ogata said toward the end of the process, "CIREFCA has been a key formative experience in many respects, breaking new ground in...demonstrating the important linkages between solutions, the consolidation of peace and development."[29]

The EC and its member states were by far the most significant donors to CIREFCA. In financial terms, the EC provided US$110 million for CIREFCA projects between 1989 and 1993, 45 percent of the total mobilized during that period. Of this, $30.4 million was for programs implemented by UNHCR, making up 47 percent of the total contributions channeled through UNHCR. This was in addition to the related $115 million that Italy provided to support mainly IDPs through PRODERE. This important European role contrasted notably with the limited contribution made by the United States. Until the fall of the Sandanista regime, the Ronald Reagan administration avoided any multilateral commitment to the region, preferring instead to channel money bilaterally in accordance with its geostrategic interests. This meant that, until the end of the Cold War, the European states were the most important donors to CIREFCA. The commitment of the Central American states was also imperative to the success of the initiative. It relied on the countries of origin and host countries' being willing to implement the projects and programs of CIREFCA,

---

29. Sadako Ogata, "Introductory Statement by Mrs Sadako Ogata," informal meeting of ExCom, 28 January 1994, Geneva, UNHCR Fonds 11, Series 3, 391.86.5, UNHCR Archives.

reintegrating returnees, locally integrating refugees, and improving legal protection standards throughout the region. Yet for neither side was this commitment to CIREFCA based on a concern with refugee protection for its own sake.

The European donor states were motivated by a range of factors. For example, it has been suggested that Italy was motivated partly by solidarity with fellow left-wing Christian democratic governments, whereas the Nordic states were concerned to promote broadly cosmopolitan values in their overseas development assistance.[30] Most important among the European motives, however, was the aim of promoting regional security and development, partly as a basis for facilitating greater interregional trade. As UNHCR noted, "the Community has regarded CIREFCA as an integral part of efforts towards peace, development and democracy in Central America."[31] Sweden openly claimed that "the support of Sweden for CIREFCA was inextricably linked to its support for the Central American peace process." The statements of the European Commission and Norway also explicitly stated that their motivation for contributing was to CIREFCA was its relationship to postconflict reconstruction and development within the Esquipulas II framework.[32] A joint UNDP-UNHCR document reiterated this, noting that the main European commitment that led the EC and a number of European states to contribute to CIREFCA was the relationship of the initiative to Esquipulas II (UN Development Programme [UNDP] and UNHCR 1995).

The EC commitment to peace and security in Central America had been evident since the 1984 San José Declaration, which established an annual forum for political and economic cooperation between the EC and Central American states. The annual San José Summit created a basis for a sustained dialogue between the foreign ministers of the regions throughout the CIREFCA process.[33] The EC had a particular concern to support

---

30. Interview with José Riera, UNHCR, November 17, 2005; interview with Mateu.

31. Jenifer Otsea (CIREFCA JSU) to UNHCR Brussels, "CIREFCA: A Strategy for Solutions," 8 February 1993, UNHCR Fonds 11, Series 3, 391.86.5, UNHCR Archives.

32. "Reunion Tecnica Informal Sobre CIREFCA," 15–16 February 1994, San José, UNHCR Archives. (On file with the author.)

33. Ruprecht Von Arnim (representative to Brussels) to Jenifer Otsea (headquarters), "The Ninth San José Summit of Foreign Ministers of the EC and Countries of Central America," memo, 3 March 1993, UNHCR Fonds 11, Series 3, 391.86/381, UNHCR Archives.

the conditions that would facilitate Central America's emerging as a viable European trading partner. Twenty percent of the regional trade was with the EC countries, and Europe therefore had a significant stake in ensuring that there was sufficient regional security to allow economic stability, growth, and development (Garoz and MacDonald 1996, 5). For the European states, CIREFCA was of value insofar as it contributed to these wider aims.

The Central American states were motivated by a desire to promote regional security and to attract development assistance to the region. Participating in the implementation of CIREFCA was worthwhile insofar as the permanent integration of refugees within either their host country or country of origin was perceived to be a means to promote peace and security or a means of attracting additional development assistance that would simultaneously benefit the citizens of the refugee-hosting states. Sergio Vieira de Mello, in his role as coordinator of the conference, commented that much of the commitment of Central American states to CIREFCA was linked directly to the peace process: "the five governments attach a special importance to having the Conference convened at the earliest possible date, if only to demonstrate that consensus is possible on the social and humanitarian components of the Esquipulas II Accord."[34] CIREFCA allowed the Central American states to demonstrate their seriousness about the peace process in a way that would attract international economic support.

Part of the reason why the North–South impasse was overcome in CIREFCA was not only that the states held these wider interests but that UNHCR was able to persuade the European donors and Central American states that refugee protection was inextricably related to these wider interests. It was able to persuade European states that targeting development assistance to refugees could contribute to peace and regional development and to persuade Central American states that supporting the implementation of CIREFCA was integral to regional peace and security and offered a means of attracting development assistance that could simultaneously

---

34. Sergio Vieira de Mello, "Preparation of the International Conference on Solutions to the Problems of Central American Refugees as a Contribution to Peace," report on a mission to Central America, Mexico and UN Headquarters, 16–18 March 1988, UNHCR Fonds 11, Series 3, 391.86.1, UNHCR Archives.

benefit the local population. This relied on CIREFCA's meeting the structural and agency conditions for cross-issue persuasion.

## Structural Conditions

Unlike ICARA, the institutional design of CIREFCA created important structural interconnections between refugee protection and other issue areas in which states had an interest. These institutional interconnections were further underpinned by a set of widely accepted ideas about the relationship between refugee protection and those wider issue areas.

### Institutional Linkages

In contrast to ICARA, CIREFCA did not attempt to address refugee protection in isolation. Rather, the UNHCR institutional design nested CIREFCA within a broader range of institutional structures. Most important, CIREFCA was conceived to be part of the wider regional peace process and postconflict reconstruction initiative for the region. Furthermore, in contrast to ICARA, CIREFCA was based on a strong partnership between UNHCR and UNDP and between UNHCR and the Office of the Secretary-General, helping to underscore institutional connections between refugee protection, on the one hand, and development and security, on the other. These structures created a contractual relationship in which a commitment to refugee protection was seen as a necessary component of the wider institutional structures.

*Esquipulas II and Special Programme of Economic Cooperation for Central America*   The most significant institutional feature of CIREFCA was the way in which it was nested within the wider peace deal and postconflict reconstruction and development initiative for the region. The Esquipulas II Declaration, which formed the normative basis of the regional peace deal, represented a strong commitment by the Central American states to work toward peace collectively and in cooperation with the international community. After late 1987, CIREFCA evolved to become structurally connected to the wider peace process. Article 8 of the declaration, for example, focused on the displaced, and CIREFCA was intended to be an integral part of PEC, the development initiative that existed to support peace and reconstruction in the region. The interconnection between the peace process and CIREFCA conferred a great deal of normative legitimacy on the latter, ensuring the commitment of states within and beyond the region. But UNHCR recognized that the most important factor drawing these elements together was the peace process. An in-house reflection piece noted:

> The most important aspect of CIREFCA is its intimate link to the concerted search by the Central American Presidents, with the support of the Secretary-General of the UN, for a negotiated peace.... A careful reading of the CIREFCA documents leads to the conclusion that Esquipulas II is the philosophical underpinning of the Conference. An analysis of the CIREFCA Declaration highlights the interrelationship of efforts in favor of refugees, returnees and displaced persons and those in favor of peace, democracy and development taking place in the regions. This interrelationship is more explicitly reaffirmed in the sections entitled Fundamentals of the Plan of Action where the affected countries link the proposals for solutions in favor of the affected groups with efforts towards regional peace and development; frame these proposals within Esquipulas II; and tie the success of the Plan of Action to economic and social development in the region.[35]

Furthermore, in addition to the explicit reference to displacement in Esquipulas II, Chapter 1 of the UNDP PEC focused specifically on displacement. It was agreed that CIREFCA would form the basis for this; indeed, as previously noted, ultimately the CIREFCA Plan of Action became that section of PEC. This nested structure served to make addressing the protracted regional refugee situation an explicit and integral part of postconflict reconstruction and also institutionally enshrined the need for interorganizational collaboration by making CIREFCA part of an explicitly UNDP-led framework.

*The Wider United Nations System*   Given that the underlying philosophy of CIREFCA was to bridge the relief-development gap, the UNHCR collaboration with UNDP was identified as central to its success. UNHCR

---

35. Mateu to Asomani, "From Conflict to Peace and Development."

noted that "The success of the CIREFCA process has its foundation in development.... a bridge thus needs to be built whereby the uprooted populations addressed in the CIREFCA initiatives are gradually incorporated into national development efforts."[36]

Within the context of Chapter 1 of the PEC, there was a focus on displacement with two separate elements: PRODERE, which focused mainly on IDPs, and CIREFCA, which focused mainly on refugees. PREDERE became the cornerstone of interagency collaboration between UNHCR and UNDP because of the significant amount of money it channeled through UNDP to address displacement.[37] Funded with a US$115 million donation from Italy, it aimed to benefit, either directly or indirectly, 443,000 (mainly) IDPs in six states (excluding Mexico) by focusing on providing basic needs and socioeconomic integration for war-affected populations.[38] When these projects focused on returnees or refugees, UNDP contracted UNHCR to take on the role of implementing partner for PRODERE. This helped to underpin a simultaneously collaborative relationship with CIREFCA. The attempts to foster UNHCR-UNDP collaboration led to mixed results. Although successful collaboration took place at the headquarters level or when there was sustained personal contact, as in the case of the JSU, there were particular difficulties experienced at the field level.

At the headquarters level, UNDP actively participated from the very start of the process, attending the San Salvador meeting that convened CIREFCA in September 1988 and pledging US$300,000 toward technical preparations for the conference. Later in the year, separate meetings were held in New York between the high commissioner and the general administrator of UNDP and between the director of the Regional Bureau for Latin America and the Caribbean (RBLAC) and the UNDP regional director, and the basis for a UNHCR-UNDP collaboration began to emerge.[39] The cooperation between New York and Geneva continued such that

---

36. "Progress Report on the Implementation of the CIREFCA Plan of Action," 1 June 1990, UNHCR Fonds 11, Series 3, 391.86.5, UNCHR Archives.

37. "Joint Statement of the Delegation of the Government of Italy and UNDP on PRO-DERE," 25 April 1991, New York, UNHCR Fonds 11, Series 3, 391.86.4, UNCHR Archives.

38. J. Rierato to Ana Liria-Franch, "Project Brief for the Action Committee Meeting," memo, 6 June 1990, UNHCR Fonds 11, Series 3, 391.86.5, UNCHR Archives.

39. "Update on International Conference Developments: Internal Paper 2," 16 November 1988, UNHCR Fonds 11, Series 3, 391.90, UNCHR Archives.

Leonardo Franco, as head of RBLAC, and Augusto Ramirez-Ocampo, as the UNDP PEC coordinator, were able to agree on the establishment of a CIREFCA JSU to jointly coordinate the followup to CIREFCA from San José.[40]

The JSU, which combined two staff members from each of the two organizations, was widely regarded as the most successful aspect of the interorganizational collaboration, largely because of the sustained contact and mutual understanding it fostered within the unit. The JSU, as the secretariat of the Follow-Up Committee, played a crucial role in coordinating the national and international mechanisms that sustained the momentum of CIREFCA. The report of a UNHCR regional seminar noted, "The most tangible experience of this collaboration is the CIREFCA Joint Support Unit. Participants insisted to place on record the appreciation of Headquarters and field staff for excellent work accomplished by the JSU."[41] The official UNHCR review identified the JSU as playing a crucial role in the CIREFCA followup in terms of offering inspiration and coordination and of forming a bridge between UNDP and UNHCR (UNHCR 1994b, 69–74).

The UNHCR-UNDP collaboration was not without difficulty. At field level, in contrast to headquarters and the JSU, interorganizational collaboration proved more difficult. These coordination problems were highlighted by a RBLAC meeting on PRODERE. The messages from Werner Blatter, the UNHCR Costa Rican representative, to headquarters highlight the difficult working relations and suspicion between the two organizations at field level:

> Since the very first PRODERE meetings, UNDP has constantly questioned UNHCR's role.... UNDP [is] still convinced that UNHCR has the responsibility for protection and assistance in camps only.... While UNDP has so far adopted the attitude of incorporating UNHCR into their PRODERE project as junior partner with no authority, they want to reduce UNHCR's role in PRODERE. UNHCR wants its share of CIREFCA and this not

---

40. Joint UNDP/UNHCR letter on support unit, 6 December 1989, UNHCR Fonds 11, Series 3, 391.86.5, UNCHR Archives.

41. "Report on UNHCR Regional Seminar for Northern Latin America, 20–22 February, 1991, Guatemala City," UNHCR Fonds 11, Series 3, 391.86.5, UNCHR Archives.

only for displaced persons but also for returnees and eventually also for refugee projects.... [The] above comments might sound alarming, but analyzing the PRODERE process since it started in 1988...make[s] us think that
UNDP has a long term strategy in mind and that PRODERE for them represents a test case and a vehicle for future enlargement of UNDP's field of
action...to the detriment of UNHCR.[42]

Blatter also suggested there was a disjuncture between headquarters-
level participation and the field: "UNDP and PRODERE at the regional
[and] local levels are not tuned into the new concept of the established cooperation between UNDP New York and UNHCR." He cited the example
of the Achiote project in Costa Rica in which he argued that UNDP and
the government were excluding UNHCR, in contradiction of the agreement reached at the New York level concerning the UNHCR position as
the lead agency.[43]

A particular difficulty resulted from the ambiguity about the division
of responsibility between the two organizations. This was most clearly
exemplified in the division of labor in PRODERE and CIREFCA, with
UNDP assuming responsibility for IDPs and UNHCR assuming responsibility for refugees. In practice, this division proved untenable due to the
difficulties of distinguishing between the two groups. There was also difficulty defining how the transition would actually take place in terms of
the envisaged handover from UNHCR to UNDP of the lead-agency role
at a designated phase in the CIREFCA process. It was not entirely clear to
either UNDP or UNHCR which projects qualified for a developmental
cluster.[44] Nevertheless, despite these operational challenges, collaboration
reached a sufficient level to allow UNDP to formally assume the lead-
agency function from mid-1993, and the collaboration is widely recognized as representing the most successful historical example of meaningful
UNHCR-UNDP collaboration.[45]

---

42. Werner Blatter to Philippe Lavanchy, memo, 17 August 1989, UNHCR Fonds 11, Series 3, 391.86.5, UNCHR Archives.

43. Werner Blatter to Leonardo Franco, memo, 9 July 1989, UNHCR Fonds 11, Series 3,
391.86.5 cos/hcr/0523, UNCHR Archives.

44. "Draft: Report on Joint UNDP/EOSG Task Force Meeting, Geneva, 6–7 May 1991,"
8 July 1991, UNHCR Fonds 11, Series 3, 391.86.5, UNCHR Archives.

45. Interview with José Riera, UNHCR, October 24, 2005.

In contrast to ICARA, one of the reasons for the relative success of UNHCR-UNDP collaboration was that it was part of a wider collaborative endeavor that was overseen by the Office of the Secretary-General. This oversight role ensured that UNDP and UNHCR were wiling to collaborate. Furthermore, it served their mutual organizational interests: UNDP simply could not implement PRODERE without UNHCR input; UNHCR could not implement CIREFCA without UNDP input.

In addition to UNHCR-UNDP collaboration, the peace agreement brought an immediate commitment from the secretary-general to the issue of displacement. Five days after the signing of the Esquipulas II agreement, Leonardo Franco, the head of the UNHCR regional bureau for Latin America, met with the assistant executive of the secretary-general, who emphasized the secretary-general's commitment to the preparatory work for the regional conference on refugees in the context of the peace plan.[46] The decision to make the Concerted Plan of Action into Chapter 1 of the PEC created an immediate institutional link between CIREFCA and the Office of the Secretary-General given that Augusto Ramirez-Ocampo had been appointed as the secretary-general's special representative for the preparation of the PEC.[47] It is in part because of this wider interconnection that the high commissioner was able to call on the secretary-general to formally convene CIREFCA.[48] Indeed, from within the Office of the Secretary-General, prominent UN civil servants such as Alvaro de Soto and Francesc Vendrell were primarily concerned to ensure the success of the Esquipulas II peace process. This commitment to the wider process translated into an interest in CIREFCA insofar as the Office of the Secretary-General wished to ensure that the role of UNHCR complemented rather than detracted from Esquipulas II.[49]

---

46. L. Franco to High Commissioner, "Meeting with M. de Soto, Executive Assistant of the S-G, in New York," memo, 13 August 1987, UNHCR Fonds 11, Series 3, 386.86 cos/hcr/0483, UNCHR Archives.

47. "Report to the Conference by UNHCR," prepared for the International Conference on Central American Refugees (CIREFCA), Guatemala City, 29–31 May 1989, UNHCR Fonds 11, Series 3, 391.86.3 HCR/Mex/0375, para. 157, UNCHR Archives.

48. Jean-Pierre Hocké to Javier Perez de Cuellar, letter, 20 December 1988, UNHCR Fonds 11, Series 3, 391.86.3 HCR/NYC/1553, UNCHR Archives.

49. Interview with José Riera, UNHCR, October 24, 2005.

Ideational Linkage

Beyond the institutional design, CIREFCA took place at a historical junc-
ture at which a dominant set of ideas about RAD (which had been highly
contested during ICARA) on the causal relationship between refugee protection and development assistance were becoming accepted by consensus
(UNHCR 1994a). These wider sets of ideas contributed to reinforcing the
belief of states that development assistance could be a means of enhancing refugee protection and that refugee protection could be a means of
promoting economic development. A number of the states involved in the
process also held ideas about the close relationship between refugee protection in Central America and security.

*Refugee Aid and Development*    During the late 1980s, and in the aftermath
of the failure of ICARA, the RAD literature grew to recognize the role
that refugees could play as agents of development. The argument was that
refugee issues should not be seen purely in humanitarian terms but that
both durable solutions and protection could be seen in terms of development. The concepts of sustainable reintegration supported by development
assistance and of local integration and self-sufficiency based on integrated
community development models are found in the work of, for example,
Robert Gorman (1986, 1987, 1993) and Jacques Cuenod (1989). It was repeatedly argued that refugees need not been viewed as passive and dependent burdens but might instead benefit their host states if they were
empowered to play an active part in the development process. By the time
CIREFCA was launched, the academic literature on RAD had developed,
notably in light of the ICARA experience. In particular, Gorman's work
attempted to draw lessons from the African experience to clarify many of
the earlier conceptual ambiguities of RAD, such as its definition and the
relationship of self-sufficiency to durable solutions.

　　This conceptual relationship between refugees and development was
consistently drawn on by UNHCR as the basis for CIREFCA. For the first
and last time in its history, UNHCR argued that the long-term encampment of refugees was not an acceptable norm and that beyond a certain
point local integration should be facilitated through integrated development. The summary of the Consultative Group Meeting in 1987 noted that
"los campamentos son por definicion transitorios y no deben perpetuarse

[camps are, by definition, temporary and must not be lasting]" and that "despues de un tiempo razonable, este tipo de campamentos deberen gradualmente abrirse a reubicarse para pasar a otro esquena de inserción local mas apropiado [beyond a reasonable length of time, this type of camp must gradually be opened to moved towards other more appropriate forms of local integration]."[50]

*Refugees and Security*     The ideas held by the main actors in CIREFCA about the relationship between refugee protection and security were shaped by the end of the Cold War and the immediate post–Cold War context. During the 1980s, the civil conflicts in the region had generally polarized along left-right and East-West lines, with both the governments and guerrilla movements being supported by the superpowers. Those displaced by conflict, especially those beyond the borders of their country of origin, had been viewed primarily in terms of national security and thus seen as the potential combatants or supporters of combatants on one or other of the left-right divide. The role and standpoint of the major stakeholders in CIREFCA—the United States, the regional actors, and the European states—were significantly shaped by this wider context. The influence of the Cold War context is especially clear in the change in direction of CIREFCA once the Esquipulas II plan acquired legitimacy and the Cold War came to an end, leading to a notable shift in the position of the United States.

The position of the countries in the region was largely shaped by their ideological positions in the Cold War context. At the time that CIREFCA was emerging, the Nicaraguan Sandinista government was a socialist state with strong alignments with the USSR and Cuba. In contrast, the right-wing governments of Honduras, El Salvador and Guatemala were strongly aligned with the United States. Meanwhile, Costa Rica and Belize held much more moderate positions—hence, the Costa Rican government was able to play a more mediatory role in the negotiations.[51]

The significance of the Cold War context for the role played by the United States is particularly apparent because of the way in which its role

---

50. Sergio Vieira de Mello to High Commissioner, memo, May 29, 1987, UNHCR Fonds 11, series 3, 391.86A, UNHCR Archives.
51. The Arias Peace Plan was named after President Arias of Costa Rica.

changed before and immediately after the end of the Cold War. The U.S. government adopted an anti-Sandinista stance and supported the Contras in Nicaragua; this made the Reagan administration extremely lukewarm toward CIREFCA and the linked peace process in its early stages. Reagan himself had described Esquipulas II as "fatally flawed" and, rather than offering political backing for the preparatory stages of CIREFCA, had continued to focus on channeling resources to the Contras in an attempt to overthrow Daniel Ortega's Sandinista government in Nicaragua.[52] The *New York Times* ("Who's Living Up to the Arias Plan?" March 11, 1989) even suggested that the Reagan administration might benefit from the failure of the Arias Peace Plan if it could portray its failure as being the fault of the Sandinistas and so use it to persuade Congress to restart aid to the Contras. The unconstructive nature of the U.S. preoccupation with Nicaragua was again highlighted in August 1988 when U.S. Secretary of State George Schultz met with the four Central American foreign ministers in Guatemala City. His attempts to foster an anti-Nicaraguan alliance resulted in a division between support from Honduras and El Salvador and in reluctance from Costa Rica and Guatemala.[53]

Furthermore, a UNHCR mission to Washington, D.C., in April 1989 led to equivocation and a lack of support from the U.S. government for CIREFCA. For example, following a meeting with the deputy director of U.S. Agency for International Development (USAID) it was noted that "The US Officials expressed concern about the capacity of governments to properly implement the projects and of the donors to monitor them." Furthermore, the deputy director suggested that "he did not envisage additional AID funding" and that the United States preferred to continue to channel approximately US$700 million per year to Central America states mainly through bilateral channels. The deputy assistant secretary for refugee programmes expressed particular concern about returning Nicaraguans in the context of the U.S. government support for the Contras.[54]

---

52. Muller to da Cunha, "Summary of the 42nd Session of the General Assembly of the UN on the Peace Plan for Central America," memo, 25 September 1987, UNHCR Fonds 11, 391.86, 167/87, UNCHR Archives.

53. Meeting between Secretary of State George Schultz and four foreign ministers in Guatemala, 1 August 1989, UNHCR Fonds 11, Series 3, 391.86.1/841.COS, UNCHR Archives.

54. Patricia Weiss Fagan, "A Note for the File. Exchanges of Views on CIREFCA: José Maria Mendiluce and Brian Deschamp, Mission to Washington, April 20–21 1989," 8 May 1989, UNHCR Fonds 11, Series 3, 391.86/38, UNCHR Archives.

**TABLE 3.** Structural Interconnections of CIREFCA

| Type of Structural Interconnection | Subtype of Structural Interconnection | Refugees-Development | Refugees-Security |
|---|---|---|---|
| Institutions | Internal linkages | Some conditionality between development assistance and protection standards | No formal linkages |
| | External nesting | **PEC and UNDP partnership** | **Esquipulas II** |
| Ideas | Inter-subjective | **RAD debates** | **Refugee-security nexus** |
| | Subjective | — | United States: end of Cold War security interests **EC: relationship among trade, human rights, and security** |

*Notes:* Bold represents structural interconnections that enabled cross-issue persuasion. CIREFCA, Conferencica Internacional sobre los Refugiados Centroamericanos; EC, European Community; PEC, Special Programme of Economic Cooperation for Central America; RAD, refugee aid and development; UNDP, United Nations Devolpment Programme.

The initially unconstructive U.S. role in CIREFCA prior to the re-gime change in Nicaragua was highlighted by the International Council of Voluntary Association (ICVA) statement to CIREFCA on behalf of NGOs. ICVA claimed that CIREFCA needed to place greater emphasis on "root causes" but this would require "foreign powers, especially the United States, [to] reformulate their policies towards Central America."[55] In contrast, it was only after the Cold War drew to a close and there had been a change of government in Nicaragua in 1990 that the George H. W. Bush administration really embraced CIREFCA, particularly as a means of promoting democracy under the government of President Violeta Barrios de Chamorro. Following the signing of a demobilization agreement, the U.S. government passed a law on aid for Nicaragua allowing a total of US$300 million to be allocated to the country, $30 million of which went toward the demobilization of the Contras, $10 million toward re-patriation from Honduras and Costa Rica, and $5 million directly to CIREFCA projects. Table 3 summarizes the structural interconnections of CIREFCA.

55. Jean-Pierre de Warlincourt (ICVA) to Jorge Santistevan (UNHCR representative in Mexico), "NGO Statement to CIREFCA, 31/5/89," letter, 30 June 1989, UNHCR Fonds 11, Series 3, 391.86.3, UNCHR Archives.

## Agency Conditions

Drawing on the structural interconnections between refugee protection, on the one hand, and peace-building and development, on the other hand, UNHCR was able to appeal to the interests of European and Central American states in these wider issue areas as a basis for contributing to refugee protection. Yet, for the strong institutional and ideational connections that existed between refugee protection and these other issue areas to translate into a commitment to protection, UNHCR still needed to demonstrate the leadership to recognize and effectively communicate these connections to the states.

Not only did UNHCR play an important role in the institutional design of CIREFCA, but it also played an important role in continually articulating and emphasizing the important relationships that refugee protection had to the wider interests of these states. UNHCR staff, for example, consistently drew on the way that CIREFCA was nested within Esquipulas II and PEC to legitimate the initiative or on ideas such as RAD as a basis for highlighting the role that development assistance could play in meeting the interests of donor states, host states, and countries of origin. A number of examples demonstrate the many ways in which UNHCR directly drew on these structures to appeal to the wider interests of states in peace-building and development during the CIREFCA process.

### Appealing to Peace-Building Interests

UNHCR consistently reinforced the logic that CIREFCA was a component part of the wider peace and postconflict reconstruction initiative for the region. The draft declaration of CIREFCA, which asserted that "The objectives...are based on a common foundation recognized by the countries concerned. It includes...a conviction that an inter-relationship... exists between solutions to the problems of refugees, peace in the region and development."[56] The relationship was also explicitly referred to in the Concerted Plan of Action.[57]

---

56. "Preparatory Meeting for CIREFCA, Guatemala, 12–14 April 1989," UNHCR Fonds 11, Series 3, 391.86.3, UNCHR Archives.

57. Mateu to Asomani, "From Conflict to Peace and Development."

Through highlighting and drawing attention to these interrelationships between peace and refugee protection, UNHCR was able to persuade the Central American states that a commitment to the latter was a means to achieve the former. UNHCR noted that Central American states saw refugees in the broader context of the peace process and that addressing the refugee crisis was important insofar as it was a necessary condition for regional stability:

> Massive flows of refugees might not only affect the domestic order and stability of receiving states, but may also jeopardize the political and social stability and economic development of entire regions, and thus endanger international peace and security. The solution to the problems of displacement is therefore a necessary part of the peace process in the region and it is not conceivable to achieve peace while ignoring the problems of refugees and other displaced persons.[58]

UNHCR argued that CIREFCA contributed to the peace process in a number of ways, describing it as "an instrument of political change."[59] It fulfilled this role in four ways. First, it provided a context for interstate dialogue and consensus-building. In a region in which politics had polarized along left-right and East-West lines throughout the Cold War, the humanitarian and explicitly nonpolitical light in which UNHCR portrayed CIREFCA gave states an area in which they could begin to build trust and interaction. Second, CIREFCA dealt directly with an issue that was perceived as an obstacle to security by the states in the region. José Riera, for example, noted how the Central American states viewed the issue of displacement: "Ten years of negotiations with Central American Governments, culminating with CIREFCA, have provided invaluable insights into the way the problem of uprootedness is perceived (linked to national security) by the governments of the region."[60] Refugees and the

---

58. CIREFCA Juridical Committee, "Principles and Criteria for the Protection and Assistance of Refugees, Repatriation and Displaced Persons," 1991, UNHCR Fonds 11, Series 3, 391.86.3 HCR/Mex/0890, UNCHR Archives.

59. Chefeke to all SMC members, "CIREFCA Process: External Evaluation."

60. José Riera (programme officer of the JSU) to Juan Amunategui, "Some Reflections on a Potential UNHCR Role with IDPs within the Framework of CIREFCA,"6 February 1991, UNHCR Fonds 11, Series 3, 391.86.5, UNCHR Archives.

displaced were often seen less as passive victims than as parties to the conflict. Nicaraguan refugees were associated with the Contras; Salvadoran and Guatemalan refugees were perceived as left-wing guerrillas. This meant that working toward solutions for the displaced was itself a means of reducing security concerns. Third, the integration or reintegration of refugees through a community development approach helped to contribute to national reconciliation on a local level. Incorporating the displaced within national development plans enabled the uprooted to play a productive economic and social role. In addition, shared services provided by the QIPs in Nicaragua, for example, fostered sustained interaction over time. Fourth, the mobilization of resources for the states, both through PEC and CIREFCA, increased the opportunity cost of any state undermining the peace process.

## Appealing to Development Interests

UNHCR persuaded the Central American states that implementing the CIREFCA projects could represent a means of simultaneously promoting development for the benefit of the local population. UNHCR argued that development assistance represented a means through which European donor states could facilitate refugees' access to durable solutions and hence achieve lasting peace and security. In particular, UNHCR promoted the idea that local integration and self-sufficiency could be a means of promoting development because refugees might be regarded as "agents of development"[61] and because the development assistance might simultaneously support host communities. Drawing on the language of RAD, UNHCR highlighted how this could be achieved through a developmental approach. In setting out its preparatory activities, UNHCR identified the important role that linking solutions with development initiatives for the local community can play in mobilizing host-country support for local integration, self-sufficiency, and reintegration. It argued that refugee assistance and development have an important relationship: "[CIREFCA] focuses on zones affected by the impact of refugees, returnees and displaced persons and also naturally benefits the local population. By doing so,

---

61. Chefeke, "Reunion Tecnica Informal Sobre CIREFCA," comment, 15–16 February 1994, San José, UNCHR Archives. (On file with the author.)

CIREFCA ensures a sustained link with development efforts on a larger scale, which otherwise would not be possible, and avoids the perpetuation of emergency schemes isolated from local communities such as closed or precarious refugee camps."[62]

This illustrates the awareness of UNHCR of the role that the promise of *additional* development resources directed toward the local host population can play in promoting a commitment by host states to solutions or forms of protection that go beyond encampment. The strategic centrality of ensuring that local populations also benefited from this approach was again highlighted in the draft declaration prepared for CIREFCA:

> All project proposals, whether aimed at refugees, returnees or displaced persons, include a component geared at redressing the adverse effects felt by the surrounding local population and ... to improve their situation. This integrated approach is a substantial part of the strategy of progressively incorporating refugees or reintegrating returnees in the countries and constitutes a key of the Plan of Action and of achieving the objectives of CIREFCA.[63]

Many host states in the region accepted this causal relationship and agreed to develop projects for the local integration or self-sufficiency of refugees who were either unable or unwilling to repatriate. Mexico, Costa Rica, and Belize, in particular, agreed to develop such initiatives to an extent that has been unprecedented. They did so because they accepted that community development projects applied in some of the most impoverished areas of the country might simultaneously benefit the local population and contribute the economic development of regions that would otherwise remain significantly underdeveloped.

One of the important principles that underpinned the CIREFCA approach to development assistance was the notion of recipient country ownership. The concept of ownership gave the regional states the scope to ensure that the developmental benefits extended beyond those available to refugees. It was highlighted throughout the preparatory activities for the conference: "The conference is an initiative of the affected countries. The preparatory work in each country is based upon proposals prepared

---

62. "Procedures for the Preparatory Activities of the Conference."
63. "Preparatory Meeting for CIREFCA, Guatemala."

by the relevant Governments.... The role of the UN system and UNHCR in particular has been one of support and orientation...special care has been taken not to impose an outside assessment on the authorities."[64]

Each state was supported in developing its own diagnostic studies and project proposals[65] and were asked to submit population statistics, an analysis of the impact of hosting or integrating, an assessment of priorities, an elaboration of specific strategies, and the formulation and presentation of projects by March 1989. UNHCR also made clear that with ownership came responsibility: "It is expected that Governments, by proposing a strategy under which basic commitments are made...will demonstrate their own responsibility towards solutions."[66] Thus, it allowed countries of origin to attract significant additional support for reconstruction. Guatemala, Nicaragua, and El Salvador, for example, benefited significantly from the funding channeled in under the auspices of UNDP because of the relationship between local development projects, on the one hand, and the return and reintegration of refugees and IDPs, on the other.

The one-year progress report on CIREFCA highlighted the extent to which the idea that there was a relationship between durable solutions and development had been normalized. In relation to voluntary repatriation, it suggested that "the process of voluntary repatriation and the reintegration of returnees should continue, *coupled with* an improvement in the absorption capacity in the country of origin in order to ensure that the battle against poverty begins with the phase of return and that the beneficiaries have a stake in development." In relation to local integration, it stated that "the situation of those who do not opt for voluntary repatriation...should receive treatment which is *in consonance with*...the development priorities of the host countries."[67] Overall, it then went on to imply that durable solutions must therefore be linked to financial support from international community and

---

64. "Procedures for the Preparatory Activities of the Conference."

65. The diagnostic studies conducted as part of the preparatory project for CIREFCA have strong parallels with the current UNHCR focus on gaps analyses and national consultations carried out as part of the Strengthening Protection Capacity Project (SPCP) and the CPA for Somali Refugees in 2004 and 2005.

66. "Procedures for the Preparatory Activities of the Conference."

67. "CIREFCA Concerted Plan of Action: One Year of Progress and Prospects for the Future." 27–28 June 1990, New York, UNCHR Archives. Emphasis added. (On file with the author.)

wider UNDP-related work: "In the face of these challenges, the sensitivity and support of the International Community are ever more necessary."[68]

The principle of ownership meant that the precise way in which local integration or self-sufficiency was implemented by the states in the region remained on their own terms and in accordance with the interests of the Central American states. For example, although Costa Rica accepted that it would engage in local integration for those refugees for whom voluntary repatriation was not possible, it did so largely on its own terms. For Salvadoran refugees in Costa Rican urban areas, who were few in number and were perceived to be hard-working, local integration took place on a larger scale than for Nicaraguan refugees, who, although they were given a degree of self-sufficiency in agricultural production, remained largely confined to these new settlements and were not given the same level of opportunities to fully integrate.[69] Nevertheless, the Costa Rican government gained from determining the location and nature of the self-sufficiency projects for the Nicaraguans who had been externally displaced. These were located in the communities of Boca de Arenal and Pocosol. Integrating the local communities within the scope of the projects allowed these areas to receive further development assistance, simultaneously improving access to jobs and health care for the local population.

UNHCR, therefore, consciously recognized and appealed to the wider interests of states in other issue areas. CIREFCA was a success precisely because both the Northern donors and Southern host states recognized that they had wider interests in other issue areas and were persuaded that there was a relationship between refugee protection and these other issue areas. The reason that, in contract to ICARA, cross-issue persuasion was possible was because there was a structural basis for connecting refugee protection to these other issue areas and because UNHCR demonstrated the necessary leadership to draw on these structural interconnections and channel them into a commitment to refugee protection.

CIREFCA represents the most successful example of North–South cooperation in the history of the global refugee regime. Its success in facilitating cooperation also translated into positive outcomes for Central

---

68. Ibid.
69. Interview with Mateu.

American refugees, leading to durable solutions for the majority of the refugees in the region. In particular, its integrated development assistance projects contributed to local integration and repatriation by benefiting not only refugees and returnees but also the local hosting communities. Success was possible only because of the dual contribution of the predominantly European donor states and the Central American states. The European states, led by the EC, provided funding for the development projects; the Central American states agreed to cooperate in implementation.

The reasons for the success of the initiative are highlighted when we contrast it to the earlier African conferences. Whereas ICARA I and II were single one-off pledging conferences, CIREFCA was a sustained political process in which UNHCR actively engaged in political negotiation, recognizing and appealing to the underlying interests of the states. Crucially, these underlying interests that underpinned international cooperation derived from other issue areas beyond refugee protection. The success of the initiative was due to the fact that, unlike ICARA, it did not address refugee protection in isolation but, instead, provided a framework within which the states involved recognized the link between refugee protection and their wider interests in relation to peace-building and development.

The interests of the European donor states in contributing to the CIREFCA projects came not from a concern with refugee protection per se but, rather, from a wider concern with security, peace-building, and post-conflict reconstruction and development in the region. This was important to the European states because it offered, in turn, a means of promoting interregional trade and also a context in which an increasingly ambitious Europe could project its values abroad. Refugee protection fitted into this only insofar as it was understood to be an essential component of these wider concerns. On the other side, the interests of the Central American states in implementing the CIREFCA projects and in engaging in offering opportunities for the integration of refugees into the countries of asylum or the reintegration of returnees who had previously been regarded as a security threat were similarly based on the extent to which implementation was understood to be inextricably linked to the success of the regional peace process and the commitment of the international community to the development and reconstruction of the region.

Significantly, UNHCR played a central role in persuading these groups of states that there is a link between these wider interests and refugee protection. It was able to fulfill this role both because there was a structural basis on which UNHCR could credibly convince states of the relationship between refugee protection and the other relevant issue areas and because it demonstrated the leadership to draw on and effectively communicate these structural relationships.

Structurally, the main connection between refugee protection and peace and development was based on the CIREFCA institutional design. CIREFCA was itself nested within the wider structures of the regional peace process and its postconflict reconstruction and development initiative. This mattered because it created a contractual relationship between the successful implementation of these and CIREFCA. The perception that CIREFCA was an essential component of these wider initiatives offered a basis for cross-issue persuasion. These institutional interconnections were further supported by the dominant ideas of the time, which served to reinforce the relationship between refugee protection and peace and development. The RAD debates and dominant ideas about the relationship between refugees and security meant that states believed that there was a causal relationship between protection and the other issue areas in which they had interests.

Even so, it was possible for the structural connections to lead to effective cross-issue persuasion only because of the leadership demonstrated by UNHCR and important individuals such as Sergio Vieira de Mello and Leonardo Franco. Not only did UNHCR contribute to creating the structural interconnections through the CIREFCA institutional design, but once the structures existed, it drew on and appealed to them in important ways, consistently articulating and reinforcing the message that there were important relationships between refugee protection and regional peace, security, and development, which were high priorities of the states.

The Central American case study highlights the importance of structural interconnections as the basis for cross-issue persuasion. In particular, it shows the important role that institutional design plays in fostering institutions connections between refugee protection and other issue areas, and the ways in which these mattered for the politics of protection. The Indochinese CPA case study (chapter 4) reinforces this argument that structural connections across issue areas matter, but there the important structural interconnections between refugee protection and other issue areas existed at the level of ideas rather than institutions.

# 4

# The Comprehensive Plan of Action for Indochinese Refugees (1988–1996)

In the aftermath of the Vietnam War and the U.S. withdrawal from Saigon in 1975, Vietnam became a united socialist country. From 1975 onward, a significant numbers of refugees fled the Socialist Republic of Vietnam, as well as its neighboring socialist states, in search of asylum. The majority fled on small, insecure boats to the shores of other Southeast Asian states or to Hong Kong. These people, frequently referred to as the "Indochinese boat people," received an inhospitable welcome from the states in the region, which often pushed back the arriving boats, refusing to allow the boat people access to their territory.

The widespread media images of the fleeing boat people drowning at sea led the international community to convene a first international conference in 1979, which resulted in an international agreement to address the mass influx of the Indochinese refugees. The agreement established that the United States, along with other Northern states, would commit to resettling all the Indochinese refugees offered asylum in the region on condition that the states in the region admitted the refugees to their territory and refrained from pushing back the arriving boats. For a while this agreement held, contributing to the resettlement of over 1 million Indochinese refugees. But the exodus showed no sign of abating, and by the late 1980s, the agreement had largely broken down. The U.S. commitment to resettlement was dwindling and the countries of first asylum were beginning to revert to pushing back the arriving boats. Meanwhile, around 150,000 Indochinese refugees were in a state of limbo, held in appalling conditions in detention centers and settlements across the region with little prospect of a durable solution.

In response to this worsening situation, UNHCR convened the second conference in 1989. By 1989, the Cold War was coming to an end and a new element was introduced to the negotiations—Vietnam was able and willing to participate the attempt to resolve the mass exodus problem. With the impending collapse of the USSR and the consequent need for Vietnam to reestablish itself in the eyes of the international community, the main country of origin was introduced into the negotiations. In July 1989, at a conference in Geneva, UNHCR successfully managed to negotiate what became known as the Comprehensive Plan of Action (CPA) for Indochinese Refugees. The CPA represented a three-way agreement between the country of origin (primarily Vietnam), the first countries of asylum in the region (the ASEAN states and Hong Kong), and third countries of resettlement (led by the United States).

Vietnam, as the main country of origin, agreed to sustainably reintegrate all of those boat people who were not found to be refugees. The first countries of asylum agreed to admit all asylum seekers to their territory and to host a screening process to determine who was a genuine refugee and who was not. The resettlement states agreed to resettle all those asylum seekers who were recognized as refugees. These three commitments were explicitly conditional on one another. Ultimately, although the CPA was criticized on human rights grounds (Helton 1993), this unprecedented three-way agreement succeeded in clearing the refugee camps and detention centers of the region and overcoming the long-standing issue of the Indochinese boat people.

In this chapter, I argue that one of the central reasons for the CPA success in facilitating international cooperation was the role of cross-issue persuasion. In addition to facilitating an interlocking three-way agreement, UNHCR was able to persuade each of the three groups of states that their wider foreign policy interests could be met through upholding their specific commitments to the CPA. I unpack those wider interests and the conditions that enabled UNHCR to channel them into a commitment to refugee protection. But first, let us review the negotiation and outcome of the CPA.

## Negotiating the Indochinese CPA

In 1979, an unprecedented multilateral agreement had been reached to address the global concerns relating to the Vietnamese boat people arriving in vast numbers in Southeast Asian countries. The agreement established a consensus to accord *prima facie* recognition to all Indochinese refugees, based on the understanding that third-country resettlement was to be the only viable durable solution. This agreement created a commitment by the ASEAN states to continue to provide asylum on the condition that states beyond the region provided sufficient ongoing access to resettlement. The agreement resulted in over 1 million Indochinese refugees being given temporary asylum in Southeast Asia and then resettled in the North between 1979 and 1988.

But by the end of 1988, the number of people fleeing Vietnam was increasing and the willingness of both host states in the region to offer protection and of third countries beyond the region to offer resettlement was declining. With resettlement quotas declining, there was a growing pool of "long-stayers" in first-asylum camps, and the countries in the region began to identify resettlement as a pull factor attracting growing numbers of economic migrants (as opposed to refugees). Despite the large number of people resettled since 1979, according to the *New York Times* roughly the same number of refugees (150,000) remained in camps in Southeast Asia as had been the case at the end of 1988 ("Vietnam and Laos Finally Join Talks on Refugees," October 30, 1988). In the words of Sergio Vieira de Mello, there was, therefore, a need for "a new solutions-oriented consensus involving the co-operation of countries of origin, first asylum and resettlement."[1]

---

1. "Procedures for the Preparatory Activities of the Conference Itself and the Establishment of Follow-Up Mechanisms," proposal submitted to the Organizing Committee Meeting, 24 January 1989, Guatemala, UNHCR Fonds 11, Series 3, 391.86.3 HCR/NYC/0102, UNCHR Archives;

In contrast to the previous decade, a new dimension emerged in this process. For the first time, Vietnam, as part of its wider attempts to repair its ties with ASEAN and the wider world, declared itself willing to engage in the process and to repatriate without punishment or persecution those who voluntarily agreed to return (*New York Times,* "Vietnam and Laos Finally Join Talks on Refugees," October 30, 1988). This new rapprochement was set in the context of improved relations between the superpowers and progress on the conflict in Cambodia that led to Vietnam's announcing the withdrawal of troops from the country. This opened a new, previously unavailable possibility—using screening to establish refugee status and repatriating those not found to have a well-founded fear of persecution in their country of origin.[2] This new element offered the prospect of a new consensus on international cooperation in relation to Indochinese refugees.

In contrast to CIREFCA, the buildup to the CPA was fairly brief and was largely a drafting exercise based on ongoing consultations with states to reach consensus. The CPA offered a focused political agreement, and the actual document was extremely concise, simply highlighting the main obligations of the three groups of states. Most of the substantive details were developed in the aftermath of the main 1989 conference, on the basis of using the CPA as a guiding political and normative focal point.

The process began with a meeting of seventeen governments from the region and beyond that was held in Bangkok in October 1988 as an informal consultation to set out the groundwork for the CPA. It was the first time since 1979 that Vietnam or the Lao People's Democratic Republic (LPDR) had been involved in talks on refugees from their countries. The initial meeting was purposefully informal, with no predetermined agenda, and explored the interests of the states as a basis for drafting a new agreement.[3] By December, Vietnam had agreed to a "Memorandum

---

Sergio Vieira de Mello to Refeeudin Ahmed (Secretary-General's Office), "Recommended Opening Speech for Kuala Lumpur Meeting, 7–9 March," memo, 22 February 1989, UNHCR Fonds 11, Series 3, 391.89 HCR/NYC/0248, UNHCR Archives.

2. Pierre Jambor, the UNHCR representative to Thailand, had first suggested using screening in a note as early as 1986 and developed the ideas through a Ford Foundation–funded study on the Indochinese. Although the idea initially met with resistance within the UNHCR Department of Refugee Law and Doctrine, it gradually gained support.

3. "Procedures for the Preparatory Activities"; "UNHCR Informal Consultations on Indochinese Asylum-Seekers in South-East Asia, Bangkok, 27–28 October 1988," 10 November 1988, UNHCR Fonds 11, Series 3, 391.89 100.Ich.gen, UNCHR Archives.

of Understanding" with UNHCR, setting out the principles to allow voluntary repatriation without punishment or persecution and allowing UNHCR to monitor reintegration.[4] It was in the aftermath of these discussions that the Forty-Third Session of the UN General Assembly requested that the secretary-general convene an international conference in the first half of 1989 to "find a comprehensive and durable solution to the problem" (UN General Assembly Resolution A/RES/43/119, 8 December, 1988).

A small Drafting Group, comprising the major stakeholders, worked on the Draft Declaration and CPA. The process of drafting was based on ongoing consultations in which the regional representatives were consulted throughout and comments were solicited from the governments at each stage.[5] The UNHCR Asia and Oceania Bureau tabulated all the comments of the states on the draft, allowing the bureau to track and input all of the amendments that were received in writing from the permanent missions in Geneva.

On the basis of this drafting process, a meeting was convened in Kuala Lumpur in March 1989, in which the participating states agreed on the draft declaration and the CPA, allowing the texts to be finalized before the main conference took place in Geneva. There, the basic principles of the agreement were set out, highlighting the obligations of each of the three main groups of states, with the high commissioner explaining the underlying ethos of the CPA, which, he said, "must...be characterized by balance and compromise between the various parties."[6]

The CPA adopted in Geneva relied on a three-way commitment by countries of first asylum in the region, countries of resettlement beyond the region, and the main country of origin. For the CPA to be successful, each group of stakeholders had to perceive that its own contribution directly underpinned the overall aim of finding a comprehensive solution to the

---

4. "Memorandum of Understanding between the SRV and UNHCR," 13 December 1988, UNHCR Fonds 11, Series 3, 391.89, UNCHR Archives.

5. Pierre Jambor (UNHCR Representative to Thailand) to Sergio Vieira de Mello, memo, 17 January 1989, UNHCR Fonds 11, Series 3, 391.89 100.Ich.gen, UNCHR Archives; Sergio Vieira de Mello (head, Regional Bureau for Asia and Oceania), "Standard Letter to Permanent Representatives," 11 January 1989, UNHCR Fonds 11, Series 3, 391.89 100.Ich.gen, UNCHR Archives.

6. "Report of the Preparatory Meeting for the International Conference on Indochinese Refugees," 7–9 March 1989, Kuala Lumpur, UNHCR Fonds 11, Series 3, 391.89, UNCHR Archives.

problem of the Indochinese boat people. The resettlement states agreed to resettle all those already in the asylum countries up to agreed-on cut-off dates and all those determined to be refugees by individual refugee status determination (RSD) after the cut-off dates. The cut-off dates varied from state to state, but began as early as March 14, 1989. In return, the ASEAN states and Hong Kong agreed to maintain the principle of first asylum. As the third party to the agreement, Vietnam committed to accept the voluntary return of the nonrefugees and to work to limit clandestine departures.

In the aftermath of the Kuala Lumpur and Geneva meetings, a Coordinating Committee, comprising a core group of states, was assembled. This met both in the immediate aftermath of the Kuala Lumpur meeting and later in April in Geneva. The committee provided a focal point to which the three subcommittees (Reception and Status Determination, Departures and Repatriation, and Resettlement) could report their work.[7] This work established the substantive details for how the CPA, as a basic political agreement, would be implemented in practice following its adoption.

In the buildup to the Geneva Conference, the main division among Northern states concerned the position of Vietnam. In particular, there was suspicion from states such as Australia about why Vietnam was insisting that return of nonrefugees be voluntary. The United Kingdom, in particular, also representing Hong Kong, insisted that those who were screened out should be returned; the British foreign secretary argued that this would be the minimum that would be acceptable to the United Kingdom and Hong Kong. In contrast, the United States argued that it shared the concerns of Vietnam and stood by the insistence on voluntary repatriation on the purported grounds that is was more humane and would facilitate better integration.[8]

Meanwhile, the Northern states saw their commitment to resettlement as what a number of states openly described as a "blank cheque"

---

7. "Report on the Meeting of the Co-ordinating Committee for the International Conference on Indochinese Refugees," 19–20 April 1989, Geneva, UNHCR Fonds 11, Series 3, 391.89 HCR/THA/0516, UNHCR Archives.

8. "Note for the File: Informal Consultations of the IGC in Kuala Lumpur," 5 March 1989, UNHCR Fonds 11, Series 3, 391.89, UNHCR Archives.

and sought particular guarantees from the asylum states in return for this open-ended commitment. First, the implementation of a cut-off date for *prima facie* determination of refugee status was seen as crucial. As Australia put it, "The blank cheque has already been signed but the figure should be the current camp population and not the tens of thousands who will come in the absence of a 'cut off.'" Second, the commitment of the states in the region to *nonrefoulement* was also seen as crucial. As the United States argued, "the principle of first asylum is an important equation in the blank cheque."[9]

These concerns reached their most divisive level in 1990. The most serious impasse concerned the issue of return for those not recognized as refugees, with the United States and Vietnam continuing to insist that return be voluntary. Douglas Hurd, the British foreign minister, wrote to the high commissioner, "My own discussions with Secretary of State Baker and President Bush in Washington on 29 January give me little hope that the United States will be willing to join in the consensus which was acceptable to all other participants in the Geneva meeting except Vietnam."[10]

Indeed, it was the failure of Vietnam to allow returns at a satisfactory rate and to reduce clandestine departures that led to crisis talks at the Steering Committee Meeting in Manila in mid-1990. Opening the meeting, Vieira de Mello suggested that "Seldom...have we been so close to a breakdown of this otherwise exemplary process."[11] Complaining about the lack of cooperation from Vietnam, the countries of asylum issued a joint statement threatening to abandon the principle of *nonrefoulement:* "In the event of failure to agree even an intermediate solution to the VBP [Vietnamese boat people] problem, countries of temporary refuge must reserve the right to take such unilateral action as they deem necessary to safeguard their national interest, including the abandonment of temporary refuge."[12] The ASEAN states placed the blame squarely on the United States: "The United States, which opposes involuntary

---

9. Ibid.

10. Douglas Hurd to High Commissioner Thorvald Stoltenberg, letter, 2 February 1990, UNHCR Fonds 11, Series 3, 391.89, UNHCR Archives.

11. Sergio Vieira de Mello, introductory remarks at Informal Steering Committee Meeting, Manila, 17 May 1990, UNHCR Fonds 11, Series 3, 391.89, UNHCR Archives.

12. "Joint Statement by Countries of Temporary Refuge," 16 May 1990, Manila, UNHCR Fonds 11, Series 3, 391.89, UNHCR Archives.

repatriation for its own reasons, has not been helpful either. In fact the United States' position provides comfort and protection to the Vietnamese intransigence.... It is the United States' insistence on treating the Vietnamese economic migrants differently that is putting the very principle of first asylum in peril."[13]

Despite all this, on the basis of the meeting in Manila, and thanks largely to the conflict-resolution skills of Sergio Vieira de Mello, a "Near Consensus Note" emerged. This provided the basis for a compromise on the issue of the return of nonrefugees, which put the CPA back on track. In the words of Dennis McNamara, "the consensus [on return] was not to call it forced and not to call it voluntary; just to say that those who were found to be refugees could not be sent back."[14] The agreed compromise was that nonrefugees would be actively encouraged to return on the basis of three months of counseling, would not be coerced, and would be monitored by UNHCR upon their return to Vietnam.[15] It further noted that, although "conditions of safety and dignity" should be upheld, "the modalities of return... would be a matter for first asylum countries to resolve with the country of origin, with the guidance and involvement of UNHCR and other appropriate agencies."[16] In other words, UNHCR passed responsibility for the return of nonrefugees over to the countries of first asylum based on the understanding that this would be a "return respecting human rights" but tacitly acknowledging that the principle of strictly voluntary return might need to be compromised for the CPA to be viable.[17] Having restored consensus, the CPA was duly reaffirmed by the Fourth Steering Committee in April 1991.[18] Although the details of the implementation needed ongoing refinement and the Vietnamese refugees remained in protracted detention in Hong Kong throughout much

---

13. Statement by Malaysian minister of foreign affairs, 23rd ASEAN Ministerial Meeting, Jakarta, 24–25 July 1990, UNHCR Fonds 11, Series 3, 391.89, UNHCR Archives.

14. Interview with Dennis McNamara, deputy director of the Department of Refugee Law and Doctrine at the time of the CPA, Geneva, November 28, 2005.

15. "Draft Consensus Note," 18 July 1090, UNHCR Fonds 11, Series 3, 391.89, UNHCR Archives.

16. "Revised Version of the 'Near Consensus Note,'" 12 July 1990, UNHCR Fonds 11, Series 3, 391.89, UNHCR Archives.

17. Interview with McNamara.

18. "Report of the Fourth Steering Committee," 30 April–1 May, Geneva, UNHCR Fonds 11, Series 3, 391.89, UNHCR Archives.

of the 1990s, the reaffirmation that followed the Manila meeting represented the achievement of a lasting consensus, which ultimately led to the resolution of the boat people issue.

From 1991, the rate of voluntary returns increased rapidly, and the number of new arrivals began to decline. As UNHCR increased the level of the reintegration grants for returnees and began implementing QIPs, Vietnam was gradually persuaded that its interests lay in supporting return and cooperating to reduce clandestine departures. This strategy, Vietnam realized, would attract the greatest bilateral and multilateral support for development assistance, trade, and political engagement. Although UNHCR attempted to uphold the CPA commitment to voluntary return for nonrefugees, in practice from around 1992 the countries in the region increasingly engaged in coerced return, an approach that UNHCR tacitly acknowledged as the process drew to a close in 1996.[19]

## Outcome of the Indochinese CPA

Countries of Asylum

As Vieira de Mello made clear, asylum countries were clearly designated responsibility for upholding the principle of *nonrefoulement:* "The crucial starting point for UNHCR in this respect is the re-establishment of first asylum for all Indochinese asylum-seekers arriving in Southeast Asia, as provided for in the CPA. We are satisfied that if properly applied, the CPA can achieve this objective while, at the same time, reducing the collective burden on first asylum states." The role of UNHCR in the aftermath of the CPA therefore focused on developing reception and RSD capacities through technical support and training courses.[20] UNHCR provided prescreening, and the asylum states then conducted the RSD hearings and appeals procedures.

19. Interview with Brian Lander, UNHCR, based in Hong Kong and Indonesia during the CPA, November 1, 2005.

20. D. McNamara (deputy director of Department of Refugee Law and Doctrine) to G. Arnaout (director of Department of Refugee Law and Doctrine), memo, 28 July 1989, UNHCR Fonds 11, Series 3, 391.89, UNHCR Archives.

The asylum states sought assurances of resettlement and return before they were prepared to provide an unconditional commitment to the principle of first asylum or countenance relaxing their approach to detention and reception.[21] There was a degree of variation in the positions of the states— Singapore was particularly obdurate, whereas the Philippines was particularly cooperative—however, collectively the states recognized that their role was contingent on the roles of Vietnam and the resettlement states.

It was because of polarization concerning the voluntary nature of return for nonrefugees that difficulties began to emerge in 1990. From the perspective of the asylum states, screening was meaningless without return. They believed that Vietnam was insisting on voluntariness as a means to reduce the rate of returns so as to extract as much economic and political advantage from the process as possible.

In this context, and partly in protest of the Vietnamese position, push-offs continued throughout 1990. UNHCR noted, for example, that some 6,000 Vietnamese were forcibly turned away by Malaysia after the cut-off date, with the police cordoning off Pulau Bidong to prevent landings. Also, UNHCR had difficulty gaining access to some areas, such as the east coast of Thailand, where forcible *nonrefoulement* may also have occurred.[22] This was exacerbated by the continuation of clandestine migration because of what UNHCR described as "rumour-mongering." For example, in 1991, the rumor that there might be a Kuwaiti guestworker program for Vietnamese asylum seekers in Hong Kong was blamed for creating a significant pull factor to Hong Kong.[23] By that point, the problem of clandestine arrivals was focused almost entirely on Hong Kong, with 98 percent of arrivals in Southeast Asia heading for Hong Kong, where approximately 20 percent of the new arrivals were found to have a well-founded fear of persecution and thus to be refugees.[24]

---

21. D. McNamara to I. Khan, "Re. Eligibility in South East Asia," memo, 11 April 1989, UNHCR Fonds 11, Series 3, 391.89, UNHCR Archives.

22. Timberlake to McNamara, "Note on Protection Concerns under the CPA," memo, 18 May 1990, UNHCR Fonds 11, Series 3, 391.89, HCR/USA/0524, UNHCR Archives.

23. High Commissioner, "Statement by the High Commissioner," Fourth Standing Committee, 30 April–1 May 1991, Geneva, UNHCR Fonds 11, Series 3, 391.89, UNHCR Archives.

24. R. Van Leeuwen (UNHCR Hong Kong) to High Commissioner, "Current and Prospective Situation in Hong Kong," memo, 6 April 1991, UNHCR Fonds 11, Series 3, 391.89, UNHCR Archives.

The asylum countries had also been concerned about the basis for re-settlement. Malaysia, which was the first state to implement the cut-off date on March 14, 1989, provides a case in point. The representative noted that the Malaysian government had wrongly assumed that early implementation of the cut-off would serve as a deterrent to new arrivals. This was not the case. In his words, "Australian officials now speak readily of the successful 'blackmail' applied to the Malaysians to get them to agree to the date," absolving the resettlement countries of direct responsibility for the new arrivals. This caused a problem for UNHCR, which was seen as "a tacit partner in encouraging the earlier date."[25]

By the Manila meeting in mid-1990, the first-asylum element of the CPA was in peril, partly because of concerns about resettlement but mainly because of concern about the role of Vietnam. Gradually, however, on the basis of the Manila meeting and the subsequent "Near Consensus Note," the asylum process became established. The incentives for voluntary return—counseling and reintegration grants—were increased, and Vietnam was persuaded that its interests lay in accepting returns at a more rapid rate. This, the declining number of new arrivals, and the early implementation of resettlement screening, reinvigorated the commitment of asylum states to work with UNHCR on RSD.

A significant and often neglected element that came to underpin the willingness of states to engage in RSD was the local dynamics it created, notably through stimulating a combination of trade and corruption. In Indonesia, for example, the presence of asylum seekers close to the town of Tanjung Pinang on the island of Bintan stimulated trade linked to the flow of remittances and the role of the Indonesian military within the area. This, in turn, generated high-level political support in Jakarta for continuing with the status quo. The presence of corruption within the RSD system and the emergence of the informal sector within refugee-hosting areas also created similar local incentives to maintain the existing asylum system. Moreover, camps such as Galang served as an example of respect for human rights, which the Suharto regime was able to exploit for political purposes in full view of the international media.[26]

---

25. Eric Morris to Sergio Vieira de Mello, "Current Situation in Malaysia," memo, 6 April 1989, UNHCR Fonds 11, Series 3, 391.89, UNHCR Archives.

26. Interview with Lander.

The screening process has been widely criticized as arbitrary, restrictive, and occasionally corrupt, and the conditions of detention and encampment often failed to meet basic human rights standards.[27] But, on the whole, once new arrivals slowed down and returns were underway after 1990, the countries of temporary refuge played the role expected of them within the CPA, tolerating the camps and detention centers, conducting RSD, and supporting the resettlement and return processes. By the end of the process in 1996, Hong Kong and the Philippines even carried out some local integration, albeit on a limited scale. Although the response of the asylum states may not always have conformed to the ideals of the 1951 Convention,[28] it did at least achieve a remarkable degree of cooperation that ultimately brought the mass exodus to an end.

## Country of Origin

Even in the buildup to the conference, there was concern that Vietnam was unable to control its borders despite implementing strict measures to deter clandestine departures (*South China Morning Post,* April 3, 1989). Nevertheless, it committed to preventing illegal departures through a combination of coastal control, reinforcing media activities, and prosecution of the organizers of clandestine departures, while building its orderly departure procedure (ODP).[29] The credibility of the Vietnamese willingness and ability to fulfill these commitments was questioned throughout the early stages of the process. Its unwillingness to accept involuntary deportation of nonrefugees and its apparent inability to prevent clandestine departures were a particular source of animosity. Nevertheless, momentum built in the aftermath of the Manila Conference so that by April 1991 8,800 nonrefugees

---

27. At the time, Arthur Helton was one of the most vocal critics from the NGO community. He wrote numerous letters to UNHCR on behalf of the Lawyers Committee for Human Rights, urging UNHCR to uphold protection principles in the implementation of the CPA. These problems have also been noted in, for example, Courtland Robinson (2004, 319–33).

28. An additional problem for UNHCR was that not all the asylum states were signatories of the 1951 Convention, which meant that UNHCR relied even more on diplomacy and goodwill than on invoking legal or moral obligation.

29. "Report on the Meeting of the Co-ordinating Committee." The ODP system, coordinated by IOM, ensured alternative channels for labor migration for nonrefugees seeking to leave Vietnam. Again, this has parallels to the contemporary recognition of the need to address economic migration alongside providing international protection to refugees.

had been returned to Vietnam under the Memorandum of Understanding, which the high commissioner described as "a beginning."[30] As Vietnam acquired greater international support for returnees, its willingness to cooperate increased. Most notably, the application of QIPs, along the lines of those applied in CIREFCA, helped provide a basic level of integrated development that facilitated return.

The willingness of Vietnam to be an active participant in the process and to issue travel documents to those who wished to return home from detention centers was crucial for the CPA. Return was both the most crucial and most sensitive element of the CPA. Indeed it was the Vietnamese desire to rehabilitate itself within the region after the decline of the USSR that opened up the possibility for the Memorandum of Understanding with UNHCR. Although the participation of the country was controversial and its arguing for voluntary returns was divisive, its active participation was the very basis of the CPA. Without this willingness, the concept of RSD would have been meaningless and agreement could not have been reached among the other stakeholders on how to overcome the impasse on the 1979 agreement.

## Resettlement States

The principles underlying the allocation of responsibility for resettlement were agreed on in the aftermath of the conference. On the basis of indicative statistics provided by UNHCR (which were based on past contributions), the states worked toward setting three-year targets for the pre-cut-off date caseload, with the intention of resettling 50 percent of the refugees in the first year. It was initially agreed that, in addition to this, there would be three further principles: (1) that refugees would be resettled in countries where they had the closest social ties, (2) that "long-stayers" would be processed first, and (3) that there would be equitable burden-sharing of the caseload without close social ties.[31] The United States played an important role in leading the resettlement process, committing to take

---

30. High commissioner, "Statement by the High Commissioner."

31. Pierre Jambor (representative to Thailand) to Headquarters, "Draft Note to the Steering Committee on the Technical Meeting on Resettlement Held in Bangkok," memo, 3 July 1989, UNHCR Fonds 11, Series 3, 391.89 HCR/Bkk/HQ/0262, UNHCR Archives.

approximately 40 percent of both pre- and post- cut-off-date refugees and making this conditional on other states' sharing the responsibility.

The resettlement process largely went as envisaged by the CPA. On the basis of the CPA priorities, UNHCR matched the resettlement criteria of states with those of the refugees in the camps. IOM also provided logistical support for resettlement. The difficulty came in resettling refugees who were less likely to make an economic contribution to the resettlement country, such as those with serious medical conditions. Norway, in particular, played an important role in providing resettlement for such groups. There was also a greater reluctance to resettle the North Vietnamese than South Vietnamese. Those from what had been North Vietnam were widely perceived to be fleeing poverty, whereas those from what had been South Vietnam were seen as refugees fleeing persecution because of their anti-communist sympathies. This partly explains why it took much longer to clear the Hong Kong detention centers, which were predominantly occupied by North Vietnamese, than the camps in other countries. Nevertheless, by 1996 the camps and detention centers in the region had been cleared in accordance with the CPA.

To a large extent, the commitment of the three principal groups of stakeholders to this cooperative success can be explained in relation to the interconnections between the refugee protection and other issues that were of concern to the states.

## The Role of Cross-Issue Persuasion

Cross-issue persuasion was crucial to the success of the CPA. The main competing explanation offered by the existing literature for the success of the initiative is the role played by U.S. hegemony (Suhrke 1998). But this explanation begs the question: Where did the interest of the hegemon in refugee protection come from? Furthermore, this explanation cannot account for how, at certain points in the process, the U.S. commitment to the CPA wavered but then reengaged through the role played by UNHCR.

The CPA was based on an interlocking three-way agreement in which all three groups of states—the resettlement states, the states of first asylum, and the country of origin—agreed to uphold their part of the bargain on condition that the other states did likewise. In other words, there were tactical linkages among the commitments. In addition, underpinning the commitment of each group of states to meeting its particular commitment—to resettle, to provide temporary asylum, or to facilitate return—was a belief that resolving the long-standing mass influx situation had an inextricable relationship to its wider foreign policy interests.

For the United States, as the main resettlement state, the CPA was seen in the context of the legacy of the Vietnam War. Following the evacuation of Saigon in 1975, the United States perceived itself to have a significant interest in regional security and the containment of communism in Southeast Asia. Admitting Vietnamese refugees represented a way of signaling its anti-communist commitment. Over time, the presence of a Vietnamese diaspora created a significant domestic interest group that underpinned this U.S. commitment to the region and its refugees.

For the ASEAN states, the CPA was primarily a means to engage in migration control. A number of the countries of first asylum were concerned that the uncontrolled mass influx would have significant negative consequences for their demographic balance. For Malaysia and Indonesia, in particular, internal stability was perceived to be closely tied to the proportion of ethnic Chinese in the population. An unfettered influx of Indochinese refugees represented a threat to this precarious demographic balance. To other less-affected states in the region, the CPA represented an opportunity to demonstrate intra-ASEAN solidarity and underpin the significance of the regional alliance.

For Vietnam, as the main country of origin, committing to facilitating the return of screened-out asylum seekers represented a mean of rehabilitating itself in the eyes of the international community and attracting new sources of overseas development assistance. The collapse of the USSR, and the tenuous diplomatic relationship of Vietnam with China, left the country with few options other than to look westward to the United States and Europe to foster new diplomatic alliances and identify sources of trade and development. Cooperating with the CPA offered Vietnam a means to do this. All three groups of states therefore contributed because they identified the success of the initiative as the overall CPA as related to their wider interests.

UNHCR also played an important brokerage role in enabling states to recognize and act on the relationship between refugee protection and their wider interests. Indeed, UNHCR and key members of staff, such as Sergio Vieira de Mello, were crucial to channeling the wider interests of states in the success of the CPA into a willingness to voluntarily uphold their end of the bargain. In the next section, I therefore unpack the structural and agency conditions that made cross-issue persuasion possible.

## Structural Conditions

Unlike CIREFCA, the CPA was not nested in wider institutional structures. On a formal level, it was not institutionally tied to any preexisting institutional framework. Nevertheless, its institutional design served to create interlocking agreements in relation to different elements of protection. This created a contractual link between the specific commitments of each group of states and the overall success of CPA. The key structural connection between the success of the CPA and the wider foreign policy interests of the states was predominantly on the level of ideas. In other words, institutional design was important for contractually linking specific state commitments to the overall CPA, but ideas were crucial in causally connecting the success of the CPA to the wider issue areas in which states had specific interests. Each of the three groups of states held certain ideas about the causal relationship between resolving the mass influx situation and their wider foreign policy interests, and these ideas underpinned the basic commitments of each group of states. These structural interconnections are illustrated in table 4.

### Institutional Linkages

In contrast to CIREFCA, the CPA was not institutionally designed to be nested within a wider institutional framework. Rather, it was conceived as a stand-alone initiative that was almost exclusively UNHCR-led and focused on refugee protection. In contrast to CIREFCA, it also relied very little on interorganizational collaboration. In the context of the CPA, UNHCR nominally developed partnerships with IOM and UNDP; however, these collaborations were very limited in scope.

During the CPA, UNHCR collaborated with IOM on a logistical level. UNHCR believed that IOM involvement on a wider level was important so that UNHCR would not become directly implicated in the deportation and return of migrants to Vietnam. According to Irene Khan, the UNHCR

TABLE 4. Structural Interconnections of the Indochinese CPA

| Type of Structural Interconnection | Subtype of Structural Interconnection | Refugees-Migration | Refugees-Security | Refugees-Development |
|---|---|---|---|---|
| Institutions | Internal linkages | **Conditional linked commitments** | Conditional linked commitments | Conditional linked commitments |
| | External nesting | No nesting or partnerships | No nesting or partnerships | No nesting and nominal role for UNDP |
| Ideas | Intersubjective | Asylum-migration nexus | — | — |
| | Subjective | **ASEAN: demographic and migration control concerns** | **United States: regional security concerns** | **Vietnam: development assistance** |

*Notes:* Bold represents structural interconnections that enabled cross-issue persuasion. ASEAN, Association of Southeast Asian Nations; CPA, Comprehensive Plan of Action; UNDP, United Nations Devolpment Programme.

employee with primary responsible for maintaining legal protection standards during the CPA, "direct involvement in the process [of deportation of non-refugees] would not only be outside our mandate but could be in conflict with it." She concluded that "UNHCR should make active efforts to help governments identify other agencies, such as IOM" that could carry out both deportation and monitoring upon return.[32] But Khan's hope that IOM would become involved in the return process if it became involuntary was contrary to Article 1 of the IOM Constitution, which clearly precludes participation in forcible-return operations. Ultimately, IOM refused to become involved in return, but, instead, worked with UNHCR on the ODP and resettlement. Irene Khan's comments highlight the concern that any UNHCR involvement in deportation could leave UNHCR complicit in *refoulement.* This became particularly problematic due to the unwillingness of IOM to collaborate on involuntary return; this left the primary responsibility for deportation to the host governments and UNHCR.

The role of UNDP in the CPA was extremely limited. Nevertheless, after 1992 and once the United States had accepted the possibility of

---

32. Irene Khan to P.-M. Moussalli, "UNHCR's Role in the Return of Non-Refugees to Vietnam," memo, 16 July 1990, UNHCR Fonds 11, Series 3, 391.89, UNHCR Archives.

nonrefugees' return and reintegration within Vietnam, UNDP became involved in the funding and implementation of QIPs for the returnees. Drawing on the model developed in CIREFCA for Nicaraguan returnees, which supported basic access to social services and livelihood opportunities, the QIPs attempted to facilitate sustainable returns through short-term integrated development projects. These, however, were a very minor and relatively belated aspect of the CPA.

Nevertheless, the CPA institutional design was important to its success insofar as it created an interlocking commitment among the obligations of the different stakeholders. The commitments of each of three stakeholder groups were proclaimed in the text of CPA and documented as being contractually connected to one another. That is, for example, the states of first asylum would only provide asylum if the resettlement states resettled all those recognized as refugees and if the country of origin agreed to accept the return of those not recognized as refugees. The interlocking and mutually conditional nature of the commitments was explicitly recognized in the UN General Assembly Resolution on the CPA, which noted that "the measures stipulated in the Comprehensive Plan of Action are interrelated and mutually reinforcing and should be implemented in their totality by all States concerned" (UN General Assembly Resolution A/RES/44/138, December 15, 1989).

## Ideational Linkages

Each of the three groups of stakeholders was prepared to commit to its part of the overall bargain because of its belief that resolving the mass influx was causally related to its other foreign policy concerns. In that sense, the most important structural basis for cross-issue persuasion in the CPA was ideational. For the United States, the success of the CPA was connected to the legacy of the Vietnam War and regional security; for the ASEAN states and Hong Kong, it was related to migration control and demographic security; for Vietnam, it was a means to rehabilitate itself politically and attract additional development assistance. Let us explore these ideas in turn.

*The United States*    The United States, as the main resettlement state and hegemonic power in the CPA, held two important ideas about the causal relationship between the success of the CPA and its wider foreign policy interests. In particular, it viewed the CPA in the context of the wider legacy of the Vietnam War and as related to, first, regional security in Southeast Asia and, second, the interests of the Vietnamese diaspora in the United States.

The U.S. position in relation to the CPA had its genesis in the Vietnam War and the evacuation of Saigon in 1975 following the victory of the Vietcong. With this victory, the advent of communism in South Vietnam, the Vietnamese invasion of Cambodia, and the alignment of China with Vietnam, the United States entered into a form of cold war with Vietnam that lasted until around 1987. In Valerie Sutter's words, "this Cold War consists of pressuring and isolating Vietnam by focusing on the plight of refugees" (1990, 87). Indeed, following the U.S. withdrawal in 1975, Gerald Ford and Henry Kissinger requested humanitarian aid from Congress as a substitute for military aid, and the *United States* began to use the refugee humanitarian issue as its main political tool for tackling communism in Southeast Asia (Sutter 1990, 61). It did so both through the resettlement of refugees and through providing political and economic support for the ASEAN states. Its commitment to resettlement was based on attempting to discredit communism by allowing people to "vote with their feet." As Sutter claims of the period before 1988, "admission levels for refugees are related to ASEAN-US relations and to the isolation of Vietnam" (1990, 85). For the United States, the refugee issue was an efficient way to meet this wider aim; "playing a leadership role in refugee matters costs little and meets little opposition at home" (Sutter 1990, 85). Even after 1988, the main U.S. interest in the region was the promotion of democracy and security—in other words, noncommunism—within the region.

For the United States, the CPA was a continuation of 1979. As Senator Edward Kennedy noted, "I am hopeful the United States will assume its traditional leadership—as we did in 1979—and support these new international efforts to address the root causes behind the continued refugee flow."[33] Similarly, as the secretary-general made clear in his opening statement to the conference, the CPA built on the prior U.S. commitment to its

---

33. UNHCR Washington, D.C., to Headquarters, "A Staff Report on the International Conference on Indochinese Refugees, 1989," prepared for 101st Congress, memo, 7 July 1989, UNHCR Fonds 11, Series 3, 391.89, UNHCR Archives.

1979 agreement: "In view of its relative proximity in time to the events that profoundly affected the three counties of Indochina, the July 1979 meeting considered that the fate of asylum seekers in that region continued to be matter of utmost concern to the international community."[34] Furthermore, this continuation from 1979 was given a great deal of impetus by domestic politics precisely because of all the Indochinese who had already been re-settled and now constituted a significant diaspora in the United States. The Council for Refugee Rights, for example, organized a conference in Westminster, California, which resulted in the Indochinese community's proclaiming: "More than one million Indochinese living in the United States are deeply concerned with the present treatment and policies of the first asylum countries for these freedom seekers."[35] Many members of the U.S. government and civil society regarded all those fleeing communism as having a right to asylum without screening. For example, individuals such as Shep Lowman and Lionel Rosenblatt, with links to the U.S. State Department and working for Refugees International, were strong advocates for regarding every Vietnamese as a refugee on the grounds that Vietnam remained a communist state. It was partly this perspective, so pervasive during the Cold War and ongoing in much of civil society even in 1989, that led to the initial U.S. insistence on *voluntary* return.[36]

Over time, however, this same underlying commitment to the Viet-namese refugees led the government to relax its stance on screening and return. This shift was echoed in the U.S. government position at the Geneva Conference, noted by the report to Congress: "If the friends of refugees had taken an unyielding stance in Geneva against the demand by the ASEAN and other countries to start a screening alternative...then the countries of first asylum would have ignored the US and perhaps have closed their doors."[37]

Tensions between the United States and Vietnam began to ease after 1987. Given the changing political situation, Mikhail Gorbachev withdrew

---

34. UN Secretary-General, "Opening Statement by the UN Secretary-General to the International Conference on Indochinese Refugees," 13 June 1989, Geneva, UNHCR Fonds 11, Series 3, 391.89, UNHCR Archives.

35. Council for Refugee Rights Conference, 7 May 1989, Westminster, Calif., UNHCR Fonds 11, Series 3, 391.89, UNHCR Archives.

36. Interview with McNamara.

37. UNHCR Washington, D.C., to Headquarters, "Staff Report."

the Soviet financial contributions to Vietnam, leading the Sixth Congress of the Vietnamese Communist Party to propose a reformist agenda in 1986. This then led to the Vietnamese withdrawal from Cambodia, announced in 1988 and implemented in 1990. In this context, there was a thaw in U.S.-Vietnamese relations. For example, agreements were reached in other areas, such as on U.S. soldiers who were missing in action (MIAs) and on the ODP, allowing Amerasians and political prisoners from reeducation camps to be resettled in the United States. This change in relations gradually opened up the possibility for the United States to consider political engagement with Vietnam, opening the prospects for the voluntary return of nonrefugees.

Despite this change, there was also a degree of continuity with respect to the position of the United States in the region. Throughout the period (both pre- and post-1987), the U.S. focus was on support for noncommunism and for security within the region. The U.S. position on return was directly related to the progress of Vietnam in the *Doi Moi* (progressive and gradual economic liberalization) reform process and emerged only because of the end of the Vietnamese alignment with the USSR, its planned withdrawal from Cambodia, and the reform announcements made by the Sixth Congress in 1986. The underlying U.S. goal of promoting democracy and capitalism within Vietnam and the wider region is evident in the report to Congress on the CPA, which noted, "It is time to take some concrete steps towards normalizing relations—of talking more directly and frequently with Hanoi.... There is ample precedence for establishing American 'interests' sections in other countries where we do not have diplomatic relations, but with which we desire more regular diplomatic contact."[38] The director of the Indochinese Policy Forum argued that the U.S. national interest lay in fostering regional stability:

> The long-term policy goal of the United States is to help bring about a peaceful and stable Vietnam that is fully integrated into the international community and is not threatening to its neighbours. As this process occurs, we shall encourage Vietnam to move increasingly towards establishing democratic institutions.... The United States should encourage conditions

---

38. Ibid.

to help Vietnam reduce its reliance upon the Soviet Union, particularly by improving its relationship with ASEAN.[39]

U.S. engagement with Vietnam was also seen as a means of influencing the prospects for peace in Cambodia, given that Vietnam had committed to withdrawing its troops from the country by 1990, and of supporting negotiations between the People's Republic of Kampuchea (PRK) and Prince Sihanouk, who for a long time had been a U.S. client. Indeed, return was a useful vehicle for achieving these ends because of the Vietnamese need to attract assistance and political legitimacy and its identification of refugee return as a means to achieve these ends. Hence, the attempted U.S. linkage proved a successful means of promoting gradual reform within Vietnam. This is most clearly illustrated in the way that Vietnam adapted its position on the ODP of political prisoners and on other areas such as the monitoring of returns after it began to receive greater political recognition and development assistance through U.S. support for return.

The U.S. commitment to resettlement was also part of its wider relationship with ASEAN, and it used the refugee issue to enhance its relationship with ASEAN in other areas of strategic importance. For example, by 1984 the region was the fifth biggest U.S. trading partner (in terms of the value of exports and imports), the United States had military bases in the Philippines and Thailand, and it relied on Indonesia for a reliable oil supply outside of the Middle East. During the Cold War, ASEAN had served as an important buffer against communism, and the ASEAN states continued to be seen as important for U.S. regional interests after the Cold War. Limiting the destabilizing effect of the mass exodus from Indochina and ensuring ongoing good relations with ASEAN were therefore crucial underlying aims of the United States, which allowed the ASEAN states a greater degree of bargaining power in demanding an ongoing U.S. commitment to providing resettlement. The United States backed ASEAN as a bulwark against communism by attempting to maintain good relations with the countries; by supporting them against destabilizing influences such as the mass influx of refugees; and through a strong military

---

39. Dick Clark (director of the Indochina Policy Forum, Aspen Institute), "Recommendations for the New Administration on United States Policy towards Indochina," November 1988. UNHCR Fonds 11, Series 3, 391.89, UNHCR Archives.

presence, especially in Thailand and the Philippines. The United States also gave support to the Coalition Government of Democratic Kampuchea (CGDK), as the remnants of the Pol Pot regime, and to Prince Sihanouck, the principal U.S. client in Cambodia.

*ASEAN and Hong Kong*     The first-asylum host countries perceived the success of the CPA as being causally connected to their migration concerns. As Courtland Robinson (1998, 193) observes, "most would agree that the CPA, first and foremost, was an effort to control migration." After 1975, the undifferentiated mass exodus of over 1 million boat people to the ASEAN states and Hong Kong led to significant regional concerns with migration.

The era of the CPA represented a departure from the way in which the causal relationship between migration and refugee status was understood. Until the CPA, refugee status had generally been accorded on a *prima facie* basis—if an individual claimed asylum, he or she would generally be regarded as a refugee. In the context of the long-standing mass influx of people in Southeast Asia, however, the causal relationship between migration and asylum began to be questioned so that the two were no longer regarded as coterminous. Instead, screening was instituted to differentiate between migrants and refugees; refugees were resettled and nonrefugee migrants were returned to their countries of origin. As Robinson (1998, 188–89) comments, "by severing the link between arrival in a UNHCR camp and presumptive refugee status, the CPA marked a fundamental break with the Indochinese programme of the previous fourteen years."

To the first-asylum host countries, the Vietnamese state and Vietnamese refugees were both seen as destabilizing influences. The mass influx of people was generally viewed in security terms, as a potential threat to the internal political stability of the ASEAN states. In many ways, the refugees were an unwelcome burden and one that remained dependent on the availability of resettlement to the United States and other Northern countries. Indeed, many of the ASEAN states perceived the refugee exodus to be an American problem, stemming from the U.S. involvement in the Vietnam War. The precise way in which this threat was perceived depended on the specific identity of the states. The principal concerns of Thailand stemmed from it geographical proximity to Indochina. Because it bordered on Cambodia, it received a sizable number of Cambodian refugees and feared that many might be Vietcong infiltrators. Because of this border threat, Thailand also accepted U.S. assistance for the CGDK within its territory. For Malaysia and, to a lesser extent, Indonesia, the principal security threat of hosting refugees came from the precarious demographic and ethnic make-ups of these countries and their precarious relationship with China. The exodus of Hoa Chinese from Vietnam was seen as something that could rapidly destabilize the demographic equilibria of these states. As Sutter (1990, 135) explains in relation to Malaysia, "the refugees pose a serious security threat related to the larger context of Sino-Malaysian relations." The unique position of Hong Kong was partly defined by its not being part of ASEAN and by its being a British colony. The United States regarded Hong Kong as a British responsibility and offered it few resettlement opportunities. Given already high levels of immigration from China in the colony and the already high population density, the boat people were therefore perceived as a threat.

Another significant element of the identity of the ASEAN states at the time was their search for international political legitimacy. For both ASEAN as a regional alliance and for a number of the individual Southeast Asian states, the commitment to temporary asylum was directly related to an interest in enhancing their political legitimacy. This applied particularly to the regimes of Ferdinand Marcos in the Philippines and of Suharto in Indonesia. In the case of the Philippines, Sutter notes that "the assistance of the Philippines also contributed to international recognition for the government of Ferdinand Marcos" (Sutter 1990, 152–53). In particular, the opening of the Bataan processing center near U.S. military bases included a photographic display of the contributions of the Marcos government to the center. In the case of Indonesia, Suharto used compliance with the CPA as a means to prove his human rights credentials to the international community. There were also many local dynamics and substate interests at play, with local officials benefiting from the presence of refugees, as a source of commerce, employment, development, or corruption in areas such as Galang. ASEAN as a whole had been internationally relatively insignificant in 1975, and its adoption of a unified and collective position in the CPA offered it an opportunity to develop collective solidarity and enhanced political legitimacy. Although these underlying motives were not explicitly linked, they were cooperation-enhancing insofar as they offered an incentive for ASEAN engagement.

*The Socialist Republic of Vietnam*    After 1975, the Vietnamese domestic political agenda focused on nation-building and the socialist transformation of the south of the country. To financially support this, it aligned with the USSR in 1978, allowing it to procure an average of £2.5 billion per year in assistance. This political agenda defined the isolated position of Vietnam in the region and its difficult relations with China and the United States. After 1986, two events created a fundamental change in the position of Vietnam vis-à-vis the international community. First, the decline of the USSR impelled Vietnam to seek alternative sources of economic support. Vietnam had been financially and politically dependent on the USSR until around 1986, when the changing situation in the USSR led the Vietnamese Communist Party to consider a reform agenda. Because assistance was becoming increasingly difficult to attract, the regime began to demand aid from the U.S. and Europe as a condition for normalizing relations and for political reform. Second, the change in the role of China in the region created conditions under which it became possible for Vietnam to seek rapprochement with the United States. The United States was willing to engage with Vietnam only after Hanoi had committed to withdrawing Vietnamese troops from Cambodia, and the reduced Chinese involvement in the region and the end to border skirmishes with the Vietnamese-backed regime in Cambodia led Vietnam to commit to its withdrawal from PRK, thus opening up an avenue for dialogue with the United States.[40]

Vietnam was induced to cooperate regarding the return and orderly departure of migrants/refugees because of the potential benefits that doing so yielded in terms of development assistance. In the context of return and once U.S.-Vietnamese relations had begun to improve, the United States was able to draw on the relationship that had been developed between UNHCR and UNDP in CIREFCA to support providing QIPs in Vietnam. Recall that QIPs had been developed to promote the reintegration of returnees in Nicaragua. The projects provided short-term integrated development projects to build housing and create livelihood opportunities to promote the sustainability of refugee return. The idea of using development assistance to limit the exodus and promote return in Vietnam had first been mooted in the United States in 1988; for example, an

---

40. Interview with Ewen MacLeod, European Commission delegation to Hanoi in the negotiations that led to the 1989 Trade and Cooperation Agreement, Oxford, September 20, 2006.

Immigration and National Security Officer suggested a substitute for the unending resettlement: "Just open a consulate in Vietnam.... if Vietnam got £50bn in aid it would be cheaper than resettlement" (quoted in Sutter 1990, 176). From 1992, after the United States accepted the idea of return, UNDP was the agency used to promote this developmental approach and to try to ensure opportunities for return alongside the monitoring of human rights to prevent the United States from being accused of *refoulement*. This approach existed alongside the ongoing use of cash incentives for return (Robinson 1998, 215–16). Although the UNDP program was comparatively small, the European Community also committed to providing Hanoi with development assistance on the condition that Vietnam cooperate with the CPA. The European Community concluded a Trade and Cooperation Agreement with Hanoi on November 23, 1989, which established a range of microcredit schemes and small development projects that were both implicitly and explicitly related to Vietnamese cooperation with the CPA. The QIPs, for example, drew on the EC humanitarian funding and adopted a community-based approach that also benefited local communities, providing schools, wells, and other forms of social provision.[41] The linking of development assistance to return was successful and persuaded Vietnam to increase the rate at which it accepted returnees and to allow the monitoring of return alongside development initiatives. The linkage was therefore cooperation-enhancing because, following the end of USSR financial support, Vietnam needed to seek alternative sources of development assistance and the return of refugees offered such a means.

The main concern of Vietnam was to maximize the economic and political benefits it could derive from the CPA. As Senator Edward Kennedy put it:

> A fundamental issue at Geneva, and in the talks preceding the conference, was over Vietnam's willingness to facilitate the establishment of methods for the safe return of non-refugees to Vietnam—under international auspices and with international monitoring and assistance (all of which is a diplomatic way of saying it will be done "with cash assistance" to "ease the burdens of reintegration"—*in short, to make it worthwhile to Vietnam*).[42]

---

41. Ibid.
42. UNHCR Washington, D.C., to Headquarters, "Staff Report."

To maximize its gains, Vietnam at times obstructed the CPA by limiting the rate of return. For example, its initial insistence on voluntary return was a means to both slow down the process and to increase its bargaining power to leverage greater financial support. To a large extent, this strategy worked, and Vietnam received growing support for development assistance and reintegration as the process evolved. This underlying motivation led to Vietnam's approaching the secretary-general and signing a "Memorandum of Understanding" with UNHCR in 1988 and, ultimately, to its allowing return, monitoring, and development assistance for returnees. This growing commitment to support sustainable return was crucial for the revival of the CPA after the 1990 Manila conference, and it coincided with the increased levels of development assistance provided by the EC under the November 23, 1989 Trade and Cooperation agreement with Hanoi.[43]

## Agency Conditions

The structural connections between refugee protection and the areas of foreign policy in which states had an interest were a necessary but insufficient condition for the success of the CPA. In addition to the ideas that the various states held about the causal relationship between the issue areas, UNHCR played a crucial brokerage role in articulating to states how their contributions to the CPA would meet their wider interests.

UNHCR provided leadership throughout the CPA. UNHCR explicitly identified itself as playing a "catalytic role" in the preparatory process.[44] At every stage of the process, UNHCR and Sergio Vieira de Mello, as the high commissioner's chef de cabinet, offered political and moral persuasion to mobilize state support. Although his role should not be overstated,[45] nearly all UNHCR staff members who worked on the CPA highlight Vieira de

---

43. Interview with MacLeod.

44. "UNHCR Informal Consultations."

45. His diplomatic talents were ably supported by the legal and protection skills of people such as Dennis McNamara and Irene Khan. Furthermore, the contrasting failure of the Commonwealth of Independent States (CIS) Conference, which Vieira de Mello also led, highlights the importance of other enabling factors such as a clear set of political interests, which allowed the "de Mello factor" to be so significant.

Mello's role in persuading states that the CPA met their wider interests and see this as integral to its success. UNHCR was highly involved with managing the process, chairing meetings and engaging directly in the drafting process.

A key example of the important role of UNHCR as a broker is the Manila meeting in late 1990, the point at which the CPA appeared to be in crisis. The ASEAN states had argued that the United States should compromise and allow the nonvoluntary return of nonrefugees to Vietnam. On the other side, the United States was reluctant to countenance sending Vietnamese back to their country of origin. Eventually, the United States accepted the nonvoluntary return it had initially vehemently opposed. One of the reasons for this *volte-face* was that UNHCR worked to persuade the United States that there was a strong relationship between the commitment of the ASEAN states to asylum and U.S. support for resettlement and return. As a result, the United States backed down in its insistence on only voluntary return to some extent, and the ASEAN states received much of the support that they demanded from the United States and other Northern resettlement states.

Vieira de Mello was largely responsible for rescuing the CPA at the Manila meeting in that he got the states to meet around the table, reminding them of their commitments and interests and bringing about a renewed consensus. Implicitly, he even invoked basic notions of game theory and the Prisoner's Dilemma, highlighting that free-riding was not an option, claiming the CPA to be a "set of mutually reinforcing undertakings, which must be carried out in its totality rather than selectively," and pointing out that this was in the collective interest: "we have very little, if anything, to gain from going it alone, in isolation. We have everything to be proud of if we continue to give our full commitment to a truly balanced implementation of the CPA."[46] In the same speech, he also used moral persuasion:

> Seen from a strictly UNHCR perspective I will surprise none of you here
> if I say that first asylum—that is lives of human beings—is at risk. Our of-
> fice's strength is more than purely legal; it is moral and has a foundation in
> its impartial, neutral and strictly humanitarian mandate.... it is my duty to

---

46. Vieira de Mello, introductory remarks at Informal Steering Committee Meeting.

tell you today that the risk of a major tragedy on the high seas is very real and imminent indeed.[47]

It was on the basis of the meeting in Manila and that a "Near Consensus Note" emerged. Significantly, this provided the basis for a compromise on the issue of the return of nonrefugees, which put the CPA back on track. UNHCR attempted to convey an ethos of compromise throughout the process. As Vieira de Mello wrote, "The CPA is an attempt to provide the framework for an international consensus on an overall solution to this prolonged refugee problem. In working towards such a consensus, governments and UNHCR have agreed on a range of measures which, in themselves, may not be entirely satisfactory to any one party."[48]

Aside from Vieira de Mello's role in mediation and persuasion, one of the primary means used by UNHCR to provide leadership during the CPA was by invoking normative conceptions of equitable burden-sharing in a way which had been almost entirely absent from CIREFCA, for example. In writing to the foreign ministers of the prospective resettlement states, the high commissioner suggested, "Undertakings by resettlement countries to provide solutions for the populations comprise one of the essential and interdependent components of the CPA.... We recognize the need to share the burden of such cases more equitably among the international community, while at the same time submitting [to your state] a reasonable proportion of cases with better prospects for integration."[49] Along with this letter, the high commissioner enclosed an analysis of the resettlement statistics from previous years to offer an indicative outline of what an equitable share of responsibility might be.

Similarly, UNHCR circulated a burden-sharing distribution formula through its Resettlement Subcommittee to help identify the proportion of resettlement quotas for which each main stakeholder should be responsible.[50] For both the pre- and post-cut-off-date caseloads, UNHCR provided

47. Ibid.

48. Sergio Vieira de Mello to See Chak Mun (ambassador, Permanent Mission of Singapore), letter, 8 May 1989, Geneva, UNHCR Fonds 11, Series 3, 391.89, UNHCR Archives.

49. Jean-Pierre Hocké to resettlement states' foreign ministers, letter, May 1989, UNHCR Fonds 11, Series 3, 391.89, UNHCR Archives.

50. "Chairman's Brief for International Conference on Indochinese Refugees: Resettlement Sub-Committee," 8 April 1989, UNHCR Fonds 11, Series 3, 391.89, UNHCR Archives.

"suggested admissions levels" or "demarches to resettlement countries."[51] This is significant because it illustrates how UNHCR managed to credibly convey to states that without each contributing their fair share the whole process would fail. In other words, free-riding was not an option if states hoped to meet their individual or collective interests. This UNHCR role of leadership and persuasion on behalf of the ASEAN states again served to strengthen their position and to induce a greater contributions from the Northern states.

The Indochinese CPA represents one of the most successful examples of international cooperation in the history of the refugee regime. Although the implementation of the CPA has been criticized on human rights grounds, the CPA nevertheless led to levels of cooperation that contributed to ending the long-standing mass influx of Indochinese boat people. By 1996, after the agreement had been fully implemented, the camps and detention centers in the region had been cleared, and all of the boat people had been either resettled as refugees or reintegrated into Vietnam.

Through the CPA, UNHCR facilitated a three-way agreement among the main country of origin, the countries of first asylum, and a number of resettlement countries led by the United States. The commitments of all three of these stakeholders were made explicitly conditional on one another. The ASEAN states and Hong Kong were prepared to provide asylum on conditions that the United States and other states offered resettlement to those recognized as refugees and that Vietnam accepted the return of those who were deemed to be nonrefugees. The resettlement states, led by the United States, agreed to offer resettlement provided the countries of first asylum refrained from *refoulement* and hosted a screening process. Finally, Vietnam was prepared to facilitate return for nonrefugees on the conditions that it was politically recognized and financially supported by the United States and its allies.

The three main groups of states were willing to commit to the agreement because the CPA was conceived in a way that made their commitment interlocking. In other words, asylum, resettlement, and return were made explicitly conditional on one another. But the success of this agreement is

---

51. "Note on Statistics of Resettlement Plan," background documentation for the conference, Annex V, 1989, UNHCR Fonds 11, Series 3, 391.89, UNHCR Archives.

largely attributable to cross-issue persuasion. The reason that these three groups of states were willing to uphold their ends of the bargain was because they were persuaded that the success of the overall CPA was causally related to their wider foreign policy interests.

Cross-issue persuasion was possible mainly because of the structural interconnections between refugee protection and the foreign policy concerns of the contributing states. In contrast to CIREFCA, the CPA was not nested within a wider institutional framework; rather, it was conceived as being fairly institutionally isolated from other issue areas. Nevertheless, the CPA was connected to other issue areas through the ideas held by the main groups of states. For the United States, the CPA was inextricable from the legacy of the Vietnam War and wider U.S. interests in the security of Southeast Asia. For the ASEAN states and Hong Kong, the CPA was primarily about migration control, especially for states such as Indonesia and Malaysia, which had particular demographic concerns related to the influx of ethnic Chinese. Finally, for Vietnam, the CPA was connected to its interest in rehabilitating itself in the eyes of the international community and attracting additional development assistance following the demise of the USSR.

In addition to this structural basis for cross-issue persuasion, there was an agency basis. UNHCR played a crucial brokerage role in drawing on these structural opportunities and channeling them into a commitment to refugee protection. UNHCR played a key facilitation role both in interstate meetings and behind the scenes to persuade states to cooperate. In particular, key members of staff (such as the late Sergio Vieira de Mello) worked to ensure that states recognized both that their individual contributions were crucial for collective action to take place and that the success of the overall CPA was in their pragmatic wider interests. This brokerage role was crucial, not only in the initial conception and negotiation of the CPA but also at time of crisis such as during the 1990 Manila meeting when, without UNHCR playing this role of facilitation and persuasion through argumentation, the CPA would have collapsed.

The CPA had a notable legacy in terms of its influence on UNHCR thinking. It led to a strong belief that UNHCR could play a pragmatic political role by recognizing the wider concerns of states and attempting to channel these into a commitment to refugee protection. This legacy reemerged a decade later when UNHCR conceived its Convention Plus initiative, in which it explicitly referred to the CPA and CIREFCA as constituting the conceptual bases of the new initiative.

# 5

# UNHCR's CONVENTION PLUS
# INITIATIVE (2003–2005)

From the mid-1990s, it was widely acknowledged that there was a global crisis of asylum. In the context of increasing South–North migration, Northern states increasingly viewed the growing number of spontaneously arriving asylum seekers as a migration issue and a security threat. European states, in particular, began to impose a complex range of restrictionist measures such as carrier sanctions, interception at sea, surveillance, and deterrence measures to limit the number of asylum seekers claiming refugee status on their territory. On the other side, in the context of declining international burden-sharing and increasingly protracted refugee situations on their territories, many Southern states began to impose restrictions on the number of refugees they were prepared to host. A number of African states, such as Tanzania, which had previously been exceptionally hospitable to refugees, even resorted to forced repatriation and expulsion (Crisp 2003a; Durieux and Kelley 2004; Milner 2009).

Given this climate of state concern with border security and the reluctance of states to provide asylum to refugees, an increasing proportion of politicians and the media began to publicly question the ongoing relevance of the 1951 Convention. There were even calls my some politicians for the convention to be abolished. This led to UNHCR convening a series of initiatives to explore the ongoing relevance of the 1951 Convention and the global refugee regime, and to explore areas in which they might be improved. To mark the fiftieth anniversary of the convention, UNHCR convened the Global Consultations to engage in a dialogue with states, NGOs, academics, and refugees. The purpose of the consultations was to ascertain the ongoing relevance of the 1951 Convention. Somewhat surprisingly given the widely recognized crisis of asylum, the consultations led to the universal reaffirmation of the ongoing relevance of the 1951 Convention. In addition, it shed light on areas of asylum and refugee protection in the early twenty-first century that were not adequately covered by the convention.

This acknowledgement of the need to supplement the refugee regime in areas that were inadequately addressed by the 1951 Convention led UNHCR to convene the Convention Plus initiative. Between 2003 and 2005, the initiative attempted to develop a normative framework for burden-sharing by facilitating interstate debate on three new "soft law" agreements between states. The areas (or strands) in which these agreements were debated all related to aspects of the division of responsibility between North and South: resettlement, targeted development assistance, and irregular secondary movement. The intention was that these agreements would then be applied in practice to coordinate the burden-sharing needed to resolve specific protracted refugee situations in particular regional contexts. The chosen pilot case studies for this were the protracted situations of Somali refugees in East Africa and the Horn of Africa and of Afghan refugees in Iran and Pakistan.

Convention Plus was ultimately a failure. The debates in the three strands polarized along North–South lines, leading to little lasting legacy. Nevertheless, the initiative is conceptually interesting because it represented the first time that UNHCR self-consciously engaged in issue linkage that can be described as cross-issue persuasion. In particular, it attempted to appeal to the interests of Northern states in migration control as the basis for their committing to burden-sharing to enhance the protection for refugees in their region of origin. On the other side, UNHCR attempted to appeal to the interests of Southern states in attracting more resettlement and develop assistance as the basis for their offering a greater commitment to protection and durable solutions on their territory. The idea was that issue linkage would lead to formal agreements in which a grand bargain would link Northern concerns with irregular movements with Southern concerns with development assistance and resettlement.

The UNHCR attempts at cross-issue persuasion failed, and Convention Plus was characterized by a North–South impasse. This, of course, begs the question of why this happened. In this chapter, I argue that one of the reasons for the failure of the initiative was the absence of a structural basis on which UNHCR could base its attempts to relate refugee protection to wider issue areas such as migration and development. I begin by explaining the origins, content, and outcome of the initiative before examining the reasons for its ultimate failure.

## Recognizing the Limitations of the 1951 Convention

The genesis of Convention Plus lay in the fiftieth anniversary of the 1951 Convention on the Status of Refugees, which culminated in a debate on whether the regime should be renegotiated or reaffirmed and how UNHCR should adapt to reflect the new global environment (Curran and Kneebone 2003). In response, UNHCR initiated a process of Global Consultations (2000–2002), in which states, NGOs, and academic experts were invited to present their views on this debate (Feller, Türk, and Nicholson 2003). Paradoxically, given the many claims that the existing legal structure was anachronistic and ill-adapted, the consultations led to the universal reaffirmation of the 1951 Convention as the basis of refugee protection. The outcome of the Global Consultations was an Agenda For Protection (AfP) identifying the gaps in the existing refugee protection regime. Convention Plus was in many ways an ad hoc response to the AfP (UNHCR 2002a). It was initially suggested that the various goals set out in the AfP would be addressed through new arrangements and tools that could be debated within an International Protection Forum.[1] Based on these preliminary discussions, High Commissioner Ruud Lubbers elaborated the

---

1. Pirkko Kourula to high commissioner, "The International Protection Forum," memo, 25 October 2002, CPU Files, UNHCR Archives.

notion of Convention Plus, which he formally launched at the October 2002 ExCom session. At this stage Convention Plus was almost entirely devoid of substance, simply referring to the idea of special agreements in areas not adequately dealt with by the convention. Lubbers's early speeches on Convention Plus referred to the need to tackle the issue of secondary movements and to build on ideas such as the use of targeted development assistance to improve protection in regions of origin.[2] Nevertheless, in the context of ongoing dialogue between the high commissioner and key European donors on the problem of onward secondary movements, the label was seized on by those states as a means to legitimate their own ideas about extraterritorial processing.[3] For example, the UK proposals for extraterritorial processing directly invoked the UNHCR Convention Plus as the source of their legitimacy, claiming that "These pilots could form part of UNHCR's development of 'Convention Plus' and the structures they have set-up for Convention Plus should give us scope for moulding the organization more as we wish it to be" (UK Government 2003). These European attempts to coopt the label Convention Plus meant that UNHCR had to work reactively to define Convention Plus. It was not until the formal launch of the initiative in June 2003 that the basis of the initiative was clarified and its central focus was identified as attempting to develop a normative framework in relation to burden-sharing, particularly in pursuing durable solutions to protracted refugee situations.

Convention Plus explicitly attempted to address areas of refugee protection that were inadequately dealt with in the 1951 Convention and its 1967 Protocol. In particular, it attempted to develop a normative framework for a range of old and new problems. Its focus was on two related areas identified within the "Agenda for Protection." First, it aimed to increase the quantity and predictability of burden-sharing; in other words, it aimed to increase the level of the financial commitment of donors to host countries

2. Ruud Lubbers, "Opening Statement by Ruud Lubbers, United Nations High Commissioner for Refugees," Fifty-Third Session of the Executive Committee of the High Commissioner's Programme, 30 September 2002, CPU Files, UNHCR Archives.

3. *Extraterritorial processing* occurs when a state assesses an asylum seeker's the claim to refugee status outside the territorial boundaries of that state. The Australian government, for example, used such an approach in its Pacific Solution. In early 2003, the UK government claimed to be in discussion with the governments of Denmark and the Netherlands about the development of a similar scheme (Noll 2003).

in the regions of origin. Second, it aimed to channel this commitment into new approaches to addressing protracted refugee situations. In the words of Ruud Lubbers, "Convention Plus means a stronger multilateral commitment to finding durable, sustainable solutions to refugee problems in a burden-sharing framework."[4] These aims were to be achieved through general normative agreements and through their application to pilot CPAs, based on the precedents of the Indochinese CPA and CIREFCA. Reflecting this, Convention Plus was divided into two main areas: the generic work and the situation-specific work. Ultimately, the bulk of the interstate focus was on the development of abstract normative agreements rather than on their application to new situation-specific CPAs.

## A Process with Three Strands

Within the context of the generic work, there were three strands to the debate in which special agreements were negotiated separately and together on an interstate level: (1) the Strategic Use of Resettlement, (2) Irregular Secondary Movements (ISM), and (3) Targeted Development Assistance (TDA) to improve access to durable solutions and protection capacities in regions of origin (UNHCR 2005a). Strategic Resettlement was conceived as "the planned use of resettlement that maximizes the benefit of resettlement, either directly or indirectly, other than to those being resettled. Those benefits accrue to other refugees, the host States, other States, and the international protection regime in general" (UNHCR 2005a). It was an acknowledgement that resettlement is likely to be most effective when applied alongside other durable solutions and that, even when numerically small, it may play a catalytic role in leveraging other solutions. The ISMs debate was an attempt to define the notion of a *secondary movement* to determine the circumstances in which a state could return a refugee to a country of first asylum through which that individual has either transited or had (or should already have had) found an adequate level of protection.

The TDA debate was an attempt to develop common principles on the role of development assistance in relation to refugee protection and

---

4. Ruud Lubbers, "Opening Statement to Inaugural Forum," First Convention Plus Forum, 27 June 2003, CPU Files, UNHCR Archives.

durable solutions. It focused on three related concepts: the 4Rs, development assistance in relation to refugees (DAR) and development through local integration (DLI). The 4Rs (repatriation, reintegration, rehabilitation, and reconstruction) focused on improving the sustainability of repatriation by fostering the capacity and institutional partnerships necessary to ensure the smooth transition from emergency relief to long-term development planning within countries of origin. DAR and DLI focused on host countries of asylum by promoting self-sufficiency pending durable solutions and local integration, respectively (UNHCR 2003b). These three areas have in common that they all relate to the distribution of state responsibilities for refugee protection and providing durable solutions between North and South. As UNHCR put it, the purpose was "to clarify the apportioning and promote the better sharing of responsibilities by States, notably in the context of mass influxes and mixed migratory flows as well as for durable solutions" (UNHCR 2003a).

The initiative, therefore, had a very strong North–South dimension. As the director of the initiative secretariat put it:

> It is absolutely possible to characterize the debate in terms of North/South...because the South is where the burden is....Convention Plus is to a large extent a North-South dialogue. We are trying to depolarize it... because we try to highlight that point of convergence of interests between the North and the South...but we have to acknowledge that they start from a very different angle and situation.[5]

The North–South dichotomy throughout the debate was generally represented by the division between donor states and host states. In the words of Lubbers, "The whole exercise of Convention Plus is about burden- and responsibility-sharing, and this requires a multilateral approach. Our role is to bring together a truly multilateral coalition, to promote convergence of interests between cash donors and host countries."[6] Internal UNHCR documentation and also the statements by the states themselves used the

---

5. Interview with Jean-Francois Durieux, head of the Convention Plus Unit, UNHCR, Geneva, September 7, 2004.

6. "Chairman's Summary, Inaugural Meeting of the Forum," 27 June 2003, CPU Files, UNHCR Archives.

language of North-South, host-donor, and developed-developing countries to characterize the main actors in the debate.[7]

In particular, the three strands attempted to address the concerns of Northern state with the asylum-migration nexus and the concerns of Southern states with the security threat posed by ongoing protracted refugee situations and the absence of international burden-sharing (both economic and in terms of resettlement). Reflecting the dual concern, ISMs was an attempt to tackle concerns about spontaneous-arrival asylum seekers in the North, whereas strategic resettlement and TDA represented the means to channel these concerns into improved North–South burden-sharing.

In terms of process, the strands were to be negotiated in Geneva in core groups of interested states led by a facilitating state or group of states.[8] The main debate would then take place at the biannual High Commissioner's Forum, of which, ultimately, there were five. The Geneva-based forum provided a mechanism for intergovernmental debate on the special agreements. The intended output from each strand was a special agreement; these would be "written arrangements between UNHCR and Government that, depending on their subject matter, are either drafted to be legally binding or intended to reflect an important degree of political commitment" (UNHCR 2003a). In the words of the high commissioner, "whether they turn out to be binding instruments or 'soft law', what we have in mind is more than just vague declarations or lofty exhortations."[9] The stated intention was that the three special agreements could then be applied collectively to situation-specific or caseload-specific protracted refugee situations through CPAs. There were plans to use Somali and Afghan refugees as pilot cases.[10]

---

7. "Note on Convention Plus," distributed by M. H. Khan, 24 January 2003, CPU Files, UNHCR Archives, para. 20. "Statement on Behalf of the African Group," First Forum, 27 June 2003, CPU Files, UNHCR Archives; "Statement of South African Government," read by Laura Joyce, First Forum, 27 June 2003, CPU Files, UNHCR Archives; "Statement of Iran," First Forum, 27 June 2003, CPU Files, UNHCR Archives.

8. South Africa and Switzerland were the facilitating states for the Core Group on ISMs; Canada was the facilitating state for the Core Group on the Strategic Use of Resettlement; and Denmark and Japan were the facilitating states for the TDA strand, although no formal core group was established for this strand.

9. "Chairman's Summary, Inaugural Meeting."

10. Ibid.

The political logic underlying the initiative was that through improved North–South cooperation and burden-sharing, both Northern and Southern nations could be better off. If Northern states provided improved burden-sharing for protection in the Southern states, there would be less need for Northern states to provide territorial asylum to spontaneous-arrival asylum seekers in the North. The logic of the South "providing protection on behalf of the North" in exchange for financial compensation by the North was explained by the representative of the African Group[11] in Geneva: "Let's face it, it is cheaper to take care of a refugee on the continent than it is for them to be taken care of in Europe...the Netherlands, for example, was spending about 10,000 Euros/yr/capita just on processing and 10,000 Euros, if this were transferred to a refugee hosting country in Africa, would do a lot."[12] He went on to claim that Ghana could provide refugee protection for just $29 per month for each refugee. This argument almost exactly echoed the logic put forward by the Netherlands, in claiming:

> UNHCR had a total budget of about USD 1 billion at its disposal in 2002 for refugee protection for 20 million people worldwide. In that same year, the Netherlands spent 1.4 billion on national refugee determination procedures, personnel, reception facilities for about 80,000 refugees and asylum seekers in the Netherlands. Other destination countries spend comparable amounts of money on comparable numbers of asylum seekers, many of whom are not recognized as refugees, but are economic migrants. This phenomenon has as a result that a significant amount of the money spent worldwide does not reach genuine refugees.[13]

Despite this idea that through a form of common but differentiated responsibility sharing the North, the South, and the refugees could benefit, the initiative largely failed in its aim of facilitating greater international cooperation.

---

11. The African Group is a regional coalition of states that speaks on behalf of African states in UN debates in Geneva.

12. Interview with Sylvester Parker-Allotey, deputy permanent representative of Ghana, Geneva, September 16, 2004.

13. Ian de Jong, "Statement by Ian de Jong, Ambassador of the Netherlands," First Forum, 27 June 2003, CPU Files, UNHCR Archives.

## North–South Polarization

By the close of the Convention Plus initiative in November 2005, it had largely failed to meet its initial aims. The intended generic agreements had not been created and there were no documents with even the soft-law status intended by the high commissioner. The only output that came close to meeting this status was the "Multilateral Framework of Understandings on Resettlement" (UNHCR 2004b). Yet even this was a modest and uncontroversial statement. It entailed no binding commitments and was intended to apply only in conjunction with the agreements on the other strands, rendering its ultimate relevance extremely limited (UNHCR 2004b). The debates on TDA and ISMs polarized along North–South lines. In relation to TDA, Southern states were left disillusioned by the reluctance of donor states to offer significant additional assistance and by the exclusion of host states from most of the donor-only discussions. Northern states were left disillusioned by the apparent unwillingness of Southern host states to countenance local integration or self-sufficiency. In the ISMs debate, there was also divergence along North–South lines. Northern states wanted a definition of *effective protection* based exclusively on civil and political rights and a notion of secondary movements based on the idea that refugees should have found protection in a country of first asylum, which would lower the threshold for return and readmission of the refugees to their regions of origin. On the other side, Southern states wanted a definition of *effective protection* that would also be based on the economic and social rights of the 1951 Convention and a greater financial commitment to strengthening the refugee protection capacity of host states without this being related to readmission. The polarization of the debate meant that, rather than resulting in special agreements, the outputs of the TDA and ISMs strands were limited to joint statements by the co-chairs of the core groups consolidating the points of convergence and divergence to emerge from the debates (UNHCR 2005b, 2005c). The lack of trust and the failure to achieve consensus on a normative level meant that there were, in turn, few additional commitments made to the UNHCR situation-specific pilot programs, such as the Somali Comprehensive Plan of Action and the Strengthening Protection Capacities Project (SPCP), carried out under the auspices of Convention Plus.

The failure of Convention Plus to lead to significant levels of sustained cooperation can be attributed to a number of factors that stem from the dynamic between North and South. First, the initiative took place in a low-trust environment in which, based on past experience, North and South were mutually suspicious. For example, African states pointed repeatedly to their past experiences of dealing with the North to highlight why they were skeptical of Northern commitments within a Convention Plus framework. In interview, Omar Mapuri, the Tanzanian minister for home affairs, pointed to the experience of Tanzania since the late 1970s in using local integration:

> We have had a bitter experience in this.... We provided income generating activities and open markets to them. But immediately once we introduced that, then the international community washed its hands. So they left the whole burden with us. We fully provided education, health services, water and all other social services to these settlements. And when we invite the international community to come in they say "we are preoccupied with the asylum-seekers." True, we understand that and we have not been complaining about it. But, of late, Zambia and Uganda came with a similar arrangement and it is being treated as something new [laughter]. For the first time in the world the international community is experiencing self-reliance to help refugees.[14]

In addition, in relation to the debate on TDA, the African Group commented that, "It is our view that the current debate on this strand is taking place largely without any information on past similar practices and precedents (e.g. lessons learnt of the two International Conferences on Assistance to Refugees in Africa [ICARA I and II])."[15] This suspicion meant that many Southern states approached the language of the North in cynical terms. In the words of one member of UNHCR staff, "Ideas such a self-sufficiency was seen as synonymous with local integration; 'burden-sharing' was understood as 'burden-shifting'; and secondary movements was about readmission."[16]

---

14. Interview with the Hon. Omar Mapuri, member of Parliament, minister for home affairs, Tanzania, Geneva, October 7, 2004.

15. DRC (African Group Coordinator on Refugee Matters) to Jean-Francois Durieux (head of Convention Plus Unit, UNHCR), letter, 8 March 2005, CPU Files, UNHCR Archives.

16. Interview with José Riera, UNHCR, November 17, 2005.

Second, the suspicions of the South were exacerbated by the feeling that it was being marginalized within the debate. For example, host states were initially excluded from interstate dialogue on TDA; it was donor states only until September 2005. In response, the African Group objected: "We are disappointed that discussions relating to this strand seem to be *about* assistance to major refugee-hosting countries or countries of origin and not discussion *with* such countries.... we wish to caution that the work in this strand should be transparent and also include the participation of refugee-hosting countries."[17] The African Group further argued that "Separate discussions of groups of states unfortunately do not add to a transparent and open process,"[18] complaining that there was no Core Group on TDA as initially envisaged and that there was no consultation on writing of the "Statement of Good Practice."[19]

It was not until September 16, 2005 that a TDA meeting was convened with both donors and host states together; but by this point the African states were so disillusioned by the lack of transparency of the North that they rejected further discussions, stating, "I have to inform [you] that the African Group has come to a conclusion that the need for setting up a [Core] Group [on TDA] is not timely," partly because "several African delegations have been informed that it is not 'realistic' to expect financial or other commitment or assistance in this regard."[20]

Third, the Convention Plus process was perceived by Southern states as a vehicle of Northern hegemony. The high commissioner had initially set out his Convention Plus initiative in Copenhagen at an EU Justice and Home Affairs meeting in September 2002, and the initiative was developed largely in consultation with Denmark, the Netherlands, and the United Kingdom. The Eurocentrism of UNHCR in the process was acknowledged by members of staff in internal correspondence. Many of the initiatives were delivered as a *fait accompli* to Southern states.

---

17. "Statement on Behalf of the African Group," read by Sylvester Parker Allotey, Convention Plus Forum, 1 October 2004, CPU Files, UNHCR Archives.

18. "Chairman's Summary, Inaugural Meeting."

19. "African Group Statement to Fourth Forum," read by Sebastien Mutomb Mujing (DRC), 20 May 2005, CPU Files, UNHCR Archives.

20. "Statement by Nigeria on Behalf of the African Group on the Occasion of an Informal Meeting on Targeted Development Assistance," 16 September 2005, CPU Files, UNHCR Archives.

In commenting on the SPCP, the head of the Convention Plus secretariat stated:

> The most critical point remains...who is going to approach the authorities of Kenya (and also Tanzania etc.), and when, with a view to bringing these authorities on board even though, in fairness, they have not been the initiators of these projects? I can see a rather bad scenario developing unless UNHCR...approaches the "target countries" before the projects are a complete "fait accompli."[21]

Meanwhile, Southern requests were largely ignored. For example, the request by African states for a framework of basic principles of burden-sharing was sidelined. Ruud Lubbers initially responded to the request by stating that "The African Group's proposal to develop a framework of basic principles applying to burden-sharing is, therefore, interesting. A document of this sort could constitute a 'preamble' to any future comprehensive solutions arrangements."[22] But the idea was never taken up by UNHCR.

Despite its limited substantive legacy, Convention Plus is conceptually fascinating. Indeed, studying failures can be as revealing as studying successes. The initiative is significant because it represents a systematic attempt by UNHCR to engage in the political facilitation of a North–South dialogue across a range of areas relating to the allocation of responsibility for protection and durable solutions between North and South. Throughout the initiative, Geneva was a locus for North–South interaction, offering an ideal case study for exploring contemporary North–South relations in the refugee regime. Furthermore, and of even greater relevance, cross-issue persuasion and issue linkage were at the heart of Convention Plus.

## The Role of Cross-Issue Persuasion

The underlying ethos of Convention Plus was the attempt by UNHCR to recognize, appeal to, and channel the perceived interests of states into cooperative win-win outcomes for the North, the South, and the refugees.

---

21. Jean-Francois Durieux to Ebrima Camara et al., "Project Proposal on Somali Refugees," e-mail, 17 October 2003, CPU Files, UNHCR Archives.

22. "Chairman's Summary, Inaugural Meeting."

The work of the initiative secretariat focused on identifying the opportunities and constraints posed by globalization and the war on terror, for example, by recognizing the changing nature of the interests of the states. In the words of the director of the secretariat (the Convention Plus Unit, CPU), "what are the opportunities at hand[?].... that is the real question.... there are incentives and also obstacles in the current state of affairs.... there are mixed signals and we are just trying to seize opportunities."[23]

One manifestation of the UNHCR attempt to appeal to the interests of states is the extent to which it used the idea of plurilateralism; that is, rather than being based on an entirely inclusive, multilateral approach, the core-group structure allowed smaller subgroups of interested states to make progress on issues of mutual concern. As part of this plurilateral approach, Convention Plus incorporated a range of bilateral partnerships, allowing interested states to move ahead with the implementation of proposals. This was, for example, the case with respect to the TDA strand, in which Denmark, as the co-facilitating state of the strand, integrated its bilateral partnership with Uganda into the initiative.

This type of support for bilateral approaches and differentiated responses among the subgroups of states builds on the logic of James Hathaway and Alexander Neve's (1997) idea of interest-convergence groups. Hathaway and Neve's idea is that states should be able to contribute to the global refugee regime in different ways that are in their mutual interest. This is a particularly important idea when we recognizes that most states contribute to refugee protection selectively and in areas in which they derive some kind of supplementary state-specific benefit (Betts 2003, 288–92).

The approach the initiative took in trying to appeal to these wider interests and channel them into a commitment to refugee protection was cross-issue persuasion. As the director of the initiative acknowledged, many of the perceived interests of states were not related to the refugee issue per se; nevertheless, "maybe the commitment is not clearly in the humanitarian or the refugee area but it can be turned to the advantage of that." UNHCR recognized that the wider interests of states in contemporary migration, security, and development issues offered it an opportunity to induce them to contribute to refugee protection. In all of its Convention Plus work,

---

23. Interview with Durieux.

UNHCR therefore attempted to make the case that refugee protection might not be of so much value to the states for its own sake but could serve Northern migration interests and Southern development interests and, furthermore, that these interests could then be institutionally linked both to one another and to refugee protection through Convention Plus.

## Structural Conditions

The key problem with the initiative was that the UNHCR claims that states could meet their interests in other issue areas through a commitment to refugee protection had very little basis. The main reason for this was twofold. In the institutional design of Convention Plus, no relationship was created between these wider issue areas and refugee protection. And on an ideational level, there was no widely held belief that there was a causal relationship between refugee protection and the other issue areas. In this section, I explain the limitations of the ways in which refugee protection was structurally connected to migration and development, and how this contributed to the failure of the UNHCR attempts to engage in cross-issue persuasion.

### Institutional Linkages

The UNHCR institutional design of Convention Plus was not auspicious for enabling cross-issue persuasion. The initiative was premised on two elements of persuasion: (1) that Northern states could be persuaded to commit to additional development assistance and resettlement because this would lead to a side-payment in terms of a reduction in irregular secondary movements and (2) that Southern states could be persuaded to commit to enhancing the quality of protection in the region, thereby reducing the need for irregular secondary movements because this would lead to a side-payment in terms of increased development assistance and resettlement. The basis of the initiative was, therefore, that Northern states commit to the Resettlement and TDA strands and that, in return, Southern states would make certain commitments that would lead to a reduction in irregular secondary movements. The success of the initiative was premised on the notion of creating a contractual linkage between Northern burden-sharing and Southern protection in the region.

But the institutional design of the initiative, with its three distinct strands, separated the elements of what was intended to be a grand bargain across the strands. This separation of the different elements of the initiative contrasts notably with the way in which the Indochinese CPA created an explicitly interlocking relationship among its three elements: resettlement, first asylum, and return. In the Indochinese CPA, the side-payments for the Northern states were conditional on their contributions to the areas that would yield side-payments for the Southern states, and vice versa. In contrast, Convention Plus was structured in a way that assumed that each element could be debated in isolation and that this would still lead to the emergence of new commitments.

Furthermore, to create a viable basis on which Southern states might receive additional development assistance as a result of a renewed commitment to refugee protection or on which Northern states might acquire greater control over immigration as a result of increased burden-sharing, UNHCR attempted to develop a range of new institutional collaborations with development and migration organizations across the UN system. These were an important element of making the side-payments for North and South possible on a practical level. In reality, however, UNHCR struggled to develop the depth of interinstitutional relationships that it had hoped to create and that had been a central feature of the success of CIREFCA.

At the start of Convention Plus, UNHCR explicitly recognized the need for wider institutional collaboration. In setting itself the goal of developing comprehensive approaches to specific refugee situations, it listed its existing partners as UN organizations, such as UNICEF, the World Food Programme (WFP), and UNDP; non-UN agencies, such as the International Committee of the Red Cross (ICRC), the International Federation of the Red Cross (IFRC), and IOM; regional organizations, such as the African Union (AU) and the Organization of American States (OAS); and a range of local and international NGO partners.[24] Most of these partnerships were informal and developed at the field level in response to specific needs. One of the distinguishing features of Convention Plus was to establish more formal interorganizational partnerships at the headquarters

---

24. "Note to the High Commissioner," 12 July 2002, CPU Files, UNHCR Archives.

level, particularly linking Geneva with the wider UN system in New York. This idea builds on the UNHCR 2004 initiative, in which the organization engaged in critical reflection on its future role within the broader UN system and with respect to states and partners in light of emerging challenges such as globalization, the proliferation in global humanitarian actors, and the growing nexus between asylum and migration. In particular, the final report noted the growing links between peace, security, development, and humanitarianism (UN General Assembly 2003). It argued that UNHCR cannot do everything alone but, instead, has an important advocacy and coordination role to play, particularly in the promotion of interagency collaboration. In particular, UNHCR has attempted to create such partnerships in the area of development, with High Commissioner Ruud Lubbers recruiting Anita Bundegaard, the former Danish development minister, to work on this task. Within Convention Plus, UNHCR particularly recognized the need for partnerships with development and migration agencies. Nevertheless, the ways in which the initiative institutionally connected refugee protection to these issue areas remained weak.

UNHCR built a range of new partnerships with development agencies. Most significantly, UNHCR joined the United Nations Development Group (UNDG). The UNDG is an instrument for UN reform created by the secretary-general in 1997 to improve the effectiveness of UN development work at the country level. Through engagement with this collaborative effort, UNHCR drafted a "UNDG Guidance Note on Durable Solutions for Displaced Persons" in October 2004 (UN Development Group [UNDG] 2004). This allowed amendments to the Common Country Assessments (CCA) and United Nations Development Assistance Framework (UNDAF) to include reference to the displaced and the need for UN country teams to consider the search for durable solutions in all their future work. UNHCR also acquired observer status on Organisation for Economic Cooperation and Development (OECD) Development Assistance Committee (DAC), collaborating in its Network on Post-Conflict Development Cooperation. In collaboration with the World Bank, it carried out a systematic analysis of the World Bank Poverty Reduction Strategy Papers (PRSPs) to review the extent to which they were displacement-sensitive (UNHCR 2004c).

UNHCR has also tried to develop more formal partnerships with the World Bank and UNDP. On May 19, 2004, a meeting was held between

High Commissioner Ruud Lubbers and James Wolfensohn, the director of the World Bank, in Washington, D.C. There they reached an agreement to analyze the PRSPs and Interim Poverty Reduction Strategy Papers (I-PRSPs) to explore the extent to which displacement issues were systematically incorporated; the analysis found that only two out of twenty papers assessed included refugees and only four out of twenty include returnees. On the basis of this, an agreement was made between UNHCR and the World Bank to work to incorporate these displacement issues in consultation with the host countries and countries of origin (UNHCR 2004c). This led, for example, to a World Bank presentation at the Fourth Forum to promote the incorporation of displacement issues within the Poverty Reduction Strategy (PRS) approach.[25] In addition, there was an ongoing dialogue between UNHCR and UNDP about how to formalize their headquarters relationship and make their relationship at field level less ad hoc.

The difficulty for UNHCR has been that development governance is contingent on prior interstate agreement and that the development agencies have been willing to incorporate a consideration of the displaced only insofar as this has been based on the principle of recipient country ownership and backed by donor support. Ewen Macleod, for example, argues this has been the problem in Pakistan, where attempts by UNHCR to incorporate UNDP have failed because of the unwillingness of Pakistan to move beyond a humanitarian paradigm. As he put it, "The first step is changing the policy paradigm at government level. In parallel, of course, we have had discussions with development agencies and donors, but invariably the refrain is 'ah, we need the Government of Pakistan to come forward and say we require this.'"[26] This is particularly the case from a UNDP perspective. Betsy Lippman, for example, explained in interview that the involvement of the organization relies on a project being premised upon "recipient state ownership" and also on donor involvement.[27] At the donor meeting on TDA on the September 22, 2004, she therefore argued

---

25. World Bank Presentation, "The PRS Approach 2005: In-Depth Review," 20 May 2005, Geneva, CPU Files, UNHCR Archives.

26. Interview with Ewen Macleod, senior policy advisor, Development and Technical Cooperation, Afghanistan Comprehensive Solutions Unit, CASWANAME (Central Asia, South-West Asia, North Africa, and the Middle East), UNHCR, Geneva, September 21, 2004.

27. Interview with Betsy Lippman, senior field advisor, Bureau For Crisis Prevention and Recovery, UNDP, Geneva, October 6, 2004.

that the key to making the "Development Assistance for Refugees" and "Development through Local Integration" viable is first "to convince governments and provide more convincing studies to show to governments that refugees are not just burdens but a potential asset."[28]

The position of the World Bank was more problematic. Although it has more autonomy and a far larger budget than UNDP, host-state TDA, unlike approaches focused on refugees' countries of origin, did not fit within its existing programs or budget lines. Whereas the country of origin–focused approaches were linked to the Bank agenda on postconflict transition, refugee protection was less of a priority. The Bank representative stated at the September 22 meeting that the Bank would become involved with displacement issues only "where they constitute a binding constraint on economic and social development."[29] This was in line with the mandate of the Bank of dealing directly with recipient governments on behalf of the interests of its shareholders (Sindzingre 2004, 175). For both the UNDP and World Bank, agency involvement was therefore contingent on first achieving interstate agreement on a specific project. Hence, the extent of formalized UNHCR collaboration with these two major development agencies remained limited.

The most authoritative institutional framework on development in the context of Convention Plus was the UN Millennium Development Goals (MDGs). Given the extent to which donor states had already committed themselves to meeting the goals, UNHCR attempted to relate Convention Plus to this wider framework. Ruud Lubbers, for example, claimed, "UNHCR is continuing to integrate the Millennium Development Goals into its programmes, contributing especially to Goal number 8, which calls for a global partnership for development, by promoting multilateral partnerships on durable solutions and burden sharing."[30]

In the buildup to the Millennium Summit in September 2005, UNHCR promoted this relationship, publishing a document entitled: "Putting Refugees on the Development Agenda: How Refugees and Returnees Can

---

28. Betsy Lippman, UNDP, comments at the Informal Meeting on Issues Involved in Targeting Development Assistance, Palais des Nations, Room VIII, Geneva, September 22, 2004.

29. World Bank representative comments to the Informal Meeting on Issues Involved in Targeting Development Assistance, Palais des Nations, Room VIII, Geneva, September 22, 2004.

30. Ruud Lubbers, "Statement by Ruud Lubbers to the Third Committee of the UN General Assembly," 9 November 2004, CPU Files, UNHCR Archives.

Contribute to Achieving the Millennium Development Goals" (UNHCR 2005d). The document, launched at the Fourth Forum, drew out ways in which Convention Plus could contribute to fulfilling the various MDGs. This was based on the MDG paragraph about "Protecting the Vulnerable," which sets out the goal of "strengthening international cooperation, including burden sharing, and the coordination of humanitarian assistance to countries hosting refugees, and to help all refugees and displaced persons to return voluntarily to their homes" (UN General Assembly Resolution 55/2, 18 September 2000, para. 26) and on the report of the director of the UN Millennium Development Project, "Investing in Development," on practical means to achieve the goals, such as that "donor agencies should aim to provide ongoing MDG-based financial and technical assistance to maintain or restore basic infrastructure and the provision of social services, delivered in a way that reaches refugees" (UN Development Programme [UNDP] 2005, 186). The difficulty with this approach was that the MDGs do not explicitly refer to refugees or forced migration at any stage, meaning that the structural relationship was tenuous even though the MDGs did carry normative authority.

In relation to partnerships with migration agencies, Convention Plus had very few structural connections to draw on. Although the Global Commission on International Migration (GCIM) was launched at around the same time as the Convention Plus initiative, forced migration issues were explicitly excluded from the work of the GCIM. This had been based partly on the request of UNHCR, which had not wanted its work to be subsumed under a broader migration governance reform debate, particularly in a context in which the UN secretary-general had been promulgating a possible Global Migration Organization that might supersede UNHCR.[31] The interagency debates between UNHCR and IOM also highlighted the way in which Convention Plus weakly connected refugee protection to migration governance. For example, in debates on African-European transit migration via the Mediterranean, which was a focal point of debates in the ISMs strand, IOM largely refused to cooperate with UNHCR with regard to transit states and governments in which it already had memoranda of

---

31. Interview with Jeff Crisp, director of Policy and Research, Global Commission on International Migration (GCIM), Geneva, September 20, 2004.

understanding and over which UNHCR had little authority.[32] The largely competitive relationship between UNHCR and IOM therefore limited the scope for institutional collaboration.

## Ideational Linkages

Since the early 2000s, two principal discourses relating the refugee issue to other areas have become extremely prominent in both academia and policy: the asylum-migration nexus and the revival of the RAD debate as part of a broader debate on the migration-development nexus. Both reflect older debates but have been more rigorously explored within epistemic communities in recent years as the subjects of academic projects based within influential university departments focusing on the study of forced migration. In turn, these sets of ideas have become part of discussions in think tanks, NGOs, and international organizations. They have been further explored at a policy level to the extent that studies have been commissioned and the language of the academic debate has been introduced to define priority areas for international organizations and intergovernmental conferences. Both discourses have been explicitly invoked as the themes for European Commission Communications intended to develop a basis for EU policy on asylum and migration.[33] And both discourses were significant for Convention Plus in that they represented a body of ideas that was further developed by UNHCR and the states involved in the initiative and that was consistently drawn on by UNHCR and the states as a means of connecting different issue areas during bargaining. The difficulty, however, is that both discourses were highly contested in terms of what they implied about causal relationships and their policy implications.

*Asylum-Migration Nexus*   The asylum-migration nexus emerged to explore the way in which the categories refugee, asylum-seeker, and labor migrant have become increasingly blurred in policy and practice (UNHCR

---

32. Interview with Ruvendrini Menikdiwela, coordinator of UNHCR project on Institution Building for Asylum in North Africa, CASWANAME, UNHCR, August 16, 2005.

33. In September 2005, the European Commission adopted two communications: "Migration and Development: Some Concrete Orientations" (European Commission 2005a) and "Regional Protection Programmes" (European Commission 2005b). In many ways, the first relates to the migration-development nexus, whereas the second refers to the asylum-migration nexus.

2006, 56–58). Academic work on this has focused particularly on transit migration from the South to Europe to highlight the inadequacy of the conventional legal categories for understanding the phenomenon. In particular, the Migration-Asylum Nexus (MAN) project at Oxford University Centre on Migration, Policy and Society (COMPAS), which ran between 2003 and 2007, explored how categories of migration are formed and used by states and migrants, and how types of migration are susceptible to influence by policy instruments. As part of this work, Stephen Castles and Nick Van Hear (2005) have described the nexus in relation to the growing difficulty in separating forced migration from economic migration, their closely related causes, the similarities between the migratory processes, and the lack of differentiation in the policy responses to both categories. They argue that many economic migrants and political refugees come from the same weak, conflict-affected or underdeveloped states and take similar routes. Often, individuals will jump categories to obtain work or as they acquire new information concerning legal categories. In addition, both refugees and other migrants may use similar social networks and smugglers to facilitate transit. Stephen Castles and Nick Van Hear further emphasize the common underlying causes for movement. In particular, they argue that the wider relationships between issues such as underdevelopment, conflict, weak states, and human rights abuses often underpin the forced movement of refugees and of many other migrants (Castles and Van Hear 2005).

This idea has become increasingly influential, and it was a focal point for the work of GCIM, which ran between 2003 and 2005, concurrently with Convention Plus. The GCIM final report argues that "the governance of international migration should be enhanced....such efforts must be based on a better appreciation of the close linkages that exist between international migration and development and other key policy issues, including trade, aid, state security, human security, and human rights" (Global Commission on International Migration [GCIM] 2005, 65). Within this context, the report focuses particularly on the relationship between asylum and migration and how the two are related within the context of irregular migration (GCIM 2005, 77). Furthermore, in a GCIM working paper that informed the work of the final report, Aspasia Papadopoulou argues that, "In today's migration flows to Europe, irregular migration and asylum meet in various ways" (2005, 3). As she points out, first, refugees increasingly take the irregular migration path to reach Europe and so become irregular if their claims are rejected, and second, those not in need of international protection often use asylum systems as alternatives methods of immigration.

Two factors in particular brought the migration debates into the broad scope of the UNHCR mandate, creating a perception that, insofar as asylum and migration could be connected, UNHCR could be the legitimate focal point for addressing migration issues. First, because of the recognition of the growing difficulty in distinguishing between transit migrants and refugees, there was a recognition of the need to "ensur[e] international protection within the context of addressing mixed flows."[34] The overarching transit migration debate was initially brought within the scope of the Convention Plus debate by the early association of the initiative with the goal of a number of EU states to develop offshore transit centers for processing asylum claims. It is due to this recognition that asylum and refugee protection were directly linked to transit migration in policy and practice that, by 2005, UNHCR made the asylum-migration nexus one of its main priorities and determined that addressing the concerns of states on this issue was central to ensuring the ongoing relevance of the organization.[35] Second, and most crucially for Convention Plus, the debates on defining *secondary* or *irregular movements of refugees* also made UNHCR a legitimate site for debating certain types of migratory movement and introduced discussions on readmission and migration control to the refugee debate.

In the second of these issues, the UNHCR Convention Plus initiative contributed directly to creating an epistemic context within which the discourse on the causal relationship between migration and asylum could develop. As part of the ISMs strand, the debate on defining *irregular* or *secondary movements* was developed through a UNHCR commissioned research project conducted by the Swiss Forum on Migration (SFM). The project was entitled "Movements of Somali Refugees and Asylum Seekers and States' Responses Thereto" (Swiss Forum on Migration 2005) and was funded by Switzerland, the Netherlands, and the European Commission.

---

34. Erika Feller, "Speech on International Protection," ExCom. 7 October 2004, CPU Files, UNHCR Archives.

35. Antonio Guterres, "Introductory Speech," ExCom, 3 October 2005, CPU Files, UNHCR Archives.

It used the case study of Somali refugees to examine the reasons underlying the onward movement of Somali refugees from their region of origin toward the EU.

The explicit intention of the project was to offer an objective means of informing the ISMs debate. In particular, it aimed to (1) highlight the causal link between secondary movements and inadequate protection in refugees' regions of origin and (2) show the scale of the problem of secondary movements to determine what action might be taken by states within the region of origin. Although the validity of the eventual survey was privately questioned, the results showed that Somali refugees often move on to a secondary country due to inadequate access to effective protection and durable solutions in their region of origin, and it suggested measures that could be taken within the region of origin to change this.

The findings of the SFM project connected migration concerns with asylum by showing that inadequate access to effective protection, lack of economic opportunity, and long-term confinement in camps and settlements contributed to the choice of refugees to engage in transit migration. This report attempted to offer empirical foundation for the claim that transit migration to the EU was related to protection and durable solutions in regions of origin.

But the existence of a relationship between refugees' access to effective protection and irregular secondary movements remained highly contested throughout the initiative. Most state representatives and policymakers remained unconvinced of a strong causal relationship between inadequate protection in regions of origin and onward secondary movements to Northern states. The SFM survey was the only empirical study of the relationship, and questions were raised about its methodology, its representativeness, and the impartiality of its claims.

The results and basis of the survey provided a site of North–South debate in which the representativeness and the implications of the survey were contested to challenge the causal relationship between protection and onward movements, and the implications this had for policy and practice. Although the survey purported to be objective and scientific, it became the subject of debate. When asked about its motivation in funding the project and choosing the Somali case, and its relationship to a Swiss migration agenda, the Swiss government acknowledged, "Of course...you're right.... But I think no country would invest an amount of money if it did not also answer questions that they thought needed to be answered."[36] The European Commission also acknowledged that the purpose of the survey was instrumental rather than purely academic: "The survey will influence the relevant policy considerations of what constitutes effective protection. We would like to invite UNHCR to explore the possibility of financing the survey under the EC's [European Commission's] new AENEAS budget line" (UNHCR 2004e).

Yet, far from passively accepting the relationship between protection and onward movement, the South contested the approach of the study and how it was likely to be used. Algeria argued, "Regarding Somalis, this is just one single—and rather unique—case given the insecurity prevailing in the country of origin. Therefore no general conclusions should be drawn from the study" (UNHCR 2004e). The NGO community, which had a strong relationship with the African Group throughout Convention Plus, also contested the objectivity of the survey: "NGOs propose that there be more than one group-specific survey undertaken within the secondary movement strand.... This is especially important in order to safeguard objectivity and also to ensure that any generic conclusions derived from the results of the survey can be widely applicable."[37] Mexico used the contestation of the epistemic linkage implied by the survey to oppose the inclusion of a migration agenda within the Convention Plus debate. It argued, "Mexico considers that it is extremely important to define the concept of irregular secondary movements. We wouldn't like to enter into migratory phenomena. In the survey proposal, a number of migration-related topics, such as remittances, are included. These are not relevant to this topic. Migration management is not part of UNHCR's mandate" (UNHCR 2004e).

*Reviving the Refugee Aid and Development Debate*    The migration-development nexus emerged from academic debates and focused on the various synergies between migration and economic and social development (Refugee Studies Centre [RSC] 2005, 49; Van Hear and Sorensen 2003).

---

36. Interview with Tania Dussey-Cavassini, counselor, Humanitarian Affairs, Permanent Mission of Switzerland, September 29, 2004.

37. "Irregular Secondary Movements of Refugees and Asylum Seekers, Statement on Behalf of NGOs," Second Forum, 12 March 2004, CPU Files, UNHCR Archives.

It has encompassed discussion on whether underdevelopment contributes to emigration, on the role of remittances, on the role of diasporas and transnationalism, and on the consequences of human capital flight. The migration-development nexus was the central theme for the UN High-Level Dialogue on Migration in September 2006. It also ran through the GCIM (2005) final report and was extensively debated in the European Commission (European Commission 2005a).

A significant subtheme of this wider debate has been the relationship between forced migration and development. At the level of root causes, it has been widely recognized that displacement is closely linked to underdevelopment in that conflict correlates with underdevelopment and horizontal inequalities (Collier and Hoeffler 2004; Stewart and Fitzgerald 2001). At the level of policy responses, the transition gap between humanitarianism and development has been identified as a major obstacle for ensuring access to refugee protection and sustainable durable solutions (Lippmann 2004; Stepputat 2004a, 2004b). There has been a growing academic and policy-based recognition that refugee issues cannot be seen in purely humanitarian terms but, rather, that the prospects for repatriation and reintegration rely on development and reconstruction in the country of origin (RSC 2005, 99–100). It has also been suggested that the ability of host states to provide local integration or self-sufficiency for refugees depends on development assistance that allows both refugees and host-country citizens to benefit fully from integration (Jacobsen 2001). These ideas built on old themes in the RAD debates of the 1980s, which were revived to become a central focus of the work of UNHCR (Gorman 1993). These academic ideas were further developed by NGOs such as the U.S. Committee for Refugees and Immigrants (USCRI), which advocated for the use of targeted development assistance to promote refugees' self-sufficiency (U.S. Committee for Refugees and Immigrants [USCRI] 2004).

As with the asylum-migration nexus, UNHCR contributed to the epistemic development of the discourses on causal connections in this area. Its *Framework for Durable Solutions for Refugees and Persons of Concern* (UNHCR 2003b) set out three principal concepts: the 4Rs, DAR, DLI, with the first of these focusing on countries of origin and the last two focusing on self-sufficiency and local integration, respectively, in host countries. The *Framework* attempts to highlight the causal connections relating to how development assistance can enhance the prospects for durable solutions for refugees. UNHCR attempted to empirically support these causal connections by framing and presenting success stories such as its Zambia Initiative (ZI) and Ugandan Self-Reliance Strategy. It did so even in the absence of a formal evaluation of these pilot projects (UNHCR 2006). UNHCR also attempted to show the relationship between development assistance and protection through compiling successful examples of 4Rs, DAR, and DLI in a "Statement of Good Practice for Targeting Development Assistance" (UNHCR 2005e).

Despite this, the causal relationship between development assistance and enhanced access to refugee protection or durable solutions within the host states of first asylum remained contested throughout the initiative. UNHCR based its claims on the purported success stories Uganda and Zambia (UNHCR 2006, 136–37). Yet numerous academic studies contested the success of the Ugandan case (UNHCR 2004d), and many states claimed the Zambian case was based on a unique set of conditions that it would be difficult to replicate (UNHCR 2004a).[38] The structural interconnections of Convention Plus are summarized in table 5.

## Agency Conditions

UNHCR attempted to articulate two key relationships to states: refugee protection–migration and refugee protection–development assistance. It tried to persuade Northern states that a commitment to burden-sharing could reduce irregular secondary movements and to persuade Southern states that a commitment to protection and durable solutions such as local integration could lead to additional development assistance.

These central claims were consistently articulated in a range of different UNHCR documents and statements. Despite considerable conceptual work by the initiative secretariat, however, the absence of a structural basis for cross-issue persuasion undermined the UNHCR attempts to promote North–South cooperation.

Given the lack of a coherent institutional design and the degree to which ideas on causal relationships remained contested, UNHCR was

---

38. Interview with Mapuri; interview with Peter Kimanthi, deputy secretary, Department for Refugee Affairs, Ministry of Home Affairs, Kenya, Geneva, October 8, 2004.

**TABLE 5.** Structural Interconnections of Convention Plus

| Type of Structural Interconnection | Subtype of Structural Interconnection | Refugees-Migration | Refugees-Development |
|---|---|---|---|
| Institutions | Internal linkages | No conditionality | No conditionality |
| | External nesting | No nesting or partnerships | Limited partnerships with OECD DAC and UNDG; tenuous connections to MDGs, UNDP, and the World Bank |
| Ideas | Intersubjective | Asylum-migration nexus: contested | Revival of Refugee Aid and Development: contested |
| | Subjective | European states: concern to limit irregular secondary movements | Southern states: concern to attract additionality through TDA |

*Notes:* In contrast to the tables in the other chapters, none of the structural interconnections are in bold because none of them were sufficient to enable cross-issue persuasion. MDGs, Millennium Development Goals; OECD DAC, Organisation for Economic Cooperation and Development Development Assistance Committee; TDA, Targeting Development Assistance; UNDG, United Nations Development Group; UNDP, United Nations Development Programme.

unable to persuade states to agree on the relationships between refugee protection and migration and between refugee protection and development assistance. First, UNHCR was unable to persuade Northern states that there was a relationship between additional burden-sharing and reducing irregular secondary movements. Although UNHCR commissioned the SFM survey on irregular secondary movements to show this relationship, Northern states were not persuaded of the causal relationship. For example, despite funding the initial preparation of projects, such as the CPA for Somali Refugees and the Strengthening Protection Capacity project, Denmark, the Netherlands, and the United Kingdom, among others, were ultimately unconvinced that strengthening protection capacity in the region would lead to a reduction in the spontaneous arrival asylum seekers in Europe.

One of the key obstacles to making this claim persuasive was that causally most Northern states seemed to recognize that the intermediary variable between effective refugee protection in the South and migration control was the existence of readmission agreements. For example, the Netherlands claimed that "enhancing protection capacity is important but the ISM debate is not only about protection capacity building. It is also about readmission and return."[39] And Australia stated, "we endorse the need to ensure linkages between all three strands. We need to deal with all aspects of contemporary mixed flows of people, including those found not to be in need of international protection" (UNHCR 2004e). But Southern states were unwilling to agree to accept readmission agreements as a condition for burden-sharing. Kenya, for example, opposed the use of irregular secondary movements as a basis for readmission: "Kenya does not consider that the principles of burden-sharing and international solidarity would be complied with if refugees who end up in third countries were to be returned to the first country of asylum. For instance we do not consider that Kenya should be the automatic or natural home for asylum-seekers and refugees from Somalia."[40] In addition, Nigeria argued against readmission agreements, claiming that "discussion on Irregular Secondary Movements of refugees and asylum seekers should be to address the cause and not the effect of such movement. It should be pursued with the aim of strengthening refugee protection done in the spirit of equitable burden and responsibility sharing."[41]

Second, UNHCR was also unable to persuade Southern states that there was a relationship between enhancing protection capacity and their own national development. An obstacle here was that, for most Southern states, the causal relationship between committing to refugee protection and development depended on additionality in development assistance. For example, South Africa suggested that "We would like to see targeting of development assistance be additional and not affect poverty reduction strategies or structural development. Aid should not be based on conditionality or linked to readmission agreements" (UNHCR 2004e). But Northern states ruled out the possibility of additionality relatively early in the process. They argued that the money would need to come from existing budget lines. For example, the Netherlands stressed that "there is limited scope for the creation of new development programmes, budget lines of priorities" (UNHCR 2004e). Once Northern states made clear

---

39. "Statement of the Netherlands," Fourth Convention Plus Forum, 20 May 2005, CPU Files, UNHCR Archives.

40. Sylvester Mwaliko, "Statement by Mr Sylvester Mwaliko, Permanent Secretary, Office of the Vice-President, Kenya," Second Forum, 12 March 2004, CPU Files, UNHCR Archives.

41. "Statement of the Nigerian Delegation," Third Meeting of the Forum of the High Commissioner on Convention Plus, 1 October 2004, CPU Files, UNHCR Archives.

that development resources allocated to protection were unlikely to be additional but, instead, would have to come from existing budget lines (UNHCR 2004e), the perspective of the Southern states polarized and the causal relationship between refugee protection and national development was contested within the South. The potential beneficiary states continued to advocate for linking development assistance to protection, whereas the potential losers contested the link. For example, Zambia and Uganda, as the major recipients of additional development assistance stemming from the ZI and the Ugandan Self-Reliance Strategy, embraced including refugees in national development plans and their PRSPs. Zambia proclaimed in the Forum: "The Zambia Initiative Development Agenda is thus regarded as an instrument of the Zambian PRSP and has been incorporated in the Country's Transitional National Development Plan 2002–2008."[42] Ethiopia was initially critical of the link, stating, "Targeting development assistance for refugees should not be at the expense of existing development aid. Any funding here should be additional" (UNHCR 2004e); however, by the Third Forum, once the Japanese government had committed to providing additional assistance to the country, it welcomed organizational linkage, stating:

> In Ethiopia, UNHCR is closely working with the United Nations Country Team (UNCT) under its Development Assistance for Refugees (DAR) initiative. The DAR initiative, in this particular situation, is linked to the overall Recovery Programme for the Somali Regional State of Ethiopia and provides synergy to the overall recovery effort. A funding proposal is submitted by the UNCT to the UN Human Security Trust Fund.[43]

Yet, because of the absence of additional resources for the majority of states, the link was resisted by many states. Based on its concern that development assistance for refugees in the country might be a substitute for that afforded to citizens, Pakistan, for example, argued that "We have viewed all assistance to refugees as humanitarian assistance. This should continue to be the case. Establishing a link to development would only distract the

---

42. "Talking Notes for Use by Peter Mumba, Permanent Secretary for the Ministry of Home Affairs, Zambia," First Convention Plus Forum, 27 June 2003, CPU Files, UNHCR Archives.

43. Ayalew Awoke, "Statement by Ethiopian Delegation," Third Meeting of Convention Plus Forum, 1 October 2004, CPU Files, UNHCR Archives.

focus from the legitimate needs of refugees. These gaps should not be filled with development assistance" (UNHCR 2004e). The African Group highlighted its fear that assistance would be provided on a highly selective basis, with some states standing to gain at the expense of others: "How will the bilateral nature of targeted assistance, which may possibly be earmarked for projects in so-called 'favoured nations' impact on the humanitarian mandate of UNHCR and its related programmes? Could selective targeted assistance be used by donor states for 'containment' rather than protection and how would the UNHCR react to such notions?"[44]

The failure to achieve additionality further eroded the North–South consensus on other issues such as including displacement in PRSPs because states feared a substitution of development assistance previously intended for citizens. Nevertheless, the small number of Southern states prepared to offer self-sufficiency or local integration—Zambia, Uganda, and Ethiopia, for example—were able to use this organizational linkage to effectively leverage additional assistance from existing development budget lines. Ethiopia attracted additional resources from the Japanese government Human Security Trust Fund; Uganda from Danish International Development Assistance (DANIDA); and Zambia from a range of bilateral and multilateral donors, partly via the World Bank and UNDP. The use of development as a carrot for refugee protection was therefore effective only insofar as it worked within the constraints of appealing to clear Northern interests in containment and competed for existing resources against other Southern states.

Convention Plus aspired to address a major gap in the global refugee regime and facilitate the development of a normative framework for burden-sharing. This was an extremely ambitious aim that required significant ability in terms of political facilitation and persuasion by UNHCR. Ultimately, the initiative failed. Nevertheless, it offers important lessons for international cooperation in the refugee regime.

Convention Plus was explicitly based on the idea of appealing to the wider interests of states and channeling these into a renewed commitment to refugee protection. UNHCR recognized that many of the same reasons

---

44. "Chairman's Summary, Inaugural Meeting."

for the crisis of asylum in North and South—concerns with migration and security in the North and underdevelopment and competition for resources in the South—also represented potential opportunities. It, therefore, tried to appeal to the interests of Northern states in migration control as a means of inducing them to commit to supporting refugee protection in the South. On the other side, UNHCR appealed to the interests of Southern states in development as a means of inducing them to commit to improving refugee protection and refugees' access to durable solutions on their territories.

The UNHCR attempt to persuade states that these wider interests could be met through a commitment to refugee protection was, however, ultimately unconvincing. The main reason for this was the absence of a structural basis for claiming that committing to refugee protection would lead to payoffs in the issue areas in which the groups of states had interests. Without a structural basis derived from the institutional design of the initiative or the prevailing ideas held by states, UNHCR could not convince states that agreeing to additional commitments to refugee protection was in their interests.

On an institutional level, Convention Plus was designed in such a way that it failed to create conditional relationships among the component parts of the initiative. Negotiating burden-sharing in the TDA and Resettlement strands separately from the definition and implications of *irregular secondary movements* (which took place in the ISMs strand) undermined the contractual basis on which Northern states may have been willing to provide additionality in development resources and on which Southern states may have been willing to consider readmission agreements. The potential for international cooperation relied on mutual compromise by both North and South across these different areas, and so negotiating them separately made little sense. Furthermore, UNHCR was unable to develop the depth of institutional partnerships with actors such as the World Bank, UNDP, and IOM; if it had done so, such partnerships may have made action in relation to development or migration a practically viable outcome of state cooperation within the refugee regime.

On an ideational level, the causal relationship between refugee protection, on the one hand, and migration and development, on the other, remained highly contested. The purported relationship between the irregular secondary movements of refugees and the quality of refugee protection provided in refugees' regions of origin was not accepted by Northern states. Even the results of the SFM survey, which claimed to objectively highlight this relationship, did little to convince Northern states that their interests in migration control could be met through a commitment to protection in the region of origin. In addition, the revived RAD debates (which posited a relationship between refugee protection and development) also remained contested. Although UNHCR claimed that refugees could constitute agents of development rather than a burden to host states, Southern states contested the conditions under which this would be the case. In particular, they were reluctant to accept that local integration or self-sufficiency might benefit their own citizens and contribute to national development in the way that UNHCR claimed.

These structural constraints meant that the UNHCR attempts to engage in cross-issue persuasion were untenable and amounted to assertions that committing to a new normative framework on burden-sharing was in the interests of the states. Northern states simply did not accept that, in the absence of readmission agreements, building protection capacity in the South would reduce the spontaneous arrivals of asylum seekers. On the other side, Southern states did not accept that, without a clear Northern commitment to additionality in development assistance, a greater commitment to refugee protection would contribute to their national development. In the absence of successful cross-issue persuasion, Convention Plus was, therefore, ultimately characterized by a North–South impasse.

# CONCLUSION

## *Cross-Issue Persuasion and World Politics*

The international politics of refugee protection cannot be understood by looking at the refugee regime in isolation. Although political science and IR tend to look at individual issue areas such as the environment, trade, and human rights as single discrete entities, this approach is simply inadequate to explain the international politics of refugee protection. To understand how states respond to refugees, when and why they contribute to refugee protection, and the conditions under which international cooperation has taken place in the refugee regime, it is necessary to look at the way in which refugee protection is interconnected with other issue areas such as migration, security, development, trade, and peace-building.

The concept of cross-issue persuasion sheds light on the conditions under which UNHCR has been able to appeal to the interests of states to induce them to contribute to refugee protection. Northern states have generally had few incentives to engage in burden-sharing, but they have done so insofar as they have been persuaded that there is a relationship between refugee protection in the South and their wider interests in other issue areas. This conclusion teases out from the case studies the role of substantive linkages in cooperation, the conditions under which UNHCR has been able to use cross-issue persuasion to facilitate cooperation, and further implications for policy and theory.

## The Role of Substantive Linkages

The main cooperation problem in the refugee regime can be described as a North–South impasse, which can be illustrated by the game theoretical analogy of a Suasion Game. Due to their greater proximity to conflict-ridden and human rights–abusing states, Southern states have historically had the responsibility for hosting the overwhelming majority of world refugees. The norm of asylum has obliged those states to open their borders to these refugees. Meanwhile, Northern states have had no corresponding obligation to contribute to the protection of refugees hosted by Southern states. This has meant that Northern states have had little interest in contributing to refugee protection in the South and that Southern states have had little option other than to accept the very limited discretionary contributions made by the North. This impasse has had significant human consequences, contributing to protracted refugee situations and low protection standards in the South.

Under certain albeit rare conditions, the North–South impasse has been overcome. In the conferences convened by UNHCR to facilitate North–South burden-sharing, issue linkage has been a necessary condition for cooperation. In the two successful case studies presented, refugee protection was credibly linked to Northern interests in other issue areas; in the two failed case studies, linkages were either absent or tenuous.

These findings are consistent with the predictions of the existing IR literature: that Suasion Games can be overcome through issue linkages creating side-payments that provide incentives for North–South cooperation. The existing work on Suasion Games, however, focuses mainly on tactical issue linkage—in other words, how substantively unrelated issues are grouped together in bargaining through horse-trading and conditionality. Tactical linkage has played a part in the UNHCR conferences—for example, in the way in which the Indochinese CPA created interlocking conditional commitments between its main stakeholders and in the way

ICARA tried, but failed, to negotiate a trade-off between burden-sharing and durable solutions. But, in practice, explicit tactical linkage plays only a small role. Generally, Southern refugee-hosting states have little to offer Northern states for horse-trading and exchange. The more important linkages in the refugee regime have been substantive linkages, which are far more neglected in the existing IR literature.

Northern states have voluntarily contributed to burden-sharing insofar as they have believed that there is a substantive relationship between refugee protection in the South and their interests in security, trade, and immigration, for example. Without these interests, Northern states would not have contributed. In ICARA and Convention Plus, there were very few Northern contributions, but the very limited contributions that were made were based on a relationship between security and immigration. In CIREFCA, European contributions were based on the belief in a relationship among protection, regional security and development, and interregional trade. In the Indochinese CPA, the important contribution of the United States was based on the relationship between protection and regional and global security at the end of the Cold War.

The causal relationships on which Northern contributions were based are illustrated in figure 3. In each case, these substantive linkages offer the strongest explanation for Northern contributions to burden-sharing. There is little evidence for alternative competing explanations. Altruism, the main possible alternative explanation, appears to be excluded based on the selective nature of the contributions, both within each case and across cases, and the way in which the contributions correlate with interests.

The existing literature on the four case studies offers alternative explanations of the relative success and failure other than issue linkage. In the case of CIREFCA, we could suggest that European values contributed to the willingness of the European states to contribute to protection. But this explanation would not account for Europe selectively focusing its resources on refugees in the Central American region at time when there were other geographical regions with refugees for which similar levels of burden-sharing were not forthcoming (such as the Indochinese situation). In the case of the Indochinese CPA, the existing literature identifies U.S. hegemony as a major factor underlying its success (Suhrke 1998). This explanation is entirely consistent with the role of substantive linkages, but

**ICARA I and II**

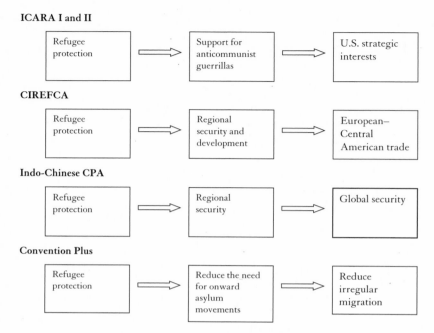

**CIREFCA**

**Indo-Chinese CPA**

**Convention Plus**

**Figure 3.** The substantive linkages between refugee protection in the South and other issue areas in which the North has an interest. CIREFCA, Conferencica Internacional sobre los Refugiados Centroamericanos; CPA, Comprehensive Plan of Action; ICARA, International Conferences on Assistance to Refugees in Africa.

the explanation based on linkage also contributes to explaining the source of hegemonic interest in refugee protection.

In Convention Plus and ICARA, there are few alternative explanations for the limited contributions that took place other than the interests of European states in control of irregular migration in Convention Plus and the interests of the United States in supporting Cold War allies in ICARA. The more challenging question is whether the *absence* of substantive linkages provides a sufficient explanation for the failure of these initiatives. In the case of ICARA, a range of explanations for its failure have been put forward, including the emergence of the famine and drought in sub-Saharan Africa in 1984, which is said to have drawn away international attention, and the limited role played by development actors such as UNDP (Gorman 1993). But these explanations matter precisely because of the absence of a clear connection between refugees in Africa and wider Northern interests. In the case of Convention Plus, competing explanations for its failure, such as the lack of conceptual coherence of the initiative and the lack of UNHCR leadership, were important because they made substantive linkages less credible. Initially, European states had supported the initiative because they believed there would be a payoff in term of reducing irregular migration; on the other side, Southern states believed there might be a payoff in development assistance. The lack of UNHCR leadership mattered in that it undermined, rather than reinforced, the credibility of these substantive linkages.

## The Conditions for Cross-Issue Persuasion

The concept of cross-issue persuasion highlights when and how these substantive relationships become relevant to and influence the politics of refugee protection. On the one hand, cross-issue persuasion needs to have a structural basis. There needs to be an ideational, institutional, or material[1] relationship between refugee protection and other issue areas.

In CIREFCA, refugee protection was primarily connected to regional peace, security, reconstruction, and development on an institutional level. The existence of the Esquipulas II peace process and the UN PEC for the region created an opportunity for UNHCR to connect CIREFCA to these wider structures. In the Indochinese CPA, refugee protection was mainly connected to issues relating to regional security on an ideational level. The way in which the refugee issue was perceived by the United States, the ASEAN countries in the region, and Vietnam all created a structural basis for cross-issue persuasion. Without this structural basis, attempts to engage in cross-issue persuasion have been ineffective. This is what happened in Convention Plus; the UNHCR attempt to appeal to European interests in controlling irregular migration as a basis for contributing to protection in the region of origin had very little structural basis and so did not lead

---

1. For the reasons explained in chapter 2, the empirical chapters do not examine structural interconnections on a material level. But this is not to say that such interconnections do not represent an important aspect of the structural relationship between two issue areas and cannot and should not be explored as part of future research. Furthermore, it is possible to speculate that many of the ideational relationships highlighted in the case studies are indicative of the existence of an underlying material relationship.

to significant contributions. Similarly, in ICARA, the UNHCR attempts to solicit greater burden-sharing by appealing to the concerns of Northern states in developing durable solutions as a means of reducing the long-term drain on humanitarian budget was ineffective because it had little structural basis. Cross-issue persuasion has therefore depended on the existence of a structural relationship between issue areas.

But the existence of these structural interconnections is an insufficient condition for the substantive linkages to influence the behavior of Northern states. In addition to requiring a structural basis, cross-issue persuasion also requires agency. There are lots of substantive linkages in the world; not all of them matter or are perceived by all actors. Which ones are recognized and how they are understood depends on the agency of actors to engage in persuasion. The actions of UNHCR have been important in altering, drawing on, or simply recognizing and effectively communicating substantive linkages to persuade other actors to change their behavior. Without this UNHCR role, the substantive linkages would not have influenced state behavior in the ways that they did. The case studies point to four mechanisms through which UNHCR has been able to change or recognize and effectively communicate substantive issue linkages: institutional design, an epistemic role, argumentation, and the provision of information.

### Institutional Design

Given the absence of a clearly defined normative or legal framework regulating burden-sharing, UNHCR has had to convene ad hoc bargaining processes to address specific regional refugee situations. Each of these has had its own unique institutional design. Crucially, however, the different initiatives have connected to deeper institutional structures in very different ways. UNHCR has not been able to radically alter the broader international institutional landscape within which it has had to work; however, it has had significant control over the institutional design of its own initiatives.[2] This has meant that it has been able to create tactical linkages between the different elements of the initiative, as it did successfully in the Indochinese CPA but failed to do in ICARA and Convention Plus. This

---

2. For an overview of the literature on institutional design, see, for example, Koremenos, Lipson, and Snidal (2003).

has also meant that it has been able to decide how far to nest the initiative within wider institutional structures. In some cases, UNHCR has, therefore, been able to connect its own conferences to deeper preexisting institutional structures. By plugging into these existing structures, UNHCR has helped to complete the institutional causal chain that connects refugee protection in the South to interests in the North.

UNHCR did this most effectively in CIREFCA, in which it nested the conference within the broader peace deal and postconflict reconstruction and development initiatives for the region. Institutionally nesting CIREFCA within these structures helped to causally connect refugee protection to regional security and, hence, to European donor interests in development interregional trade relations. In contrast, ICARA, for example, was institutionally conceived in isolation from any deeper institutional structures that linked to Northern donor interests. ICARA I was a stand-alone donor-pledging conference; although ICARA II integrated UNDP into its work, the component that dealt with development was institutionally separated from the component that addressed refugee protection. In Convention Plus, UNHCR tried but failed to create the kinds of interinstitutional partnerships that may have reinforced the substantive linkages. These observations highlight that questions of institutional design in IR should include considerations of how issue areas are nested within other issue areas because nesting may influence the payoffs from cooperation in a given regime.

## Epistemic Role

UNHCR has, alongside other actors such as NGOs and academics, played an important role in contributing to the development of ideas about the causal relationship between actions in one issue area and outcomes in another. Because ideas on causal connections are subject to a range of influences and are developed in the context of broader knowledge communities, they are difficult for any single actor to control. Nevertheless, UNHCR has played an important role in creating, developing, and disseminating ideas such as the RAD debates, the asylum-migration nexus, and the relationship between refugees and security. This suggests that one way in which it can create, change, or highlight substantive linkages is by playing an active part in what has been described in IR as an epistemic community (Adler 1992; Drake and Nicolaides 1992; Haas 1989/1994).

In the case studies, this has sometimes been effective, as it was in the use of the RAD debates, for example. Between the ICARA conferences and CIREFCA, High Commissioner Jean-Paul Hocké's ideas about the relationship between development assistance and refugee protection were built on and developed by a range of academics. UNHCR was able to draw on and use these ideas to credibly argue that donors could use targeted development assistance to Central American states as a means of facilitating refugees' access to durable solutions.

At other times, however, UNHCR attempts to play this kind of epistemic role have been ineffective. For example, during Convention Plus, despite commissioning an academic study by SFM, UNHCR was unable to establish a clear consensus on the relationship between South-North irregular migration and the absence of effective refugee protection in the South.

## Argumentation

At times, UNHCR has used argumentation to induce states to change their beliefs about the causal relationship between issue areas. In some cases, this appears to have influenced the understanding of states about those causal relationships; in other cases, it appears to have had little impact. In the Indochinese CPA, Sergio Vieira de Mello, for example, was able to effectively use argumentation to persuade the participating states of the link between the CPA and their wider interests. At the point when the Indochinese CPA was in crisis during talks in Manila in 1990, Vieira de Mello highlighted the various interests that states had in the success of the CPA and the consequences of its failure. This type of argumentation and charismatic leadership brought the Indochinese CPA back from the brink. Similarly, throughout CIREFCA, UNHCR, in general, and specific individuals such as Leonardo de Franco and High Commissioner Sadako Ogata consistently argued that there was an inextricable relationship among security, development, and refugees. UNHCR provided very little empirical evidence for this relationship but relied instead on argumentation to persuade states that it did, in fact, exist. That these arguments were repeated in the language and statements of European donors and Central American host states implies UNHCR had some success in this type of argumentation.

At other times, UNHCR was less successful in it arguments about the causal relationship between issue areas. In ICARA II, Soren Jessen-Petersen, the conference convener, consistently made arguments about the relationship among burden-sharing, development assistance, and durable solutions. Similarly, in Convention Plus, High Commissioner Ruud Lubbers made numerous statements in Europe about the relationship between protection and durable solutions in the region of origin and irregular South-North migration. In both cases, Northern donor states retained significant skepticism about these causal relationships.

## The Provision of Information

There is a fine line between argumentation and the provision of information. Argumentation is generally considered to be based on speech acts that involve giving reasons. In contrast, the provision of information may exclude an attempt to engage in reasoning and may simply involve providing empirical data. In the context of substantive linkages, there are times when UNHCR has simply played a role in recognizing and effectively communicating the existence of structural interconnections between issue areas and this information role was all that was required. Nevertheless, the provision of information may be extremely important when there is imperfect information about substantive linkages or when those relationships are ambiguous.

In all four of the initiatives, the UNHCR field presence and missions from headquarters to the field gave it an authoritative position in providing empirical information on the relationship between the projects and programs and the wider political context. In CIREFCA, the secretariat based in San José was able to provide constant information to European donors on the relationship among refugees, development, and security. Likewise, in the Indochinese CPA, UNHCR was uniquely placed to provide information on states on the scale of the mass influx from Indochina and its impact on the countries of first asylum in Southeast Asia.

## Implications for UNHCR

The case studies presented here highlight the significant role that UNHCR can play in politically facilitating international cooperation in refugee protection. Far from being a passive actor, it has played a historically important role in influencing the willingness states to contribute to refugee protection. In situations in which it has been able to recognize and effectively appeal to the wider interests of states in other issue areas, it has been able to facilitate international cooperation. CIREFCA and the Indochinese CPA demonstrate that, by being aware of the wider political context of its work, UNHCR has been able to draw on and channel the wider interests states into a commitment to refugee protection, even when this has been based on their own self-interest rather than an altruistic commitment to refugee protection per se. This implies that, if UNHCR is to influence the responses of states to refugees, it needs to be politically engaged. This does *not* mean that it needs to compromise its nonpolitical character in terms of its neutrality and impartiality. But it does mean that it needs to acquire a greater analytical and practical capacity to recognize and exploit the wider political context of its work.

Issue linkage is a tool that UNHCR can use to facilitate burden-sharing. It may be able to use tactical issue linkage in bargaining processes to connect Northern and Southern interests. And even in the absence of clear trade-offs and the possibility for negotiated conditionality across issue areas, it may be able to draw on and use substantive linkages. Cross-issue persuasion is a key means by which UNHCR can appeal to and channel the wider interests of states into a commitment to protection and durable solutions. Making use of cross-issue persuasion requires that UNHCR be aware of the broader substantive linkages that connect refugee protection to other issue areas.

The world in which UNHCR works has become increasingly complex since the 1950s. The range of institutional, ideational, and material interconnections between refugee protection and other issue areas has rapidly grown. As the scope of the work of UNHCR expands to address issues such as internal displacement, environmental displacement, and the protection of vulnerable irregular migrants, its being aware of these broader interconnections will become increasingly important. UNHCR needs to engage with the politics of other issue areas such as migration, climate change, security, terrorism, peace-building, and development.

Institutional interconnections matter not only for practical and operational reasons but also because they affect the politics of protection. The institutional partnerships that UNHCR has with other actors such as UNDP, IOM, the UN Department of Peacekeeping Operations (DPKO), the Peacebuilding Commission, the Office of the Secretary-General, and the World Bank matter not only because they practically enable refugee protection to take place but also because these institutional connections shape how states perceive and respond to refugee protection. Addressing refugee protection within a broader collaborative institutional context has contributed to maximizing the scope for issue linkage and, hence, cross-issue persuasion.

Ideational interconnections matter for the work of UNHCR because they frame the context within which states understand the relationship between refugee protection and their wider interests. The RAD debates, the asylum-migration nexus, and understandings about the relationship between refugee movements and security are not merely academic debates. Rather, they are the context in which states make assumptions about the role that contributing to refugee protection will play in meeting their wider interests. UNHCR can and needs to play an active epistemic role in the creation and dissemination of knowledge, alongside NGOs and the academic community, to influence these debates.

Material interconnections matter because of the way in which they allow certain claims about the relationships between issue areas to be validated. It is important that UNHCR be aware of the material relationships that connect refugee protection to other areas. In particular, if UNHCR hopes to facilitate North–South burden-sharing, it needs to be aware of the complex interdependencies that connect refugee protection in the South to interests in the North. The empirical relationships between refugees and issues such as conflict, terrorism, regional and international security, development, and peace-building are crucial for UNHCR to credibly articulate to states why refugees matter.

In the past, UNHCR has been able to alter or highlight these structural interconnections through institutional design, its epistemic role, argumentation, and the provision of information. UNHCR can do a number of things to enhance its capacity to draw on structural interconnections to effectively channel the wider interests of states into a commitment to protection. In CIREFCA and the Indochinese CPA, UNHCR demonstrated significant political leadership and analytical capacity, which was lacking in ICARA and Convention Plus. By having high-level staff with political expertise working full-time on the conceptualization and negotiation of CIREFCA and the Indochinese CPA, UNHCR was able to identify the wider political motives underlying the positions of the Northern and Southern states and to persuade these states that meeting the needs of refugee protection was a central component of addressing their wider interests.

It is important to be aware that not all forms of cross-issue persuasion, or even all forms of international cooperation, will be protection-enhancing or liberal in purpose. Cross-issue persuasion may entail risks as well as opportunities. On the one hand, the focus of states on security and terrorism in the post-9/11 era presents myriad opportunities for issue linkage and cross-issue persuasion; on the other hand, appealing to interests in security may serve to define refugees in terms of security and thereby legitimate the implementation of restrictive and illiberal asylum policies by states. This makes it all the more important that UNHCR has the capacity to judiciously distinguish between political strategies that will be protection-enhancing and those that will be protection-diminishing.

If UNHCR is to replicate the success of CIREFCA and the Indochinese CPA and to effectively use cross-issue persuasion to shape the responses of states to protection, it needs to develop personnel structures that recruit and promote staff members with the necessary political and analytical skills. UNHCR might also consider creating a permanent unit within headquarters that can work full-time in identifying its organizational political strategy and respond effectively to wider political constraints and opportunities. Whether or not these organizational changes take place, it is clear that the future capacity of UNHCR to fulfill its mandate will depend on its ability to effectively engage with politics beyond the refugee regime.

## Implications for International Relations

Aside from insights into the role of UNHCR in the global refugee regime, the analysis of the international politics of refugee protection presented here has wider conceptual implications for IR. In particular, it offers insights into the conditions under which substantive issue linkages come to matter for the politics of a given issue area and how they can be used by a nonstate actor to influence the behavior of states. The politics of refugee protection represents a methodologically useful case study for exploring this wider question because of the way in which, in the absence of a normative framework for burden-sharing, each of the ad hoc UNHCR initiatives was created in a different context and hence connected refugee protection to other issue areas in different ways. In addition, the insights of this analysis in this area arguably have practical implications that go far beyond just explaining the politics of refugee protection.

## Cross-Issue Persuasion and Issue Linkage

In this book, I build on the existing IR literature on issue linkage. The main types of issue linkage in that literature are tactical linkage, which looks at how issues are grouped together within interstate bargaining on the basis of horse-trading, and substantive linkage, which looks are how issues are grouped together on the basis of an empirical or perceived relationship between those issues. Issue linkage has been examined as a dependent variable to explain how issues come to be grouped together and as an independent variable to explain international cooperation, for example.

The work on linkage as an independent variable focuses mainly on the role of tactical issue linkage. It explores the way in which issues are made formally conditional on one another at the level of instrumental bargaining. There has been far less work examining the role that substantive linkages play in, for example, contributing to international cooperation. The concept of cross-issue persuasion builds on the existing work on substantive linkages to highlight the conditions under which substantive linkages can be used by an actor to influence the behavior of another actor.

There is an increasingly complex array of substantive linkages in the world that connect issues on institutional, ideational, and material levels. Globalization, interdependence, and institutional proliferation, for example, have contributed this increase in the array of relationships that connect issue areas. Given the range of interconnections that exist in a complex world, not all of these linkages will be recognized or acted on. The obscurity, ambiguity, and malleability of many of these relationships offer an opportunity for actors such as UNHCR to influence the behavior of states. By changing these substantive relationships, or by simply recognizing and effectively communicating their existence, an international organization or another nonstate actor may be able to influence the behavior of a state.

The typology in table 6 highlights where cross-issue persuasion fits into the existing IR literature on issue linkage. Tactical and substantive linkages have very different bases. The basis of tactical linkage is horse-trading based on instrumental bargaining; the basis of substantive linkage is a structural relationship between issues or issue areas (ideational, institutional or material). But identifying the basis of linkage tells us very little about the conditions under which linkages come to influence actor behavior or under which they can be used as a resource of power. Tactical linkage serves as a resource of power insofar as it enables or constrains actor A to use conditionality to influence actor B. Similarly, substantive linkage serves as a resource of power insofar as it enables or constrains actor A to influence actor B through cross-issue persuasion. Cross-issue persuasion is an important concept because it highlights the important role of agency—through, for example, institutional design, playing an epistemic role, argumentation, and the provision of information—in drawing on and using structural interconnections as a resource of power.

## Substantive Linkages and Power

This analysis of the international politics of refugee protection sheds light on a neglected source of power. It demonstrates that structural interconnections between issue areas represent a resource of power, insofar as recognizing and using them can allow actor A to induce actor B to do something that actor B would otherwise not have done. If an actor is able to recognize and effectively communicate the existence of a structural interconnection (institutional, ideational, or material), this represents a means of influencing the

**TABLE 6.** Typology of Issue Linkage and How Cross-Issue Persuasion Relates to Substantive and Tactical Linkage

| Type of Linkage | Basis for Linkage | Mechanism by Which Linkage Influences Actor Behavior |
|---|---|---|
| Substantive | Structural interconnections: material, ideational, institutional | Cross-issue persuasion |
| Tactical | Horse-trading | Conditionality |

behavior of other actors by persuading them to see their interests differently. Similarly, if an actor is able to create or influence structural interconnections, this represents a means of influencing the behavior of other actors.

Once structural interconnections exist, they can be used by any actor to influence the behavior of another actor, provided that the actor is capable of recognizing and effectively communicating their existence. In that sense, structural interconnections can be thought of as a resource of power. They represent a structure that an actor can draw on to influence the behavior of another actor.

Examining resources of power is a different level of analysis compared to the dominant typology of power in the work of Michael Barnett and Robert Duvall (2005). They examine what might be called the mechanisms of power—in other words, how actor A relationally influences actor B—whether the relationship between A and B is direct or diffuse, or constraining or constitutive. In contrast, structural interconnections refer to a resource of power—something that can be drawn on instrumentally by actor A to influence actor B. This is on the same level of analysis as Joseph Nye's (2004) concept "soft power." In Nye's terms, structural interconnections might also be thought of as an important and neglected resource of soft power insofar as they enable and constrain cross-issue persuasion and cross-issue persuasion represents a nonmilitary means of influencing other actors.

Identifying structural interconnections as a resource of power is of particular significance because it has particularly low barriers to use. That is, drawing on and using structural interconnections to influence the behavior of another actor does not rely on how much military or economic power an actor has. In IR, the most important resources of power are assumed to be military and economic capabilities, and IR offers little explanation of how actors without significant military or economic strength influence world politics. Irrespective of how many guns or how much money an actor has, if two issue areas are structurally interconnected, that actor will have a basis on which to persuade another actor that action in issue area X could meet its interests in issue area Y. This is because using structural interconnections to influence the behavior of another actor relies on persuasion and an appeal to interests rather than coercion.

The low barriers to using structural interconnections as a resource of power mean that it represents a potentially significant means through which relatively weaker actors such as Southern states, international organizations, and nonstate actors can influence relatively more powerful states in world politics. Provided they have the analytical and communication skills to articulate to a more powerful state the structural relationship between two issue areas, this may create a basis for inducing action in issue area X on the basis of interests in issue area Y. This implies that cross-issue persuasion offers a means through which relatively weaker actors in world politics are partly able to offset power asymmetries.

## The Concept of Persuasion

IR rightly identifies persuasion as an important causal mechanisms of influence. Nevertheless, the concept of cross-issue persuasion challenges two common assumptions about the nature of persuasion in world politics. On the one hand, it calls into question the relationship between persuasion and argument; on the other hand, it highlights the way in which persuasion is not only the consequence of agency but also has an important structural dimension.

A significant proportion of the IR literature sees argument and persuasion as being very closely related (Risse 2003). It analytically defines *persuasion* as influence designed to change beliefs, which it correctly distinguishes from other forms of influence such as coercion, bargaining, and emulation (Keohane 2003). The existing literature, however, frequently assumes that the only mechanism through which persuasion takes place is argument (i.e., through speech acts involving giving reasons). Argument is indeed one mechanism through which an actor can engage in action to change the beliefs of another actor; however, it is not the only one. Persuasion is a broader concept than argument. It is not necessarily limited to the use of argument; it may also involve other actions that change beliefs.

In practice, actions designed to change beliefs can take a variety forms. The provision of information might be considered to be a form of persuasion when it is used to change beliefs. Furthermore, actions that are designed to change the structural basis on which beliefs are formed can also be considered to be persuasion. If beliefs are formed in a given ideational or institutional context, then actions that change or influence the beliefs of another actor will also amount to persuasion. In the case studies, UNHCR was able to engage in cross-issue persuasion through a combination of information provision, argumentation, institutional design, and playing an epistemic role.

In addition, persuasion is commonly assumed to involve a broker (in this case, UNHCR) communicating and arguing in a manner that leads to a change in the underlying beliefs of a target (in this case, a state). In other words, persuasion is often seen as based purely on the actions and agency of a broker in bringing about a change in the perception of a target. In contrast, the case studies presented here from the global refugee regime highlight that persuasion has not only an agency dimension but also a structural dimension. Perception changes as a result of the role of both structure and agency. In the absence of a structural basis for a certain perception, agency must do more work in persuasion; in the absence of agency, the structural basis for the claim of a relationship between two issue areas must to be stronger for a given actor to be convinced of a certain relationship.

Structure and agency are, therefore, both important elements of an actor's being persuaded to believe that there is a relationship between issue area X and issue area Y. An analogy that captures this is the recognition that security comprises both threat and vulnerability—in other words, it has a structural element and an actor-specific element. Similarly, persuasion cannot be seen as just a product of the agency of the persuading actor; it is also a function of the extent to which the preexisting structures lend themselves to a given perception.

## Securitization as Cross-Issue Persuasion

There has been a burgeoning literature on securitization (Buzan, Wæver, and de Wilde 1998; Campbell 1992; Wæver et al. 1993). This work is diverse but generally explores the conditions under which an issue comes to be designated a security issue. It examines how labeling or describing an issue or issue area such as migration, climate change, or contagious disease as a security issue changes how it is perceived. Securitization thereby legitimates certain types of political response and may be an incentive for states to prioritize an issue that they might otherwise neglect.

In many ways, securitization represents a special case of the broader phenomenon of cross-issue persuasion. It concerns the conditions under which an actor can persuade another actor that an issue area is linked to security as a means of inducing that actor to act in the particular issue area. Securitization can be analyzed on many levels, but it involves both structure and agency as means of altering the perceived relationship between security and another issue area held by an actor. The parallel between cross-issue persuasion and securitization is useful because it opens up the possibility for future research that draws on these similarities. It might enable research on securitization to be informed by the literature on substantive issue linkage and also allow future work on cross-issue persuasion to draw on ideas within the securitization literature.

Cross-issue persuasion broadens the focus of securitization to consider how other issue areas may take on a similarly pervasive and influential quality across a number of issue areas. For example, in addition to security, we might observe a trend of other issue areas, such as development, playing a pervasive role in influencing the politics of a range of issue areas. For example, there are widespread debates on the relationship between migration and development, the environment and development, and human rights and development. In this context, it might be appropriate to examine developmentization as well as simply securitization. In a similar way to securitization, developmentization may induce a sense of urgency and, in particular, makes an issue of greater priority for developing countries.

This, in turn, begs the question of whether there is something unique about securitization as distinct from other forms of cross-issue persuasion. Is security an issue area like all others, or does it have a ubiquitous quality and is inherent in all other issue areas? Irrespective of how we answer this question, cross-issue persuasion challenges the existing literature on securitization to examine how other forms of substantive linkage take place and offers new analytical tools for identifying mechanisms of securitization.

## Further Research

The potentially significant role of cross-issue persuasion in world politics and the structural and agency conditions for its use require further empirical exploration. A number of other issue areas can also be characterized by a North–South impasse. For health, the alleviation of poverty, intrastate conflict, and certain environmental issues, the most significant negative consequences are often largely regionally confined in the South

Northern states frequently have inadequate incentives to contribute to addressing the problem for its own sake. But Northern donors may often contribute to solving the problem because of their wider interests in other issue areas. For example, in the case of health, Northern donors are frequently motivated to earmark contributions in situations in which they identify their wider interests in security or trade. Similarly, much overseas development assistance is rendered on the basis of wider interests in trade, human rights, and security. In these issue areas, the concept of cross-issue persuasion may similarly shed light on the conditions under which the North–South impasse has been overcome.

Beyond its role in North–South cooperation, cross-issue persuasion could be explored in relation to its use by a range of international organizations as an instrument of political facilitation. It might also be applied in the examination of how NGOs or private actors attempt to influence international political negotiations. For example, given the low barriers to the use of cross-issue persuasion, it may be usefully applied to understand how NGOs and multinational corporations influence international standard setting. Cross-issue persuasion may be a particularly important source of influence for nonstate actors because it enables them to influence the behavior of states while working within the constraints of their preexisting interests.

One area in which the concepts developed in this book have particular relevance is the international politics of migration. There is currently very little institutionalized cooperation on migration and no coherent multilateral architecture regulating the migration policies of states. In the context of the Global Forum on Migration and Development (GFMD), however, there is a growing academic interest in international cooperation and migration. Like the politics of refugee protection, the politics of migration divides along North–South lines. Like burden-sharing in the refugee regime, migration also lacks a clear normative and legal framework regulating the behavior of states at the international level. Migrant-receiving countries generally have the power to autonomously determine their immigration policies, whereas migrant-sending countries are generally forced to be the takers of these policies, working within the constraints defined by receiving countries. In that sense, the politics of migration can also be characterized by the analogy of the Suasion Game described in this book.

Issue linkage has an important role to play in facilitating international cooperation on migration. On one level, this involves tactical linkage. It may be conceivable that a multilateral regulatory framework on migration could emerge as the result of a North–South grand bargain based on linking development and security. For example, Northern states might offer Southern states development assistance or privileged access to labor markets in exchange for the cooperation of Southern state on the control of irregular migration. Indeed, much bilateral cooperation on migration occurs in the context of tactical issue linkage.

Beyond tactical linkage, this book highlights the important role of substantive linkages in facilitating international cooperation on migration. There are significant material, ideational, and institutional connections between migration and a range of other issue areas, including development, security, and the environment. These relationships offer a means through which states may be induced to cooperate on migration on the basis of their wider interests. A range of actors, including states, international organizations, NGOs, and academics, may be able to draw on these structural interconnections and use cross-issue persuasion to change the behavior of states in relation to migration. Indeed, there is evidence that cross-issue persuasion is increasingly prevalent in the politics of migration. Southern states are being induced to engage in international discussions, such as the GFMD, on the basis of the structural relationship between migration and development. For the range of international actors aspiring to facilitate enhanced cooperation on migration, influencing or drawing on substantive linkages to development and security will probably be the most effective means of persuading states to cooperate.

Within the wider empirical exploration of the role of and conditions for cross-issue persuasion, there are a number of further hypotheses and research questions that require exploration. In particular, what is the relationship between power and cross-issue persuasion? Under what conditions does its use reinforce or offset power asymmetries? What are the barriers to use of structural interconnections as a resource of power? How are structural interconnections between issue areas created, and how do they change and evolve over time?

Until now, there has been little work from a political science or IR theory perspective that has explored the international politics of refugee protection. This book highlights the importance of understanding the international politics of refugee protection both for refugees' access to their human rights and for the work of UNHCR. Only by understanding the conditions under which states contribute to refugee protection can actors such as UNHCR work to ensure that refugees have access to effective protection and durable solutions. Further, this book highlights how integrating the study of the politics of refugee protection within the mainstream study of IR can generate new concepts with much wider relevance for world politics.

# References

Adler, Emanuel. 1992. "The Emergence of Cooperation: National Epistemic Communities and the International Evolution of the Idea of Nuclear Arms Control." *International Organization* 46 (1): 101–45.

Aggarwal, Vinod. 1998. "Reconciling Multiple Institutions: Bargaining, Linkages, and Nesting." In *Institutional Designs for a Complex World,* edited by V. Aggarwal. Ithaca: Cornell University Press.

———. 2006. "Reconciling Institutions: Nested, Horizontal, Overlapping, and Independent Institutions." Paper prepared for workshop on Nesting and Overlapping Institutions, Princeton University, 24 February.

Alter, Karen, and Sophie Meunier. 2009. "The Politics of Regime Complexity." *Perspectives on Politics* 7 (1): 13–24.

Axelrod, Robert. 1984. *The Evolution of Cooperation.* London: Basic Books.

Barratt, Scott. 2008. *Why Cooperate? Understanding Global Public Goods.* Oxford: Oxford University Press.

Barnett, Michael, and Robert Duvall. 2005. "Power in Global Governance." In *Power in Global Governance,* edited by M. Barnett and R. Duvall. Cambridge, UK: Cambridge University Press.

Barnett, Michael, and Martha Finnemore. 2004. *Rules for the World: International Organizations in Global Politics.* Ithaca: Cornell University Press.

Barutciski, Michael, and Astri Suhrke. 2001. "Lessons from the Kosovo Refugee Crisis: Innovations in Protection and Burden-Sharing." *Journal of Refugee Studies* 41 (2): 95–115.

Benz, Sophia, and Andreas Hasenclever. 2008. "The Global Governance of Forced Migration." Lecture presented at University of Oxford, November 24.

Betts, Alexander. 2003. "Public Goods Theory and the Provision of Refugee Protection: The Role of the Joint-Product Model in Burden-Sharing Theory." *Journal of Refugee Studies* 16 (3): 274–96.

———. 2004. "International Cooperation and Targeting Development Assistance For Refugee Solutions." New Issues in Refugee Research Working Paper no. 107. Geneva: UNHCR.

———. 2008. "Historical Lessons for Overcoming Protracted Refugee Situations." In *Protracted Refugee Situations: Politics, Human Rights and Security Implications,* edited by G. Loescher, J. Milner, E. Newman, and G. Troeller. Tokyo: United Nations University Press.

———. 2009. "Institutional Proliferation and the Global Refugee Regime." *Perspectives on Politics* 7 (1): 53–58.

Betts, Alexander, and Jean-François Durieux. 2007. "Convention Plus as a Norm-Setting Exercise." *Journal of Refugee Studies* 20 (3): 509–35.

Betts, Tristram. 1981. "Documentary Note: Rural Refugees in Africa." *International Migration Review* 15 (53–54): 213–18.

———. 1984. "Evolution and Promotion of the Integrated Rural Development Approach to Refugee Policy in Africa." *Africa Today* 31 (1): 7–24.

Bhagwati, Jadish. 1984. "Introduction." In *Power, Passions and Purpose: Prospects for North-South Negotiations,* edited by J. Bhagwati and J. Ruggie. Cambridge, Mass.: MIT Press.

Boyer, Mark. 1993. *International Cooperation and Public Goods: Opportunities for the Western Alliance.* Baltimore: Johns Hopkins University Press.

Bull, Hedley. 1977. *The Anarchical Society: A Study of Order in World Politics.* New York: Columbia University Press.

Buzan, Barry, Ole Wæver, and Jaap de Wilde, eds. 1998. *Security: A New Framework for Analysis.* Boulder: Lynne Rienner.

Calleo, David. 1987. *Beyond American Hegemony: The Future of the Western Alliance.* New York: Basic Books.

Campbell, David. 1992. *Writing Security: United States Foreign Policy and the Politics of Identity.* Minneapolis: Minnesota University Press.

Carlsnaes, Walter. 1992. "The Agency Structure Problem in Foreign Policy Analysis." *International Studies Quarterly* 36 (3): 245–70.

Castles, Stephen. 2004. "The International Politics of Forced Migration." *Development* 46: 11–20.

Castles, Stephen, and Nick Van Hear. 2005. "The Migration-Asylum Nexus: Definition and Significance." Lecture given at COMPAS, University of Oxford, January 27.

Chambers, Robert. 1979. "Rural Refugees in Africa: What the Eye Does Not See." *Disasters* 3 (4): 381–92.

Chimni, B. S. 1998. "The Geopolitics of Refugee Studies: A View from the South." *Journal of Refugee Studies* 11 (4): 350–74.

———. 1999. "From Resettlement to Involuntary Repatriation: Towards a Critical History of Durable Solutions to Refugee Problems." New Issues in Refugee Research Working Paper No. 2. Geneva: UNHCR.

Clark, Lance, and Barry Stein. 1985. "The Relationship between ICARA II and Refugee Aid and Development." *Migration Today* 13 (1): 33–38.

Cohen, Roberta. 2006. "Developing an International System for Internally Displaced Persons." *International Studies Perspectives* 7 (2): 87–101.

Collier, Paul, and Anke Hoeffler. 2004. "Greed and Grievance in Civil War." *Oxford Economic Papers* 56 (4): 563–95.

Conybeare, John. 1984. "Public Goods, Prisoner's Dilemma and the International Political Economy." *International Studies Quarterly* 28: 5–22.

Cornes, Richard, and Todd Sandler. 1996. *The Theory of Externalities, Public Goods, and Club Goods.* Cambridge, UK: Cambridge University Press.

Crawford, Neta. 2002. *Argument and Change in World Politics.* Cambridge, UK: Cambridge University Press.

Crisp, Jeff. 2003a. "A New Asylum Paradigm? Globalization, Migration and the Uncertain Future of the International Refugee Regime." New Issues in Refugee Research Working Paper no. 100. Geneva: UNHCR.

———. 2003b. "No Solutions in Sight: The Problem of Protracted Refugee Situations in Africa." New Issues in Refugee Research Working Paper no. 75. Geneva: UNHCR.

———. 2008. "Beyond the Nexus: UNHCR's Evolving Perspective on Refugee Protection and International Migration." New Issues in Refugee Research Working Paper no. 155. Geneva: UNHCR.

Crisp, Jeff, and Lowell Martin. 1992. "Quick Impact Project: A Review of UNHCR's Returnee Reintegration Programme in Nicaragua." Evaluation and Policy Analysis Unit EPAU Evaluation Report. United Nations High Commissioner for Refugees, Geneva.

Cuenod, Jacques. 1989. "Refugees: Development or Relief." In *Refugees and International Relations,* edited by G. Loescher and L. Monahan. Oxford: Oxford University Press.

Curran, Lisa, and Susan Kneebone. 2003. "Overview." In *The Refugee Convention 50 Years On: Globalization and International Law,* edited by S. Kneebone. Ashgate, UK: Aldershot.

Dessler, David. 1989. "What's at Stake in the Agent-Structure Debate?" *International Organization* 43 (3): 441–73.

Doty, Roxanne. 1996. *Imperial Encounters: The Politics of Representation in North-South Relations.* Minneapolis: University of Minnesota Press.

Drake, William, and Kalypso Nicolaides. 1992. "Ideas, Interests, and Institutionalization: 'Trade in Services' and the Uruguay Round." *International Organization* 46 (1): 37–100.

Duffield, Mark. 2001. *Global Governance and the New Wars.* London: Zed.

Dumper, Michael. 2008. "Palestinian Refugees." In *Protracted Refugee Situations: Politics, Human Rights and Security Implications,* edited by G. Loescher, J. Milner, E. Newman, and G. Troeller. Tokyo: United Nations University Press.

Dunne, Tim, and Wheeler, Nicholas, eds. 1999. *Human Rights in Global Politics.* Cambridge, UK: Cambridge University Press.

Durieux, Jean-François, and Ninette Kelley. 2004. "UNHCR and Current Challenges in International Refugee Protection." *Refuge* 22 (1): 6–17.

European Commission. 2005a. "Migration and Development: Some Concrete Orientations." COM 390, Brussels.

——. 2005b. "Regional Protection Programmes." COM 388, Brussels.

Fawcett, Louise, and Yazid Sayigh, eds. 1999. *The Third World beyond the Cold War: Continuity and Change.* Oxford: Oxford University Press.

Feller, Erika, Volker Türk, and Frances Nicholson, eds. 2003. *Refugee Protection in International Law: UNHCR's Global Consultations on International Protection.* Cambridge, UK: Cambridge University Press.

Garoz, Byron, and Mark Macdonald. 1996. "La Politica de Cooperacion de la Union Europa Hacia Guatemala." Estudio elaborado para Asamblea de la Sociedad Civil (ASC), Guatemala. On file with the author.

Gilpin, Robert. 2001. *Global Political Economy.* Princeton: Princeton University Press.

Global Commission on International Migration (GCIM). 2005. *GCIM Report: Migration in an Interconnected World: New Directions for Action.* Geneva: GCIM.

Goodwin-Gill, Guy. 2000. "The International Protection of Refugees: What Future?" *International Journal of Refugee Law* 12 (1): 1–6.

Goodwin-Gill, Guy, and Jane McAdam. 2007. *The Refugee in International Law.* Oxford: Oxford University Press.

Gordenker, Leon. 1987. *Refugees in International Politics.* New York: Columbia University Press.

Gorlick, Brian. 2000. "Human Rights and Refugees: Enhancing Protection through International Human Rights Law." New Issues in Refugee Research Working Paper no. 30. Geneva: UNHCR.

Gorman, Robert. 1986. "Beyond ICARA II: Implementing Refugee-Related Development Assistance." *International Migration Review* 8 (3): 283–98.

——. 1987. *Coping with Africa's Refugee Burden: A Time for Solutions.* The Hague: Martinus Nijhoff.

——. 1993. "Linking Refugee Aid and Development in Africa." In *Refugee Aid and Development: Theory and Practice,* edited by R. Gorman. London: Greenwood.

Guterres, Antonio. 2008. "Millions Uprooted." *Foreign Affairs* 87 (5): 90–99.

Haas, Ernst. 1980/1994. "Why Collaborate? Issue-Linkages and International Regimes." In *International Organization: A Reader,* edited by F. Kratochwil and E. Mansfield. New York: Harper Collins.

——. 1990. *When Power Is Knowledge.* Berkeley: University of California Press.

Haas, Peter. 1989/1994. "Do Regimes Matter? Epistemic Communities and Mediterranean Pollution Control." In *International Organization: A Reader,* edited by F. Kratochwil and E. Mansfield. New York: Harper Collins.

Haddad, Emma. 2008. *The Refugee in International Society.* Cambridge, UK: Cambridge University Press.

Hasenclever, Andreas, Peter Mayer, and Volker Rittberger. 1997. *Theories of International Regimes.* Cambridge, UK: Cambridge University Press.

Hathaway, James. 2005 *The Rights of Refugees under International Law.* Cambridge, UK: Cambridge University Press.

Hathaway, James, and R. Alexander Neve. 1997. "Making International Refugee Law Relevant Again: A Proposal for Collectivized and Solution-Oriented Protection." *Harvard Human Rights Journal* 10 (Spring): 115–51.

Helton, Arthur. 1993. "Refugee Determinations under the Comprehensive Plan of Action: Overview and Assessment." *International Journal of Refugee Law* 5 (4): 544–58.

Hurrell, Andrew. 2007. *On Global Order*. Oxford: Oxford University Press.

Jacobsen, Karen. 2001. "The Forgotten Solution: Local Integration for Refugees in Developing Countries." New Issues in Refugee Research Working Paper no. 45. Geneva: UNHCR.

Jambor, Pierre. 1992. *Indochinese Refugees in Southeast Asia: Mass Exodus and the Politics of Aid*. Bangkok: Ford Foundation.

Juma, Monica, and Peter Kagwanja. 2008. "Asylum in the Age of Extremism: Somali Refugees, Security and the Politics of 'Terrorism.'" In *Protracted Refugee Situations: Politics, Human Rights and Security Implications,* edited by G. Loescher, J. Milner, E. Newman, and G. Troeller. Tokyo: United Nations University Press.

Kanbur, Ravi, Todd Sandler, and Kevin Morrison. 1999. *The Future of Development Assistance: Common Pools and International Public Goods*. Washington, D.C.: Overseas Development Council.

Kaul, Inge, Isabelle Grunberg, and Marc Stern, eds. 1999. *Global Public Goods: International Cooperation in the Twenty-First Century*. Oxford: Oxford University Press.

Keeley, Charles. 1981. *Global Refugee Policy: The Case for a Development-Oriented Strategy*. New York: Population Council.

Keohane, Robert. 1982. "The Demand for International Regimes." *International Organization* 36 (2): 325–55.

———. 1984. *After Hegemony*. Princeton: Princeton University Press.

———. 2003. "The Causal Pathways of Persuasion." Unpublished memo written following the conference Arguing and Persuasion in International Relations and European Affairs, European University Institute, Florence, April 8–10, 2002.

Keohane, Robert, and Joseph Nye. 1989. *Power and Interdependence*. London: Harper Collins.

Kindleberger, Charles. 1973. *The World Depression 1929–1939*. London: Penguin.

Koremenos, Barbara, Charles Lipson, and Duncan Snidal, eds. 2003. *The Rational Design of International Institutions*. Cambridge, UK: Cambridge University Press.

Krasner, Stephen. 1983. "Structural Causes and Regime Consequences." In *International Regimes,* edited by Stephen Krasner. Ithaca: Cornell University Press.

———. 1985. *Structural Conflict: The Third World against Global Liberalism*. Berkeley: University of California Press.

Landau, Loren. 2007. "Can We Talk and Is Anybody Listening? Reflections on IASFM 10, 'Talking Across Borders: New Dialogues in Forced Migration.'" *Journal of Refugee Studies* 20: 335–48.

Lauterpacht, Eli, and David Bethlehem. 2003. "The Scope and Content of the Principle of *Non-Refoulement*." In *Refugee Protection in International Law: UNHCR's Global Consultations on International Protection,* edited by E. Feller, V. Türk, and F. Nicholson. Cambridge, UK: Cambridge University Press.

Lippman, Betsy. 2004. "The 4Rs: The Way Ahead?" *Forced Migration Review* 21: 9–11.

Lischer, Sarah. 2005. *Dangerous Sanctuaries: Refugee Camps, Civil War, and the Dilemmas of Humanitarian Aid.* Ithaca: Cornell University Press.

Loescher, Gil. 1986. *Calculated Kindness: Refugees and America's Half-Open Door.* London: Macmillan.

———. 1993. *Beyond Charity: International Cooperation and the Global Refugee Crisis.* Oxford: Oxford University Press.

———. 2001a. "Protection of Humanitarian Action." In *Global Migrants, Global Refugees: Problems and Solutions,* edited by A. Zolberg and P. Benda. Oxford: Berghahn.

———. 2001b. *The UNHCR and World Politics.* Oxford: Oxford University Press.

Loescher, Gil, Alexander Betts, and James Milner. 2008. *UNHCR: The Politics and Practice of Refugee Protection into the Twenty-First Century.* Oxford: Routledge.

Loescher, Gil, and James Milner. 2005. "Protracted Refugee Situations: Domestic and International Security Implications." Adelphi Paper no. 375, London, Routledge.

Loescher, Gil, James Milner, Edward Newman, and Gary Troeller, eds. 2008. *Protracted Refugee Situations: Politics, Human Rights and Security Implications.* Tokyo: United Nations University Press.

Loescher, Gil, and Laila Monahan, eds. 1996. *Refugees and International Relations.* Oxford: Oxford University Press.

Martin, Lisa. 1993. "The Rational State Choice of Multilateralism." In *Multilateralism Matters: The Theory and Praxis of an Institutional Form,* edited by J. Ruggie. New York: Columbia University Press.

McAdam, Jane. 2007. *Complementary Protection in International Law.* Oxford: Oxford University Press.

McGinnis, Micheal. 1986. "Issue Linkage and the Evolution of International Cooperation." *Journal of Conflict Resolution* 30: 141–70.

Milner, James. 2000. "Sharing the Security Burden: Towards the Convergence of Refugee Protection and State Security." Refugee Studies Centre Working Paper no. 4. Oxford: Refugee Studies Centre.

———. 2004. "Golden Age? What Golden Age? A Critical History of African Asylum Policy." Paper presented at the Centre for Refugee Studies, York University, January 1.

———. 2009. *Refugees, the State and the Politics of Asylum in Africa.* Basingstoke, UK: Palgrave Macmillan.

Morris, Eric, and Stephen Stedman. 2008. "Protracted Refugee Situations, Conflict, and Security: The Need for Better Diagnosis and Prescription." In *Protracted Refugee Situations: Politics, Human Rights and Security Implications,* edited by G. Loescher, J. Milner, E. Newman, and G. Troeller. Tokyo: United Nations University Press.

Newman, Edward, and Joanne Van Selm, eds. 2003. *Refugees and Forced Displacement: International Security, Human Vulnerability and the State.* Tokyo: United Nations University Press.

Nicaragua, Republica de. 1993. "Plan de Accion CIREFCA 1993–1996: Resumen Ejecutivo." On file with the author.

Noll, Gregor. 2003. "Visions of the Exceptional: Legal and Theoretical Issues Raised by Transit Processing Centres and Protection Zones." *European Journal of Migration and Law* 5: 303–41.

Nye, Joseph. 2004. *Soft Power.* New York: Public Affairs.

Olson, Mancur. 1965. *The Logic of Collective Action.* Cambridge, Mass.: Harvard University Press.

Olson, Mancur, and Robert Zeckhauser. 1966. "An Economic Theory of Alliances." *Review of Economics and Statistics* 48: 266–79.

O'Neill, Kate, Jorg Balsiger, and Stacy VanDeveer. 2004. "Actors, Norms and Impact: Recent International Cooperation Theory and the Influence of the Agent-Structure Debate." *Annual Review of Political Science* 7: 149–75.

Papadopoulou, Aspasia. 2005. "Exploring the Asylum-Migration Nexus: A Case Study of Transit Migrants in Europe." Global Migration Perspectives no. 23. Geneva: Global Commission on International Migration.

Phuong, Catherine. 2005. *The International Protection of Internally Displaced Persons.* Cambridge, UK: Cambridge University Press.

Power, Samantha. 2008. *Chasing the Flame: Sergio Vieira de Mello and the Fight to Save the World.* London: Penguin.

Ravenhill, John. 1990. "The North-South Balance of Power." *International Affairs* 66 (4): 731–48.

Refugee Studies Centre (RSC). 2005. *Developing DFID's Policy Approach to Refugees and Internally Displaced Persons.* Final Report. Oxford: RSC.

Risse, Thomas. 2003. "Let's Argue! Communicative Action in World Politics." *International Organization* 54 (1): 1–39.

Robinson, Courtland. 1998. *Terms of Refuge: The Indochinese Exodus and the International Response.* London: Zed.

———. 2004. "The Comprehensive Plan of Action for Indo-Chinese Refugees, 1989–1997." *Journal of Refugee Studies* 17 (3): 319–33.

Rogge, John. 1987. "When Is Self-Sufficiency Achieved? The Case of Rural Settlements in Sudan?" In *Refugees, a Third World Dilemma,* edited by J. Rogge. Totowa, N.J.: Rowman and Littlefield.

Salehyan, Idean, and Kristian Skrede Gleditsch. 2006. "Refugees and the Spread of Civil War." *International Organization* 60 (2): 335–66.

Sandler, Todd, and Keith Hartley. 1995. *The Economics of Defense.* Cambridge, UK: Cambridge University Press.

———. 1999. *The Political Economy of NATO: Past, Present and into the Twenty-First Century.* Cambridge, UK: Cambridge University Press.

Sindzingre, Alice. 2004. "The Evolution of the Concept of Poverty in Multilateral Financial Institutions: The Case of the World Bank." In *Global Institutions and Development: Framing the World,* edited by M. Boas and D. McNeil. Abingdon: Routledge.

Skran, Claudena. 1995. *Refugees in Inter-war Europe: The Emergence of a Regime.* Oxford: Clarendon.

Smith, Merrill. 2004. "Warehousing Refugees: A Denial of Rights, a Waste of Humanity." In *World Refugee Survey 2004* (online), edited by M. Smith. Arlington, Va.: U.S. Committee for Refugees and Immigrants.

Stedman, Stephen, and Fred Tanner. 2003. "Refugees as Resources in War." In *Refugee Manipulation: War, Politics, and the Abuse of Human Suffering,* edited by S. Stedman and F. Tanner. Washington, D.C.: Brookings Institution.

Stein, Arthur. 1980. "The Politics of Linkage." *World Politics* 33 (1): 62–81.

Stein, Barry. 1987. "ICARA II: Burden-Sharing and Durable Solutions." In *Refugees: A Third World Dilemma,* edited by R. Rogge. Totowa, N.J.: Rowman and Littlefield.

———. 1997. "Regional Efforts to Address Refugee Problems." Paper presented at the International Studies Association meeting, Toronto, March 21.

Stepputat, Finn. 2004a. "Dynamics of Return and Sustainable Reintegration in a 'Mobile Livelihoods'-Perspective." DIIS Working Paper no. 2004/10. Copenhagen: Danish Institute for International Studies.

———. 2004b. "Refugees, Security and Development." DIIS Working Paper no. 2004/11. Copenhagen: Danish Institute for International Studies.

Stewart, Frances, and Valpy Fitzgerald. 2001. *War and Underdevelopment.* Vol. 2. Oxford: QEH.

Suhrke, Astri. 1998. "Burden-Sharing during Refugee Emergencies: The Logic of Collective Action versus National Action." *Journal of Refugee Studies* 11 (4): 396–415.

Sutter, Valerie. 1990. *The Indo-Chinese Refugee Dilemma.* Baton Rouge: Louisiana University Press.

Swiss Forum for Migration. 2005. "Movements of Somali Refugees and Asylum Seekers and States' Responses Thereto." Neuchatel: SFM.

Thielemann, Eiko. 2003. "Between Interests and Norms: Burden-Sharing in the European Union." *Journal of Refugee Studies* 16 (3): 253–73.

Towle, Rick. 2006. "Processes and Critiques of the Indo-Chinese Comprehenive Plan of Action: An Instrument of International Burden-Sharing?" *International Journal of Refugee Law* 18 (4): 537–70.

Turk, Volker, and Frances Nicholson. 2003. "Refugee Protection in International Law: An Overall Perspective." In *Refugee Protection in International Law: UNHCR's Global Consultations on International Protection,* edited by E. Feller, V. Türk, and F. Nicholson. Cambridge, UK: Cambridge University Press.

UK Government. 2003. "New Vision." Document. On file with the author.

UN Development Group (UNDG). 2004. "UNDG Guidance Note on Durable Solutions for Displaced Persons." UNDG, New York. Available at www.undg.org.

UN Development Programme (UNDP). 2005."Investing in Development: A Practical Guide to Achieve the Millennium Development Goals." Millennium Project, UNDP, New York.

UN Development Programme and UN High Commissioner for Refugees. 1995. "CIREFCA: An Opportunity and Challenge for Inter-Agency Collaboration." May, UNDP and UNHCR, New York. On file with the author.

UN General Assembly. 2003. "Strengthening the Capacity of the Office of the United Nations High Commissioner for Refugees to Carry Out Its Mandate." 58th Session, Item 112, A/58/410.

UN High Commissioner for Refugees (UNHCR). 1983. Executive Committee Conclusion Number 29.

———. 1984. "Recommendations from the Pan-African Conference on the Situation of Refugees in Africa." Geneva: UNHCR.

———. 1993. "Summary of the CIREFCA Projects." Prepared by the Joint Support Unit. Geneva: UNHCR. On file with the author.

——. 1994a. *Returnee Aid and Development.* Geneva: UNHCR.

——. 1994b. "Review of the CIREFCA Process." Geneva: UNHCR. Available at www.unhcr.ch.

——. 1998. "Annual Theme: International Solidarity and Burden Sharing in All Its Aspects: National, Regional and International Responsibilities for Refugees." Executive Committee Report, 49th Session, A/AC.96/90, Geneva: UNHCR.

——. 1999. "Lessons Learnt from UNHCR's Involvement in the Guatemalan Refugee Repatriation and Reintegration Programme (1987–1999)." Geneva: Evaluation and Policy Analysis Unit Evaluation, UNHCR. Available at www.unhcr.ch.

——. 2002a. *Agenda for Protection.* Geneva: UNHCR. Available at www.unhcr.ch.

——. 2002b. *Statistical Yearbook 2001.* Geneva: UNHCR.

——. 2003a. "Convention Plus and Special Agreements." Geneva: UNHCR. On file with the author.

——. 2003b. *Framework for Durable Solutions for Refugees and Persons of Concern.* Geneva: UNHCR.

——. 2004a. *In Pursuit of Durable Solutions in Zambia.* Geneva: UNHCR.

——. 2004b. "Multilateral Framework of Understandings on Resettlement." FORUM/2004/6, September 16, 2004, UNHCR, Geneva. Available at www.unhcr.ch.

——. 2004c. "Poverty Reduction Strategy Papers: A Displacement Perspective." Geneva: UNHCR.

——. 2004d. "Report of the Mid-Term Review: Self-Reliance Strategy (SRS 1999–2003) for Refugee Hosting Areas in Moyo, Arua and Adjumani Districts, Uganda." Geneva: UNHCR.

——. 2004e. "Summary of Second Forum Meeting." March 12, 2004, UNHCR, Geneva. On file with the author.

——. 2005a. "Convention Plus: At A Glance." UNHCR, Geneva. Available at www.unhcr.ch.

——. 2005b. "Convention Plus Core Group on Addressing Irregular Secondary Movements of Refugees and Asylum Seekers: Joint Statement by Co-Chairs." FORUM/2005/7, November 15, 2005. Geneva: UNHCR.

——. 2005c. "Convention Plus Targeting Development Assistance for Durable Solutions to Forced Displacement: Joint Statement by Co-Chairs." FORUM/2005/8, November 15, 2005. Geneva: UNHCR.

——. 2005d. "Putting Refugees on the Development Agenda: How Refugees and Returnees Can Contribute to Achieving the Millennium Development Goals." FORUM/2005/4, May 18, 2005. Geneva: UNHCR.

——. 2005e. "Statement of Good Practice for Targeting Development Assistance." Geneva: UNHCR.

——. 2006. *The State of the World's Refugees.* Oxford: Oxford University Press.

——. 2008. 2007 *Global Trends: Refugees, Asylum-Seekers, Returnees, Internally Displaced, and Stateless Persons.* Geneva: UNHCR.

UN High Commissioner for Refugees (UNHCR) Archives. UNHCR Headquarters, Geneva.

USCRI 2004. "Warehousing Issue." *World Refugee Survey.*

Van Hear, Nick, and NinnaNyberg Sorensen, eds. 2003. *The Migration-Development Nexus*. Geneva: United Nations and International Organization for Migration.

Wæver, Ole, Barry Buzan, Martin Kelstrup, and Pierre Lemaitre, eds. 1993. *Identity, Migration and the New Security Agenda Europe*. London: Pinter.

Weiner, Myron. 1996. "Bad Neighbors, Bad Neighborhoods: An Inquiry into the Causes of Refugee Flows." *International Security* 21 (1): 5–42.

Weiss, Thomas, and David Korn. 2006. *Internal Displacement: Conceptualization and Its Consequences*. London: Routledge.

Wendt, Alexander. 1987. "The Agent-Structure Problem in International Relations Theory." *International Organization* 41 (3): 335–70.

——. 1992. "Anarchy Is What States Make of It: The Social Construction of Power Politics." *International Organization* 46 (3): 391–425.

——. 1999. *Social Theory of International Politics*. Cambridge, UK: Cambridge University Press.

Young, Oran. 1996. "Institutional Linkages in International Society." *Global Governance* 2: 1–23.

Zolberg, Aristide, Astri Suhrke, and Sergio Aguayo. 1989. *Escape from Violence: Conflict and the Refugee Crisis in the Developing World*. Oxford: Oxford University Press.

# INDEX

United Nations High Commissioner for Refugees (UNHCR) *(continued)*
mandate, 10–11, 19, 56–57
*Principles for Action in Developing Countries,* 70
responsibility for human rights, 10
responsibility for timely resolution, 10
role in world politics, 10–11, 16, 183–86
Statute of the Office of the United Nations High Commissioner for Refugees, 10
*See also* individual initiatives
United Nations International Children's Emergency Fund (UNICEF), 61, 157
United Nations secretary-general, 57, 59, 68–69, 94, 99, 116, 130–31, 138, 158, 161, 185
United States, 15, 30, 44, 50, 58, 71, 74, 91, 101–3, 112–13, 117–19, 118, 124–25, 126, 129–34, 136–37, 139, 167
U.S. Agency for International Development (USAID), 102
U.S. Committee for Refugees and Immigrants (USCRI), 15, 167
USSR, 50, 74, 101, 113, 126, 131–32, 136

Valley of Peace, 85, 88
Vendrell, Francesc, 99
Vietnam, 6, 17, 30, 49, 50, 112–13, 115, 117–26, 130–38, 142
Vietnam War, 130, 134, 142

Waldheim, Kurt, 57
Washington, D.C., 102, 159
water systems, 57, 63, 152
Wendt, Alexander, 42
Western Cayo, 85
Wolfensohn, James, 158–59
World Bank, 158–59, 160, 172, 173, 185
World Bank Poverty Reduction Strategy Papers (PRSPs), 158–59
World Food Programme (WFP), 157
World War I, 5
World War II, 1, 5, 8, 9, 10, 30

Yucatan Peninsula, 88
Yugoslavia, 5–6, 10–11

Zaire, 53, 62
Zambia, 53–54, 152, 168, 171, 172
Zambia Initiative (ZI), 168, 171